THE HUMAN WORLD: A CHANGING PLACE

THE HUMAN WORLD
A CHANGING PLACE

Robert Harshman, B.A., M.A., B. Ed.
Applewood Heights Secondary School

Christine Hannell, B.Sc., M.Sc., B. Ed.
Brampton Centennial Secondary School

 John Wiley & Sons

Toronto   New York   Chichester   Brisbane   Singapore

Care has been taken to trace ownership of copyright material
contained in this text. The publishers will gladly receive any
information that will enable them to rectify any reference or
credit line in subsequent editions.

The metric usage in this text has been reviewed by the Metric
Screening Office of the Canadian General Standards Board.
Metric Commission Canada has granted permission for the
use of the National Symbol for Metric conversion.

The case studies, "The Tran Family" and "Amerasians in
Thailand" (Chapter 8), are based on real events and people,
but names and some details have been altered to protect the
privacy of the individuals involved.

CANADIAN CATALOGUING IN PUBLICATION DATA

Harshman, Robert.
  The human world

For use in secondary schools.
Includes index.
ISBN 0-471-79796-0

1. Man—Influence on nature.   2. Human ecology.
3. Physical geography.   I. Hannell, Christine.   II. Title.

GF75.H36   1985   304.2'8   C84-098435-9

Maps and diagrams: James Loates, *illustrating*

Printed and bound in Canada at The Bryant Press Limited.
10 9 8 7 6 5 4 3 2 1

To my wife, Susan, and our daughters Michelle and Kristen

R. HARSHMAN

To Professor F.G. Hannell, our children, and my students

C. HANNELL

Contents

4. Economic Systems of the World

5. Industry in Canada Today   *134*

SECTION III   Cultural Geography

7. The Spread of Culture, Ideas, Beliefs, and Races   *194*

SECTION V   **The Future**

11. Prospects for the Future   *346*

Preface

Students in Canadian high schools today have a great interest in the world around them. This is partly the result of television and other types of media, which have made all Canadians feel the immediacy of major current events taking place in other areas of the globe. In this text, students will be able to study some of the areas of the world where these events take place. By examining economics, industry and technology, transportation, energy, global lifestyles and leisure, mass media, pollution, conservation, and prospects for the future, they will come to understand how humans are influenced by their physical environments and how the development of human cultures has affected the world around them.

The introductory chapter of this text presents a broad overview of some of the major landscapes of the world: from tropical rainforests to the cold deserts of the Arctic, from the high Andes Mountains in South America to the giant cities of Europe. Students will discover the worldwide patterns of physical and human geography and how people interact with their environment.

One major force that helps mould the landscape of the world is human economic activity. Section II explores the origins of the world's economic systems, as well as current global economic patterns. Beginning with an examination of early hunting-and-gathering economies, the origins of agriculture, and the rise of urban centres, this section goes on to the study of the industrialization of the United States, the United Kingdom, and Japan, the development of multinational corporations, the rise of the superpowers, and the establishment of world economic organizations. Then the focus turns to Canada: its industries, transportation links, resources, labour force, new technologies, and trade with other countries.

Another important factor affecting the global landscape is human cultural activity. In Section III, students will be looking at culture hearths, migration, and population shifts; languages and religions of the world; and lifestyles, leisure and mass media in Canada and North America.

Inevitably, human activity in its various forms alters the environment of the world. Such activity, however, has both a beneficial and a damaging impact on the world. Section IV deals with the environmental impact of people's activities in both the industrialized countries and the developing world. These issues are examined as they relate to everyday pollution hazards, chemical pollution, garbage disposal, and acid rain in Canada, as well as ocean pollution, desertification, and deforestation around the world. The scope of environmental damage around the world is commensurate with the variety and size of human population and the technology in use. The extent to which the people of the world solve the environmental problems they have generated will help determine the future quality of life on earth.

The last section of this text deals with projections and theories about the future. What will life be like in the twenty-first century? How important is the arms race in determining future prospects for the world? What can Canadians do today to alter the directions the world is taking? Issues such as these help students develop a thoughtful approach to current geographical concerns and their possible resolution.

Throughout the book, the main text is supplemented with current and historical case studies, including studies on Matsushita Electric; Hong Kong; Vietnamese refugees to Canada; Cubatao, Brazil; Agent Orange; and the High Aswân Dam. Each chapter contains maps, statistical information, and numerous illustrations, and a wealth of questions, activities, and research topics.

Any study of the world as a whole is a step toward increasing understanding between people of different cultures. It is hoped that this book will help students come to this greater understanding.

In developing this book, we received many useful comments and suggestions from a number of reviewers, whose contribution we would like to acknowledge here. The reviewers are:

David Alexander, Danforth Technical School, Toronto, Ontario
R.D. Arber, Sir Wilfrid Laurier Collegiate Institute, Scarborough, Ontario
J.E. Reid Barter, Upper Canada College, Toronto, Ontario
W.J. Barton, Ajax High School, Ajax, Ontario
Jim Campbell, Board of Education, Calgary, Alberta
Betty Carlyle, Sir John A. Macdonald Secondary School, Hamilton, Ontario
Eric Dowsett, Neelin High School, Brandon, Manitoba
The Reverend Rex Kearley, Avalon Consolidated School Board, St. John's, Newfoundland
Douglas C. Nesbit, Banting Memorial High School, Alliston, Ontario

Many of their recommendations were followed throughout the development of this text, for the final content of which we alone are responsible.

Robert Harshman   *Christine Hannell*
Mississauga, Ontario   *Hamilton, Ontario*

March, 1985

Organization of
The Human World:
a Changing Place

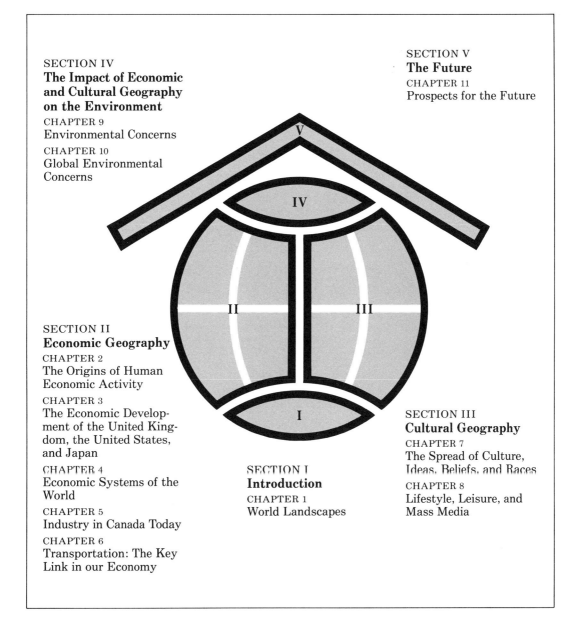

1

SECTION I | **Introduction**

 # World Landscapes

Introduction

To an astronaut returning from a journey in space, Earth appears as a bright, beautiful jewel floating in a black, endless void. The great variety of landscapes, barely visible from space, makes the home planet a place you would like to explore. You may want to visit the wild natural landscapes of the high Himalayas, the scorching Sahara Desert, the spectacular Grand Canyon, or the vast and steamy Amazon forests.

On the other hand, your interests may lie in the human landscape, the great achievements of your ancestors. You may want to see the mysterious circle of stones at Stonehenge, the Great Pyramids in Egypt, the Dome of the Rock in Jerusalem, the Palace of Knossos in Crete, or the Coliseum of Rome. You may even want to venture as far as the Great Wall of China or to explore the many pyramids built by the Aztecs in Central America.

Perhaps you would like to find out how people in various parts of the world live today. What would it be like to live in remote areas of the Arctic or the Atlas Mountains of North Africa? How would your life differ if you lived in the almost continuous **urban** (built-up) area of Washington-New York-Boston, or in the **ghettos** of Detroit? What would your day-to-day activities involve in a poor village of Bangladesh or in a war-torn area of Southeast Asia?

This book will help you to explore and understand the great variety of natural and cultural landscapes in the world. The book's major emphasis is on contemporary human life and activities. The

Figure 1.1 The
Earth Viewed
from Space

way in which history and physical factors have influenced people's
lives will also form a vital part of your study. In some areas, people
have been able to change their environments greatly. In others,
people live on the edge of poverty and starvation, and their attempts
to improve their situation are mostly futile. Why do these differences
exist?

By reading and working through the activities in this book,
you will begin to understand some of the controlling factors in the
modern world. You will also learn to what extent all the countries
in the world are dependent on worldwide forces.

1. Using photographs from magazines, newspapers, or postcards,
   construct a *collage* that illustrates the great variety of cultural
   or physical landscapes in the world. (A collage is a grouping of
   pictures on a sheet of paper or bristol board.)

2. Write a one- to two-page account listing at least four places in
   the world that you would like to visit. In each case, explain why
   you want to visit that place and what you would like to see there.

Today's World: Its Physical and Cultural Landscapes

Scientists claim that the earth's physical landscape has been changing for over four thousand million years, and that it continues to change very slowly. Figure 1.2 illustrates the distribution of the major physical regions: mountains, plains, shields, plateaus, lowlands.

The distribution of different physical regions may appear to have no pattern. However, **geologists**, who study rock formations, have been able to research the long history of our earth to explain the ordering of these landscapes. In the study of human geography, you will be considering the influence that these varied landscapes have upon people's activities.

**Figure 1.2
The World's
Major Physical
Regions**

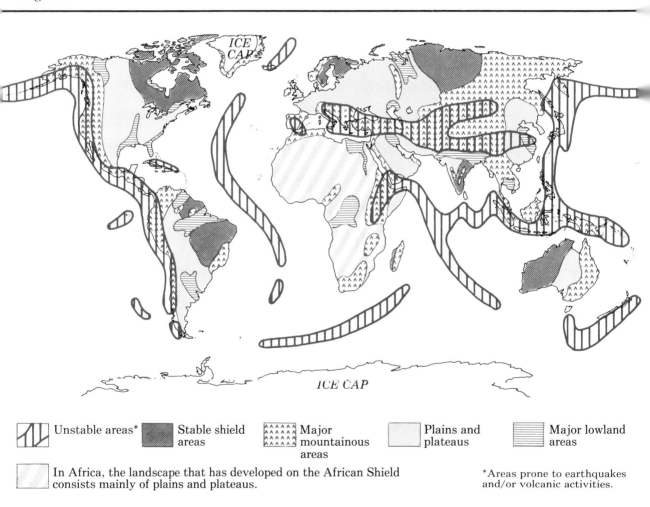

ICE CAP

ICE CAP

Unstable areas*   Stable shield areas   Major mountainous areas   Plains and plateaus   Major lowland areas

In Africa, the landscape that has developed on the African Shield consists mainly of plains and plateaus.

*Areas prone to earthquakes and/or volcanic activities.

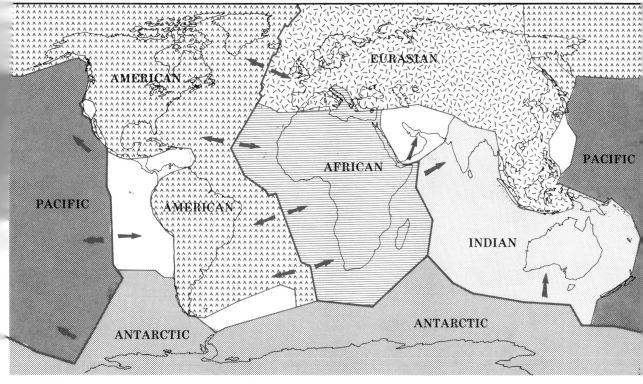

NOTE: The six major plates are named. Minor plates are unnamed.

 Zones where the plates are spreading apart very actively

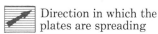 Direction in which the plates are spreading

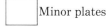 Minor plates

Figure 1.3 The Major Plates of the Earth

Areas Prone to Volcanoes and Earthquakes

Perhaps the most spectacular physical landscapes are those where the surface of the earth is very unstable, where there are many earthquakes and active volcanoes. Figure 1.2 shows that these areas occur in definite bands. The Mid-Atlantic Ridge in the Atlantic Ocean and the "Ring of Fire" which surrounds the Pacific Ocean are two volcanic areas. People living in these areas know that they could lose their property, way of life, and even their lives, in a few minutes.

Earthquakes occur where there are cracks between the rigid plates of rock that support the crust of the earth. These plates are moved slowly about by the currents within the lower layers of the earth. (See Figure 1.3.) As the plates move, tremendous vibrations and heat are created, resulting in volcanic eruptions and in more earthquakes.

Despite the known dangers, many people choose to stay in areas that are prone to earthquakes and volcanic eruptions.

3. Imagine that you are interviewing a Sicilian whose house has recently been buried beneath a flow of lava. You ask, "Do you intend to stay in the same village?"

   Write about 100 words, outlining at least three reasons why the Sicilian might wish to remain near his or her old home.

4. Many cities and towns in California have been built on or near the active San Andreas Fault. It caused the earthquake that destroyed much of San Francisco in 1906.
   (a) Why do you think that cities have grown up in western California, where the danger of earthquakes is well known? Look at a map of California to prepare your answer.
   (b) Imagine that a major earthquake takes place in the largest city of your province or territory. List the facilities that would probably be damaged or destroyed.
     • How would this damage affect the economic activity of the city after the earthquake?
     • How would the earthquake change your life?

The Shields: Areas of Stability

The oldest and hardest rocks of the earth are found in the great shields. The rocks themselves contain many valuable minerals. Thus, even in cold or dry climates, these areas are very important. The immense gold and diamond mines of South Africa are located within the African Shield. The Canadian Shield is our country's greatest source of metallic minerals. Figure 1.4 shows two types of mines used to extract metallic minerals from shield areas.

5. Using a map of Canadian *natural resources*, list the kinds of minerals mined in the Canadian Shield. (A natural resource is naturally existing material used by people, such as water, iron, timber.)

6. In what ways is the *exploitation* of these mineral resources vital in opening up the northern areas of Canada? To exploit means to make use of a substance (or person).

7. Compare the map of world population, Figure 1.8, with Figure 1.2, which shows the world distribution of shields.
   (a) Do the shields coincide with areas of *dense* or *sparse* population? (In an area of dense population, many people live close together. If very few people lived in that same area, it would be described as having a sparse population.)
   (b) Are the shield areas of the world important food-producing areas? Give the reasons for your answer.

a

b

The Mountains: Regions Inhospitable to Human Settlement

Generally speaking, few people live in the mountainous regions of
the world. These regions tend to be **inhospitable**, providing little
shelter or means of survival. Although the mountains contain valuable mineral and hydro-electric resources, and are often covered
by great forests, there is a limit to where settlements can be established. In Switzerland, for example, small settlements tend to be
located in valleys, on south-facing slopes, where there is sufficient
land to grow a few crops and raise some animals, and the sun shines
more intensely and for a longer period each day than on the other
slopes. (See Figure 1.5.)

**Figure 1.4 Mining
in the Shields of
the World**
(a) A Silver Mine,
No Longer in
Use
(b) An Open-Pit
Mine

**Figure 1.5
A Settlement in a
Valley in the
Swiss Alps**

NORTH   SOUTH

Sun's rays

SHADOW

Land cleared
for agriculture

River

Land left
in forest

**Figure 1.6
Terracing a Slope
for Agriculture**

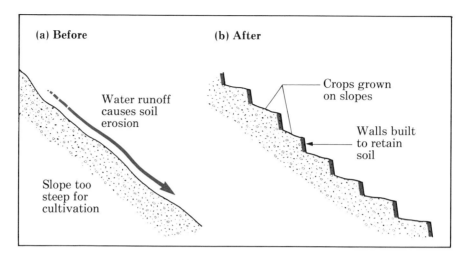

(a) Before

Water runoff
causes soil
erosion

Slope too
steep for
cultivation

(b) After

Crops grown
on slopes

Walls built
to retain
soil

In Japan, there is such a shortage of land suitable for agriculture that mountain slopes have been used for this purpose extensively. **Terracing** the slopes, by fashioning them into a series of steps, makes agriculture possible and reduces the rate of **soil erosion**. The effect of terracing is shown in Figure 1.6. Soil erosion is the loss of soil by wind or by moving ice or water.

**Figure 1.7 The
Pattern of
Settlement and
Communications
in a Mountainous
Area of Canada**

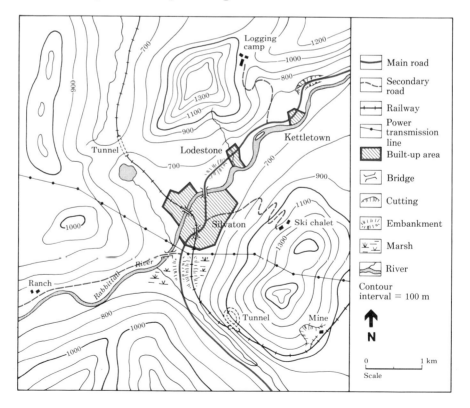

8. The map in Figure 1.7 represents a mountainous area of western Canada.
   (a) Put a piece of tracing paper over the map.
      • Mark all the settlements in red.
      • Mark all the roads in red and the railways in black.
      • Shade in, in brown, the areas higher than 700 m above sea level.
   (b) Look at your map. Describe
      • how physical features have affected where settlements, and transportation and communications lines, are located.
      • how people have crossed or overcome some of the physical barriers in the area.

The Plateaus and Plains: Moderately Populated Areas

There are large areas of the earth's surface that are fairly flat, but are still at a high or moderate elevation. These are the plateaus and plains. The rocks underlying these areas were usually formed from loose sediments which were deposited at the bottom of the sea that covered the plateaus and plains millions of years ago. They are now valuable as sources of **fossil fuels** such as oil and natural gas.

Salt, gypsum (used in making moulds and in construction), and potash (used for fertilizer) are other valuable minerals that were often buried in the layers of the rocks as the water slowly evaporated. Chemical industries and **petrochemical industries** (those that make products from petroleum) develop near these buried resources. Such industries are a vital part of the modern world, as they produce fertilizers for agriculture, chemicals for industry, and synthetic fibres.

Many of the plains and plateaus are also valuable agricultural areas. The degree of agricultural activity, of course, depends upon climatic and soil conditions. Where these factors are favourable, such as in the Great Plains of North America, grain crops are grown extensively. Drier areas are often used to raise cattle and other livestock for food for human consumption. In Canada, the United States, and the U.S.S.R., there are plains where grain is grown for local use and for export.

The Productive, Densely Populated Lowland Regions

Over millions of years, rich alluvial deposits have built up on the beds of great rivers such as the Nile, Amazon, Parana, Mississippi, Congo, Tigris, Euphrates, Ganges, Irrawaddy, Mekong, and Yangtze. Alluvial deposits are composed of layers of fine soil particles that are left on lakebeds, riverbeds, and the bottoms of ponds, or where rivers flow into the sea.

In other areas, rich deposits have resulted from the recent elevation of land from beneath the sea, and from the advancing and retreating action of the glaciers, which moved large quantities of topsoil from one area to another.

Some of the lowland regions formed in this way also had a good climate, which led to a high level of agricultural production. The growth of early civilizations, such as those around the Nile, Tigris, and Euphrates rivers, and in northern India, was the direct result of an abundance of food. Food surpluses led to the development of trade between settlements. Since some people did not have to spend any time obtaining food, they were free to do other things. People began to invent better tools and devices and eventually built great cities and temples. Five thousand years ago, in Sumer, located in the valley of the Tigris and the Euphrates, the first use of the wheel and money was recorded. This was also the first civilization to use writing as a means of recording. This is known as cuneiform writing.

Figure 1.8 World Population Distribution

Today, many of these lowland regions remain areas of dense population. Figure 1.8 shows the distribution of people in the world.

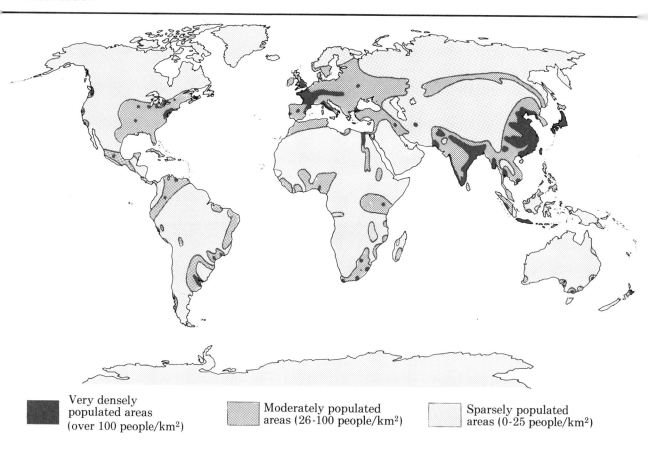

Very densely populated areas (over 100 people/km²)

Moderately populated areas (26-100 people/km²)

Sparsely populated areas (0-25 people/km²)

a

b

c

Figure 1.9 Some of the World's Great Lowland Areas
(a) The Great Lakes–St. Lawrence Lowlands
(b) The Netherlands
(c) The Mississippi River Lowlands

9. There are many reasons why population is often dense in low areas near large rivers. One reason is agriculture. List and briefly explain five other reasons.

10. There are several large river valleys in the world where the population is not dense. Using an atlas, explain what factors discourage the concentration of population in the following river valleys: the Amazon in Brazil, the Congo in Zaire, the Mackenzie in Canada, and the Ob-Yenisei in the U.S.S.R.

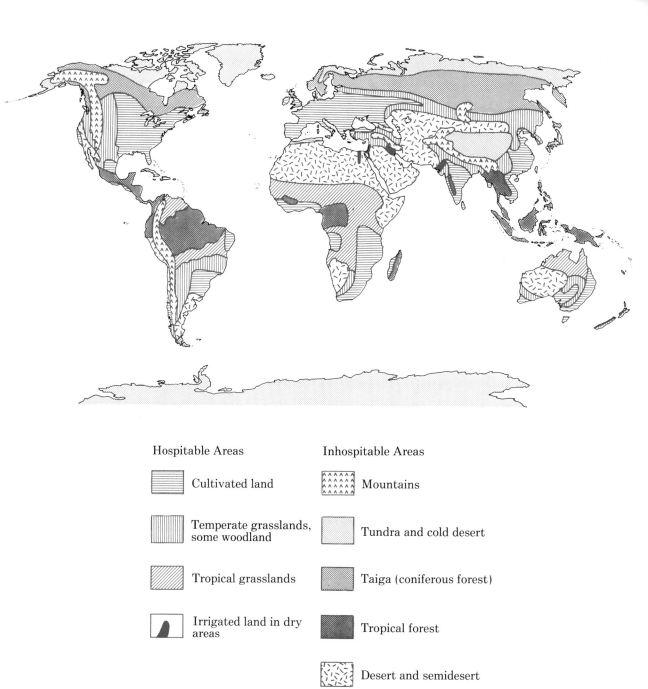

Hospitable Areas

| | Cultivated land |

| | Temperate grasslands, some woodland |

| | Tropical grasslands |

| | Irrigated land in dry areas |

Inhospitable Areas

| | Mountains |

| | Tundra and cold desert |

| | Taiga (coniferous forest) |

| | Tropical forest |

| | Desert and semidesert |

Figure 1.10 Hospitable and Inhospitable Areas of the World

a

b

c

d

Hospitable and Inhospitable Areas

The earth's land surface can be classified into hospitable and inhospitable areas, according to the nature of rock formations, soil, and climate (see Figure 1.10). The hospitable areas, where people can find or produce the means to survive with reasonable ease, make up about 47% of the land surface. The inhospitable areas can support few people, who probably have to struggle to survive.

**Figure 1.11
Contrasts in the Way of Life in Hospitable and Inhospitable Areas**
(a) Hospitable
(b) Hospitable
(c) Inhospitable
(d) Inhospitable

Pie Graphs

A **pie graph** is a circular diagram in which the "slices of the pie" represent the proportions that make up the whole item. For example, of the earth's surface, 71% is covered by water and 29% by land. This could be represented by the following pie graph:

The Relative Proportions
of the Earth's
Surface Covered
by Land and
Water

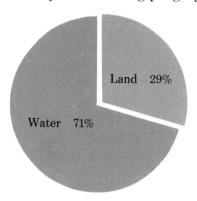

In this diagram, the circle represents the entire area of the world. The water sector occupies 71% of the circle and thus 71% of the earth. The angle to plot this sector is calculated as follows:

$$\frac{71}{100} = \frac{\text{water angle}}{360}$$

$$\text{water angle} = \frac{360 \times 71}{100} = 256°$$

Instructions for Drawing a Pie Graph

1. Draw a circle. Draw one radial line from the centre to the top.
2. Calculate the angle of the first sector to be plotted. If the value is 30%, the formula is:

$$(\frac{30}{100} \times 360) = 108°$$

3. Measure the calculated angle from the radial line in a clockwise direction. Label the sector.
4. Use a similar method to calculate subsequent sectors. Always plot the angle from the last line you have constructed.
5. If your calculations and plotting are correct, the final sector will bring you back to the first line.

11. Construct two pie graphs, using the data given below. Remember to plot each sector or "slice" in a clockwise direction from the previous sector. Colour and label each sector. Give each pie graph a title.

(a) Hospitable and inhospitable areas of the world: hospitable areas cover 47% of the land surface and inhospitable areas cover 53%.

(b) The proportions of the various categories of land in hospitable areas:

	%
Cultivated land	49
Temperate grasslands and woodlands	20
Tropical grasslands	20
Areas of high urban concentration	8
Irrigated land	3

The Oceans

Much of the earth is covered by oceans. The oceans have a significant influence on human life. The variety of uses to which oceans have been put is suggested in Figure 1.12. For example, they help control

a

b

c

d

Figure 1.12 The Oceans: Their Many Uses
(a) Seawater Distillation Plant in Aruba, Netherlands Antilles
(b) Shipping in Vera Cruz, Mexico
(c) Fishing on the Bosporus in Istanbul, Turkey
(d) Pleasure Boat in the Caribbean

the climate. They also contain many resources necessary for survival. The oceans have supplied food for coastal communities for thousands of years, and in the future they may prove to be a vital source of food and mineral resources. Today, however, the oceans are being overfished and are being polluted by the wastes from rivers, lakes, and coastal activities.

By international agreement, control over the seas and oceans is divided among the nations of the world. Figure 1.13 outlines the major proposed divisions.

12. In what ways do you consider the oceanic divisions shown in Figure 1.13 to be fair and/or unfair to the various peoples of the world?

13. Why do you think the nations involved considered it important to have possession or control of a certain portion of the ocean?

14. Why are the oceans so difficult to explore?

Figure 1.13 A Proposal for the Distribution of Oceanic Control

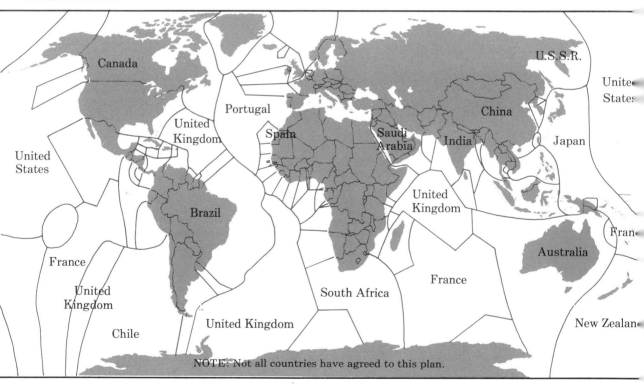

NOTE: Not all countries have agreed to this plan.

Cultural Landscapes

Just as there are hospitable and inhospitable areas of the natural landscape there are also different degrees of **affluence** among the people of the world. (Affluence refers to the amount of wealth people have.)

Figure 1.14 shows the economic situation of various areas of the world. The figures used are referred to as the **Gross National Product per capita** (GNP per capita or GNP per person). (This term refers to the average value of goods and services produced in a country by each person in one year.) A detailed breakdown of GNP per-person values can be found in an atlas.

Figure 1.14 The Major Economic Divisions of the World

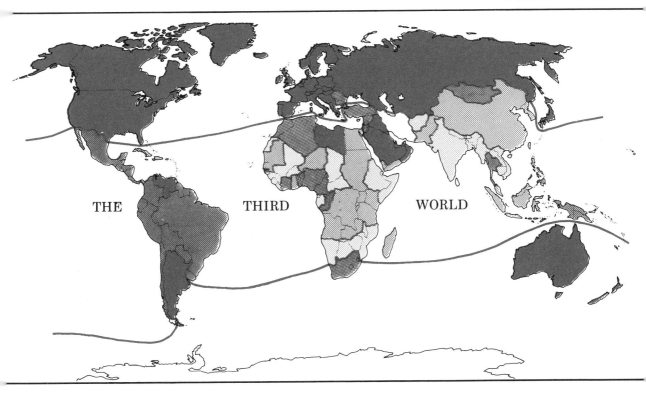

THE   THIRD   WORLD

GNP per Capita, 1979

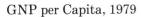

Over $9000 $251-$500

$2001-$9000 $80-$250

$501-$2000

NOTES: South Africa is not included in the Third World because it has a highly developed industrial economy. White people have relatively high incomes. The Bantu, however, are very poor.

Wealthier nations within the Third World depend on extra income from oil exports. Kuwait has a GNP per capita of $17 100.

	GNP PER PERSON (US $)	% OF TOTAL POPULATION LIVING IN CITIES	AVERAGE LIFE EXPECTANCY	DAILY PER CAPITA CALORIE SUPPLY AS A PERCENTAGE OF THAT REQUIRED	NUMBER OF PEOPLE PER DOCTOR	NUMBER OF PASSENGER CARS PER 1000 PEOPLE	ANNUAL CONSUMPTION OF ENERGY PER INHABITANT (In Kilograms of Coal Equivalent)
Canada	10 180	76	74	127	550 ('79)	419.0 ('81)	10 547
U.S.	11 590	74	74	139	549	520.0	10 415
Japan	9 020	72	76	124	761 ('81)	209.0 ('81)	3 669
India	230	20	52	86	2 517	1.6 ('81)	183
Kenya	390	10	55	89	10 134 ('78)	6.0 ('82)	136

NOTE: Figures shown are for 1980 unless otherwise indicated.

Figure 1.15
Indicators of the Degree of Development of Selected Countries

The degree of development of an area is indicated by a number of different factors. Figure 1.15 compares the degree of development of five selected countries.

15. In Figure 1.15, seven factors are shown as indicators of the degree of development of various countries. Explain what the following statistics reveal about each country and its level of development.
    (a) Annual Consumption of Energy per Inhabitant
    (b) Number of People per Doctor
    (c) Average Life Expectancy

16. (a) Rank the factors in Figure 1.15 in order of importance as indicators. Start with the most important.
    (b) Explain the reasons for the order you chose in (a).

Figure 1.16
Contrasts in Health Care Facilities
(a) Heart Surgery in a Hospital in a Wealthy Nation
(b) Minimal Care in a Poor Nation

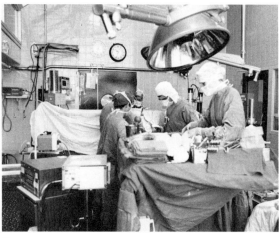

a

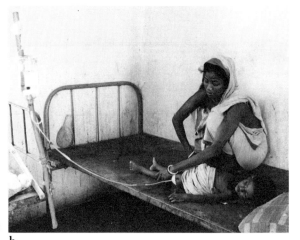

b

Figure 1.17
Development
Assistance from
OECD and OPEC

OECD (1981) ORGANIZATION FOR ECONOMIC CO-OPERATION AND DEVELOPMENT			OPEC (1980) ORGANIZATION OF PETROLEUM EXPORTING COUNTRIES		
COUNTRY	ASSISTANCE (US $ Millions)	% OF DONOR GNP	COUNTRY	ASSISTANCE (US $ Millions)	% OF DONOR GNP
Australia	649	0.41	Algeria	83	0.27
Austria	317	0.48	Iran	3	0.00
Belgium	574	0.59	Iraq	829	2.12
Canada	1 187	0.43	Kuwait	1 188	3.88
Denmark	405	0.73	Libya	281	0.92
Finland	135	0.28	Nigeria	42	0.05
France	4 022	0.71	Qatar	319	4.80
Federal Republic of Germany	3 182	0.46	Saudi Arabia	3 040	2.60
Italy	670	0.19	United Arab Emirates	1 062	3.96
Japan	3 170	0.28	Venezuela	130	0.22
Netherlands	1 510	1.08			
New Zealand	67	0.29			
Norway	467	0.82			
Sweden	916	0.83			
Switzerland	236	0.24			
United Kingdom	2 194	0.43			
United States	5 760	0.20			

The more-developed nations of the world give millions of dollars in aid to the less-developed countries (see Figure 1.17). In spite of this financial aid, the less-developed nations still find it very difficult to improve their situation. The reasons for this are summarized in Figure 1.18, which illustrates the situation in Bangladesh, one of the world's poorest countries.

Bangladesh gained its independence from Pakistan as a result of a devastating civil war. Political instability continues to make the country weak and to make long-term planning difficult. Despite receiving $2000 million in aid since gaining independence in 1971, Bangladesh remains a desperately poor nation with little prospect for significant improvement. Natural disasters such as hurricanes and flooding, which destroy life, property, and crops, frequently occur in Bangladesh.

Without the ability to buy sufficient energy supplies, raw materials, or technology, countries such as Bangladesh will remain poor. **Inflation** affects all nations of the world, but its greatest effects are felt in the poor nations. (Inflation is indicated by rising prices and a decrease in a currency's purchasing power.)

Figure 1.18 The Cycle of Poverty in Bangladesh

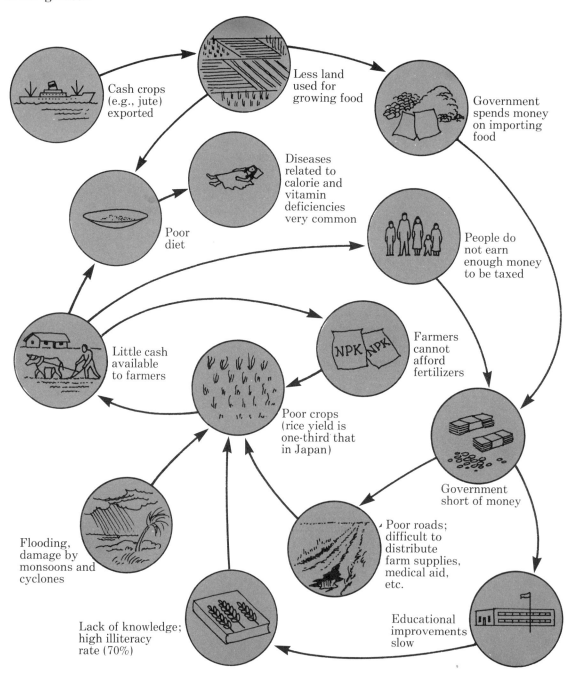

Cash crops (e.g., jute) exported

Less land used for growing food

Government spends money on importing food

Diseases related to calorie and vitamin deficiencies very common

Poor diet

People do not earn enough money to be taxed

Little cash available to farmers

Farmers cannot afford fertilizers

NPK NPK

Poor crops (rice yield is one-third that in Japan)

Government short of money

Flooding, damage by monsoons and cyclones

Poor roads; difficult to distribute farm supplies, medical aid, etc.

Educational improvements slow

Lack of knowledge; high illiteracy rate (70%)

Exceptions are the oil-producing countries that are members of **OPEC** (Oil Producing and Exporting Countries). The organization has formed a **cartel** that has forced oil prices up. (A cartel is an organization of producers who agree to control the amount they produce and the price they charge for a **commodity** such as oil.) The increased income from oil that OPEC has brought to these countries has enabled them to make enormous changes. For example, Kuwait, at the head of the Arabian gulf, is among the wealthiest nations. Here are some indicators of Kuwait's prosperity:

- There are no taxes on income, gasoline, or houses.
- There is a free telephone service.
- One in three citizens has a car.
- There is a hospital bed for every 80 people.
- There is one teacher for every ten students.
- Only one percent of the people are involved in agriculture.
- Forty-four percent of the people are involved in service industries.

A Worldwide System

World Economic Ties

No country can be completely isolated from events that take place in the rest of the world. And no individual on earth is unaffected by the activities of others. The way of life of people all over the world depends in part upon worldwide trade and mass communications.

Instant communications around the world inform us of events taking place thousands of kilometres away. These events affect what goods are available to us and determine the value of our money. We are all part of a worldwide system so that what happens in one area has repercussions or effects elsewhere — like the ripples created by a rock thrown into a pond. (Figure 1.19 shows the worldwide influences on something as familiar to you as a piece of toast.)

Figure 1.19 Worldwide Influences on Your Breakfast Toast

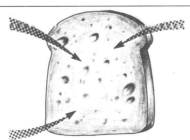

Weather conditions, political conditions, and trading agreements at home and abroad determine the cost of the ingredients used in manufacturing (flour, sugar, fats, oils, yeast, preserving chemicals).

Canada's energy policy, which is influenced by events abroad, determines the cost of energy (electricity, petroleum) used in obtaining raw materials, and in manufacturing and transportation.

Labour conditions and agreements, which vary greatly around the world, determine the cost of the labour involved in providing raw materials, and in manufacturing, transportation, and retailing.

Worldwide Environmental Ties

Pollution is spread by wind and water. As a result, pollutants produced in one country may well affect neighbouring countries. Prime examples of this are occurring in North America and Northern Europe (see Figure 1.20).

The industrial pollutants sulphur dioxide and nitrogen oxides, when mixed with moisture in the air, become mild acids. This acidic moisture is blown by the prevailing winds until it falls as rain or snow. Acid rain kills fish and damages plants, soil, and even the bricks and cement of buildings.

Sources of Sulphur Dioxide and Nitrogen Oxides in North America (In millions of tonnes)

	U.S.	CANADA	TOTAL
Sulphur dioxide	24	5	29
Nitrogen oxides	19	2	21

Canada produces less pollution than the United States, as can be seen from the above table. The prevailing winds, however, result in most of the acid rain and snow falling in Canada. Sweden is in a similar position with respect to other industrialized European nations. Attempts to reduce the problem of acid rain will depend on international agreements. Only time will tell whether such agreements can be made and enforced.

The underwater explorer Jacques Cousteau has said, "There is only one pollution, as all toxic (poisonous) substances end up in the sea."

17. Explain how all toxic substances (in the air, water, and on land) eventually end up in the sea. A diagram may help you answer.

18. Ocean pollutants are transported by ocean currents.
    (a) Using an atlas, draw a map of the North Atlantic Ocean. Mark and name the major ocean currents and show their directions of movement.
    (b) The pollution entering the North Atlantic has many sources. The cities of the northeastern United States are one source. List the countries that border the North Atlantic and would eventually share in North America's pollution. Mark them on your map.

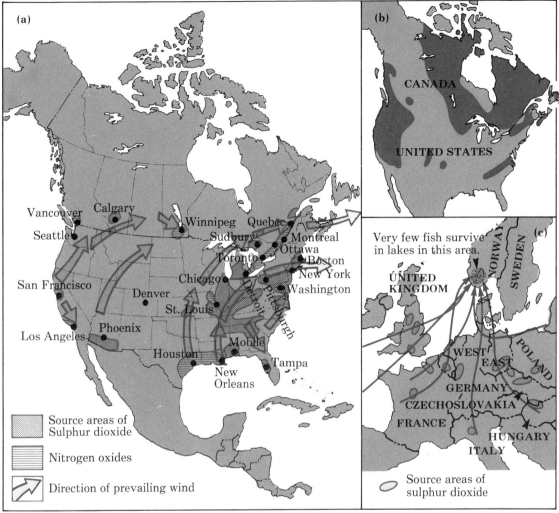

(a) Sources of Sulphur dioxide

Nitrogen oxides

Direction of prevailing wind

Very few fish survive in lakes in this area.

Source areas of sulphur dioxide

(c) Which current(s) would carry this pollution? Include them on your map.

19. What effects will increased concentration of pollutants in the ocean have
   (a) directly on marine life, such as fish, plants, and shellfish?
   (b) indirectly on the economic life of coastal communities?

Nature produces its own kind of pollution. For example, on May 18, 1980, Mount St. Helens in Washington State erupted with the power of a 10 Mt-bomb. Complete destruction was confined to within about 1500 km² of the volcano itself. Within three days,

Figure 1.20
(a) Sources of Acid Rain in Canada and the United States and Direction of Prevailing Wind
(b) Areas Susceptible to Damage from Acid Rain
(c) Sources of the Acid Rain That Falls in Norway

however, the ash had entered the earth's upper atmosphere and had spread across most of North America, driven by high-level winds (Figure 1.21). In seventeen days, the ash had circled the world, and was falling on many countries.

The spread of ash from Mount St. Helens illustrates the dangers that would result from human activity such as the explosion of nuclear devices or, ultimately, a nuclear war. When a hydrogen

Figure 1.21 The Areas of North America Where Ash from Mount St. Helens Fell in May 1980

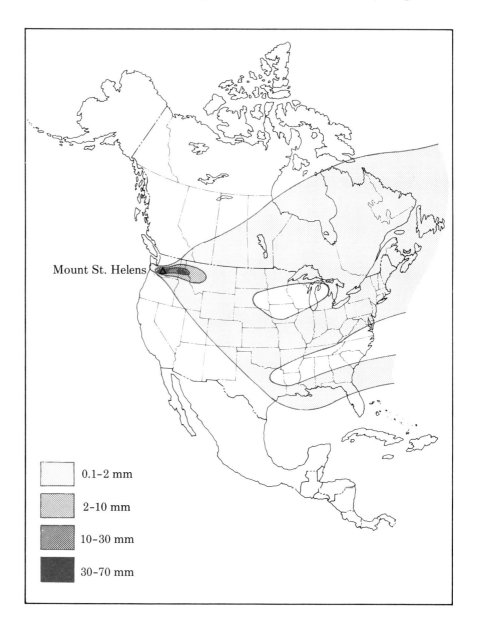

Mount St. Helens

0.1–2 mm

2–10 mm

10–30 mm

30–70 mm

bomb explodes on or near the earth's surface, there is complete destruction to the immediate area. In addition, great quantities of radioactive material are sent into the upper atmosphere, where they are distributed by high-level winds. (See Figure 1.22.)

Controlled tests of nuclear arms on the earth's surface have affected many thousands of people in the following way. Strontium 90, which is radioactive, is released into the air. Eventually it enters people's bodies, where it replaces some of the calcium in their bones. Radioactive materials cause genetic disorders and cancer. A person with severe radiation poisoning suffers diarrhea, vomiting, and general weakness and dies within one day to two weeks.

Never before have people had the capability of destroying all life on this planet. This fact in itself makes a study of the world important.

**Figure 1.22
Results of a
20-Mt Explosion**

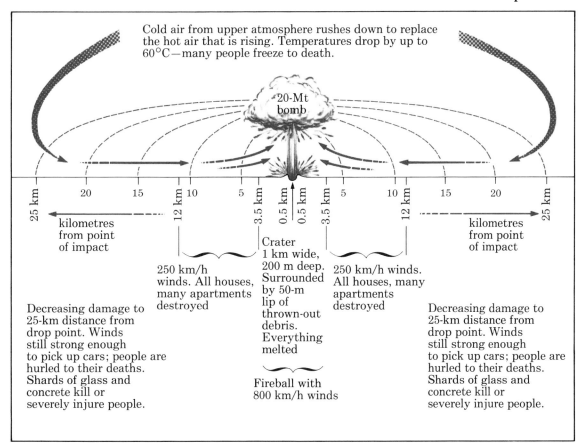

Cold air from upper atmosphere rushes down to replace the hot air that is rising. Temperatures drop by up to 60°C—many people freeze to death.

20-Mt bomb

25 km | 20 | 15 | 12 km | 10 | 5 | 3.5 km | 0.5 km | 0.5 km | 3.5 km | 5 | 10 | 12 km | 15 | 20 | 25 km

kilometres from point of impact

kilometres from point of impact

250 km/h winds. All houses, many apartments destroyed

Crater 1 km wide, 200 m deep. Surrounded by 50-m lip of thrown-out debris. Everything melted

250 km/h winds. All houses, many apartments destroyed

Decreasing damage to 25-km distance from drop point. Winds still strong enough to pick up cars; people are hurled to their deaths. Shards of glass and concrete kill or severely injure people.

Fireball with 800 km/h winds

Decreasing damage to 25-km distance from drop point. Winds still strong enough to pick up cars; people are hurled to their deaths. Shards of glass and concrete kill or severely injure people.

20. Figure 1.22 shows the degree of damage resulting from the explosion of a 20-Mt hydrogen bomb, which is an average-sized nuclear bomb.
    (a) Obtain a map of your city or of a nearby city. A highway or *large-scale* atlas map will do, one that shows the detail of a small area.
    (b) On tracing paper, draw four concentric circles (i.e., circles that share the same centre). Their diameters should be equivalent to 0.5, 3.5, 12, and 25 km. Be sure to use the scale of the map that you obtained in (a).
    (c) Place the tracing paper on the map of the city from (a), with the centre of the circle at the centre of the city.
    (d) Estimate the percentage of the city that would be completely devastated if a 20-Mt hydrogen bomb hit the city centre.
    (e) List six facilities that would be destroyed or damaged by such an explosion (e.g., a hospital). In each case, explain the effects this would have on the survivors in the area.

21. Assume that radioactive material is forced into the high layers of the atmosphere. Using specific examples (and the example of Mount St. Helens as a guide), explain why nuclear war would affect all life on earth.

The Worldwide Spread of Disease

The worldwide community in which people live affects you in a number of other ways. One of these is the way in which diseases spread around the globe.

Diseases can be spread by direct contact such as by parasites or mosquitoes, or indirectly by **contaminated** (infected or polluted) soil, water, or food. Some diseases, such as sickle cell anaemia, are inherited. The causes of others, such as cancer, are not fully understood, although they may be related to toxic substances or pollutants.

Cholera is an example of a disease spread by drinking contaminated water. Cholera causes severe diarrhea and vomiting,

Figure 1.23 Life Cycle of Cholera Bacteria

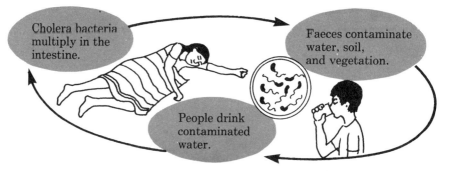

Figure 1.24
A Cholera Victim
in India

which in turn causes **dehydration**, or extreme loss of water from
the body. This condition often results in death within a few hours
or days. Cholera has caused millions of deaths all over the world.
However, following a worldwide campaign to improve water supplies,
sanitation, and vaccination, cholera remained only in India.

In 1961, however, a new strain of cholera called El Tor was
found in the Celebes Islands. As people travelled by sea, air, and
land, the disease spread quickly around the world, and it is still
a problem in some countries. The path of the disease can be followed
in Figure 1.25

Figure 1.25 The
Spread of El Tor
Cholera

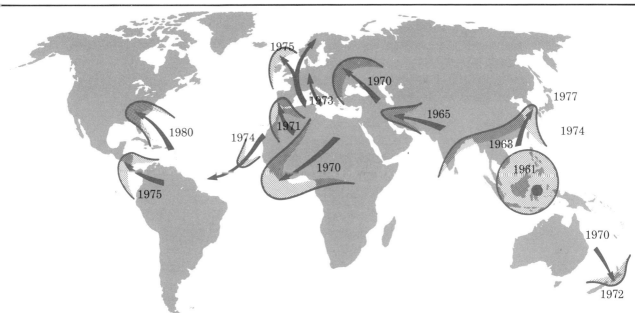

Cholera is just one example of diseases that travel around the world. Others include the numerous viruses that cause influenza and the common cold. Such viruses are commonly named for their area of origin, such as the Hong Kong or Victoria flu.

As recently as 1965, smallpox was still considered a major killer in the world. Having caused deaths in the tens of millions, this disease has earned a deadly reputation. It has recently been **eradicted** (eliminated). Until a few years ago, Canadians travelling to other countries had to have proof of smallpox vaccination within the preceding three years. Now, smallpox viruses exist only in a few medical laboratories throughout the world. This achievement resulted from worldwide vaccination of travellers and careful tracking and control of the disease.

22. **What steps must be taken to control and eventually eradicate cholera?**

23. **Of the countries where cholera is still a problem, many (but not all) are very poor. What five steps would you suggest that a poor country take in order to obtain the supplies, money, and specialists necessary to combat cholera?**

24. **In what ways is the control of cholera dependent on international co-operation? Why can one nation not succeed alone?**

CASE STUDY

The Mediterranean Fruit Fly Invasion of California

Just as the spread of a human disease from another part of the world can devastate a country, so too can the spread of disease or insects that harm the food supply.

In the summer of 1981, the Mediterranean fruit fly invaded some of California's most productive farmland and ruined millions of dollars worth of fruit. Oranges, almonds, dates, figs, and olives were among the 200 farm products infested. The fruit fly had arrived with a shipment of imported fruit.

Despite its small size (see Figure 1.26), the fly has a large impact by turning fruit into a "mush". The fruit fly is also able to reproduce quickly and move swiftly to carry on its destruction. Under ideal temperature conditions, one mature female fly can produce 1000 eggs during its two-month life. Within one year, at least six generations of fruit flies can be born. Assuming every egg hatched, one fertile female fly could lead to the production of over 60 million flies in one year!

Shown about eight times larger than actual size

Figure 1.26 A Mediterranean Fruit Fly

To combat the Mediterranean fruit fly, fruit was stripped from infested trees and buried. The government of California then faced the dilemma of whether or not to have helicopters spray the insecticide malathion to destroy the fruit fly. If spraying was not carried out farmers stood to lose up to $4000 million from ruined produce. If helicopters did spray malathion, however, this poison would be spread across densely inhabited land. Any poison used on such a large scale would be certain to influence the environment and present some danger to human and animal life.

The government decided to use malathion; mixed with molasses, sugar, and yeast, it came down in tiny droplets. The dangerous insecticide was used across a wide area of California in both farm and city areas. The fruit fly was effectively eliminated.

25. (a) **Which specific groups in southern California would oppose the spraying of malathion? (List at least five.)**
    (b) **Which groups in southern California would support the spraying program most strongly? (List at least five.)**

26. **Write one-half page to describe the spread of the fruit fly throughout the world since the early 1900s. Refer to Figure 1.27.**

27. **Why has Canada not yet been invaded?**

28. **How could a country ensure that it would not be invaded by the Mediterranean fruit fly from California?**

Figure 1.27 The Spread of "Medfly" around the World

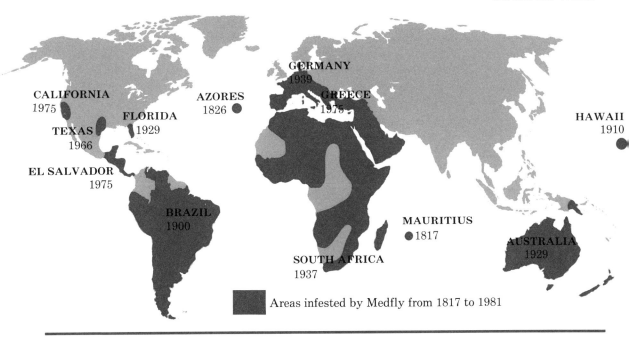

Areas infested by Medfly from 1817 to 1981

The Worldwide Spread of Skills and Knowledge

Information concerning most aspects of most countries is readily available at your school. Thus, in geography, you can acquire a reasonably accurate picture of China, the Australian desert, or Hong Kong without stepping from the classroom or library. You can get this information quickly and inexpensively by referring to films, photographs, television, magazines, and books.

Figure 1.28 Helping Each Other in the Classroom

When you face a problem, the fastest method of finding a solution is to look to others who have faced the same problem. Sharing skills and knowledge with others is also useful in solving worldwide problems. When you look at the world at large, you can see that there are many important problems to be tackled. Perhaps the most pressing one is to improve the living conditions of the poorer peoples of the world. Reaching this goal will be very difficult, if not impossible, to achieve. It will involve

- improving food supply, storage, and distribution
- controlling the rate of population increase
- making radical changes in the political and economic structure of nations so that wealth is spread more evenly among the people of a country

Experiments being conducted throughout the world are already leading to some improvements in food supplies and population control. The poorer countries will benefit greatly if they are able to use this knowledge.

DISCOVERY AND DEVELOPMENT	TEACHING	LEARNING AND APPLYING IDEAS
(Research leads to better results.) →	(Ideas are transmitted to area in need.) →	(Methods are explained to workers, so that they in turn can apply them.)

Figure 1.29 Blueprint for Improvement

Continued progress in poorer nations will depend to some extent upon the ability of their citizens to learn and apply new ideas. Learning depends largely upon the degree of **literacy**. Figure 1.30 shows that a country's degree of literacy is an important indicator of its stage of industrial development.

Changing the social and economic structures of the poorer nations will probably come only after the degree of literacy improves. Literate people are better able to influence their governments to make improvements.

Figure 1.30 Literacy Rates around the World

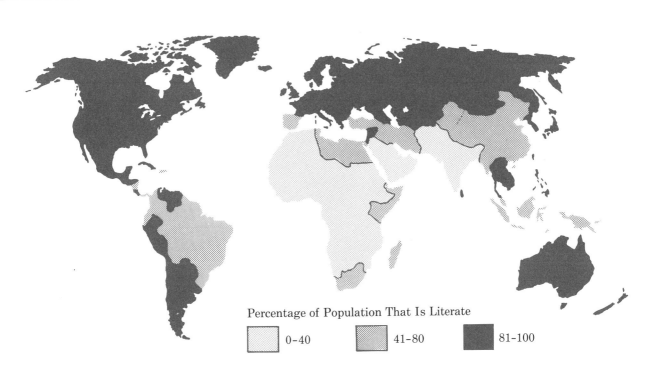

Percentage of Population That Is Literate

0–40   41–80   81–100

People's Response to Their Environment

People have three ways of responding to their environment.

1. They can adapt to it.
2. They can change it.
3. They can move to a more acceptable environment.

Adapting to the Environment

In winter, when outside, Canadians wear warm clothing. In summer, a T-shirt and shorts are normal. Environment dictates the clothing worn.

Farmers have learned to use the environment to their advantage by planting crops most suited to it. For example, spring wheat is grown in the Prairie provinces, whereas winter wheat is grown in parts of southern Canada where the winters are not so severe. Peaches are grown only in the warmest parts of the country, but apples can be grown in much cooler areas.

Figure 1.31 Rainwear: An Adaptation to the Environment

CASE STUDY

The Tasaday People of Mindanao

The 20 to 30 people of the Tasaday group live in the remote rain forests of the Philippines (see Figure 1.32). They inhabit one large and several small caves in a cliff face. Wearing only loincloths or skirts made from leaves, they scramble down a steep slope each morning to a nearby stream in search of food. Their food consists of what they can catch or find in or near the stream: small fish, crabs, frogs, berries, fruits, roots.

Through limited contact with people from the "outside world" the Tasaday have acquired steel knives, which they call "bolos", and which have replaced their old stone and wooden axes. (See Figure 1.33.)

Apart from a few blankets given to them by a local hunter, they have rejected all other offers of assistance. They are now protected from modern intruders by strict laws, and the government has created a 20 000 ha preserve for their exclusive use. Despite this protection and their apparently happy existence, it is unlikely that the Tasaday will survive for many generations. This is owing to several factors:

• There are few females in the group, and most of the children are males.

Figure 1.32 Where the Tasaday People Live

- Many babies and young children die because there is a poor level of nutrition and no modern means of controlling diseases and infections.
- Pressure on the government to exploit valuable timber resources may eventually lead to the destruction of the Tasaday homeland.

29. Reread the information about the Tasaday.
    (a) Write 150 words to explain why they should be protected.
    (b) Write 150 words explaining why the Tasaday should be helped by outsiders.
    (c) What is your opinion on whether or not the Tasaday should be left alone? Explain your answer.

30. Assume that you are to spend two weeks with the Tasaday and that your guide cannot stay with you.
    (a) How would you communicate with them? Give four specific examples.
    (b) Would you attempt to explain modern life to them? Why or why not?

(a)

Rattan-tied stone axe

0   10 cm
Scale

(b)

Steel bolo

Figure 1.33 Old and New Cutting Tools

Changing the Environment

Controlled environments can be created through the use of modern building techniques. Enclosed shopping malls are an example of this kind of control. Some downtown city developments include underground or above-ground walkways between buildings, which allow

Figure 1.34 The Renaissance Center of Detroit

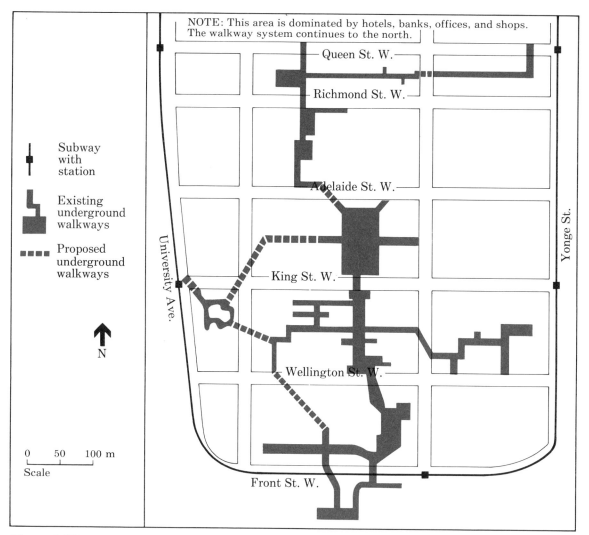

NOTE: This area is dominated by hotels, banks, offices, and shops. The walkway system continues to the north.

Queen St. W.

Richmond St. W.

Adelaide St. W.

King St. W.

Wellington St. W.

Front St. W.

University Ave.

Yonge St.

Subway with station

Existing underground walkways

Proposed underground walkways

N

0   50   100 m

Scale

**Figure 1.35
Toronto's
Underground
Walkways**

people to walk for several kilometres without ever going outside. Underground developments often house offices, stores, hotels, movie theatres, restaurants, and subways. (One plan of underground development is shown in Figure 1.35.)

31. (a) What controlled environments have you lived in or visited?
   (b) Explain the ways in which each environment was controlled and the extent of that environment.
   (c) What were the advantages of controlling each particular environment?
   (d) What drawbacks are there to building a large, artificially controlled environment?

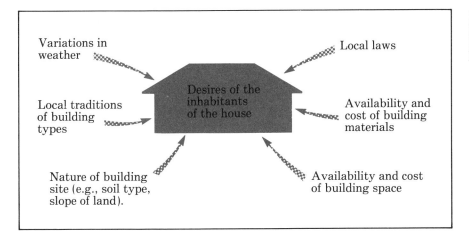

**Figure 1.36
Factors
Determining
Housing Types**

Variations in weather

Local laws

Local traditions of building types

Desires of the inhabitants of the house

Availability and cost of building materials

Nature of building site (e.g., soil type, slope of land).

Availability and cost of building space

All houses, whether large or small, complicated or simple, are designed to make a comfortable living environment. Figure 1.36 outlines the factors that determine the types of housing found within a city or in different parts of the world.

Figure 1.37 illustrates the variety of housing available in Canada.

a   b

c   d

Figure 1.37 Types of Housing in Canada
(a) Large De-
 tached Home
(b) Town Houses
(c) Apartments
(d) An Older
 Home

32. (a) Examine Figure 1.37. In which type of housing do you live? If you do not live in any of the types of housing shown, choose the one that is most like your type of housing and then explain how yours is different.

(b) Describe your housing by referring to its building site, types of materials used, and style relative to other housing nearby.

33. Rank the houses shown in Figure 1.37 according to their probable value. Start with the most expensive. Exclude the apartment buildings.

34. In which type of housing shown in Figure 1.37 would you like to live? Why?

In Canada, our houses are usually made of combinations of brick, stone, metal, glass, and wood. Local building laws control the types that may be built in an area. Similar types of houses tend to be grouped together. In areas that predate building laws, different types of houses can be found together. Where land is in short supply and expensive, houses are built "one on top of the other": apartments, condominiums.

35. Look at the photographs in Figure 1.37.

(a) List the features these houses have in common.

(b) Explain why all houses in Canada require the features that you have listed in (a).

36. (a) List four differences that you can see among the houses in Figure 1.37. In each case make sure that you identify the houses about which you are writing.

(b) Account for these differences, relating them, where relevant, to
   • wealth of the occupants
   • local laws and traditions
   • building materials
   • availability and cost of building materials and nature of the site (the land on which the house is built).

There is a great deal more variety in housing types in other parts of the world than there is in Canada. But wherever houses are located, the type of housing is still determined by the factors illustrated in Figure 1.36.

Figure 1.38 shows distinctive types of housing in various parts of the world.

a

b

c

Figure 1.38
Housing around
the World
(a) Mud Hut in
    Kenya
(b) Poorer Neigh-
    bourhood in
    Barcelona,
    Spain
(c) Flat-topped
    Houses in
    Niger
(d) Row Houses
    in Emmelvord,
    the
    Netherlands
(e) Luxury House
    in Nassau, The
    Bahamas
(f) Chalet in
    Switzerland

d

e

f

37. (a) Set up a table as shown below for the seven types of housing illustrated in Figure 1.38. Using the photographs in the figure and climatic maps in an atlas, fill in the table.

TYPE OF HOUSING	CLIMATE OF AREA	BUILDING MATERIALS	STYLE (SHAPE, SIZE, ETC.)	APPARENT WEALTH OF INHABITANTS
Mud huts Row houses etc.		SAMPLE ONLY		

(b) Choose two of the houses that you have described in (a) and explain the ways in which the people have changed their living environment.

(c) In what ways would the two houses in (b) be suitable or unsuitable for where you live? Be specific about such things as weather, laws, and materials.

38. Design the house of your dreams. Imagine that you have won a million dollars on condition that it is to be used to buy land and to build a house.

(a) Describe where your house would be built. Include information about geographic location, site, and views.

(b) Draw a plan of your house and property showing
   • the dimensions of your lot
   • the outside shape of your house
   • any other significant features *outside* the house (swimming pool, driveway, etc.)
   Use 150 words to explain why you want specific features.

(c) Draw a picture showing what the front of your dream house would look like. List the building materials used and explain why you have chosen them.

(d) Sketch the interior of the house, showing the arrangement of the rooms. Explain the features that you like about your plan.

Changing the Climate and Weather

At present, it is beyond our capabilities to control or change the weather on a large scale. On a small scale, greenhouses enable people to grow limited quantities of plants that might otherwise not develop and survive.

In cities, the buildings, roads, traffic, and heating keep temperatures higher than in surrounding rural areas. Our urban way of life has also affected worldwide climates by pumping pollutants into the air. These pollutants trap heat or reflect energy from the sun and thus change temperatures on the earth's surface.

39. **In the future, it may be possible to control the weather.**
    (a) **What are four advantages?**
    (b) **Control of weather might result in conflict between groups. For example, farmers might want rain whereas cottagers might want continuously sunny weather. List three other possible conflicts.**

Changing the Land

Earlier in this chapter, terracing was discussed—a technique the Japanese use to increase the amount of agricultural land. This method is used in many other mountainous areas of the world. Another approach to the shortage of land is to create land where there was none before.

CASE STUDY

Reclaiming Land in the Netherlands

One of the most spectacular examples of how people can change their environment on a large scale is in the Netherlands, a small country in Western Europe. Over the past thousand years, the

**Figure 1.39
Growth of the
Land Area of
the Netherlands**

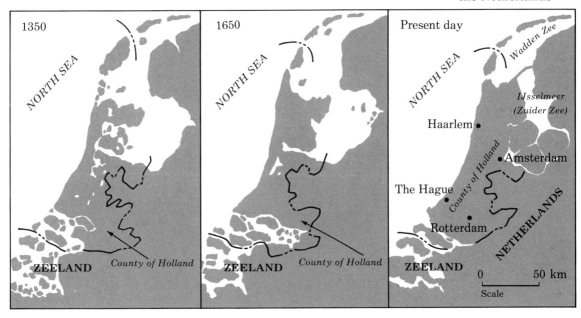

people of the Netherlands have faced many problems. The most pressing of these have been a shortage of land for agriculture and building, and repeated flooding of the low land by rivers and the sea.

The Dutch started to reclaim marshes and small ponds in the ninth century by building **dikes**—banks of earth—around them and draining out the water. Windmills helped to pump out the water—these were later replaced by steam and electrical pumps. Larger, improved dikes were built along the coast to protect the land from the sea.

Between 1927 and 1932, a great dam was completed across the entrance to what was then called the Zuider Zee. The salt water behind the dam slowly became fresh as rivers flowed into IJsselmeer, the lake that was formed (see Figure 1.40).

Dikes were built, surrounding large areas of the lake, and the water inside the dikes was pumped out to expose the lake bed. These areas of reclaimed sea floor are called **polders.** With careful treatment, they were developed into very valuable farmland.

The process of draining the polders of IJsselmeer is a slow and extremely expensive project. People have continued to move into these low-lying areas, and now over 60% of the population of the Netherlands lives below sea level.

Fourteen hundred Dutch people drowned during the storms of 1953 in the southern Netherlands. To protect other members of the population and the land on which they live, a project called the Delta Plan is being undertaken. It involves building many huge

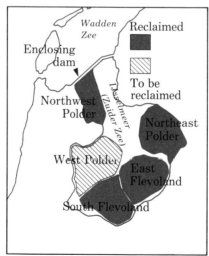

Figure 1.40 Land Reclaimed from the Zuider Zee

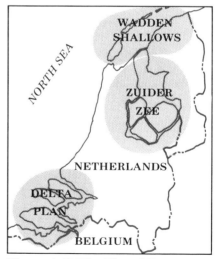

Figure 1.41 The Three Major Land Reclamation Projects in the Netherlands

sea walls and dikes. A future plan involves the reclamation of the shallow waters of the Wadden Zee. Figure 1.41 shows the locations of these projects.

40. Describe the way in which the Dutch people have changed the environment where the polders are now found. Include a description of the area before and after it was reclaimed, and a brief explanation of how the reclaiming was done.

41. (a) Using information from an atlas, list the population densities of Canada, the United States, Hong Kong, Japan, the U.S.S.R., and the United Kingdom.
    (b) In which countries would you expect some land reclamation to be taking place? Give reasons for your answers.

Moving to Another Environment

People have been moving from one place to another for thousands of years. These movements may have been short or long, temporary or permanent, voluntary or forced.

Each day, millions of workers travel to and from their jobs—a relatively short, repeated movement. Similarly each day you get up, go to school, and return home. You may also take part in longer, less frequent movements when you go on vacation.

Much of the movement that goes on in the world is in search of food. Fishing boats follow schools of fish as they swim from one feeding ground to another. In many countries, people herd their animals in search of better pasture. The **nomadic herders** usually repeat the same journey each year, returning to a home base for part of the year.

Other people's **migrations** are permanent. During the last ice age, animals migrated in search of better grazing as the climate changed. Following the herds, people migrated to new areas.

Permanent migrations that have taken place in the last few centuries fall into two main categories: **forced** and **voluntary.** It is estimated that between 12 million and 30 million Africans were forced by the slave trade to move to the Americas during the 1700s. In the latter part of that same century, thousands of British convicts were **deported** and sent to Australia. More recently, some countries have forced certain groups of people to leave because of their racial origin, political views, or religious beliefs.

Sometimes natural disasters, such as earthquakes, erupting volcanoes, and hurricanes, force people to move. Drought and war in the world during the 1970s caused 11 million **refugees** to migrate in search of food and safety. The United Nations spends hundreds of millions of dollars to relieve the miseries of these refugees, but many still die. (Figure 7.11, later in this book, shows where the greatest numbers of refugees are found in the world today.)

The plight of refugees is illustrated by the millions who began fleeing from Ethiopia to Somalia in 1977. On some nights, as many as 2000 people, mostly women and children, would cross the border. Many died, 70% to 80% had tuberculosis, and all of them were starving. Somalia, however, is one of the world's poorest nations and could do very little to help the refugees. The Somalians provided each refugee with a handful of rice and a mug of milk each day, approximately one-quarter of the normal daily requirement of food.

42. **Imagine that enemy forces have invaded a densely populated area of Canada, killing millions of people. You decide to escape by going to a remote area. You have two days to prepare for the move.**
    (a) **Where would you go? Why did you choose this place?**
    (b) **How would you get there? Assume that all sources of fuel are controlled by the occupying army, and that there is no public transport.**
    (c) **Whom would you choose to take with you, and why?**
    (d) **What would you take with you? Remember that you may never be able to return, and that somehow you have to transport these articles!**
    (e) **Choose books to take with you and explain the reasons for your choice.**
    (f) **How would you survive in your new environment? Think carefully about getting food, constructing and maintaining shelter, making clothes, and keeping healthy and happy.**

During the last 300 years, millions of people have moved from densely populated, war-torn Europe to all parts of the world. These people were subjected to push and pull factors. The **push factors**, which encouraged people to leave Europe, included poverty, war, and religious and political oppression. The **pull factors**, which attracted people to other countries, included the possibility of a better standard of living.

	1851–1870	1871–1890	1891–1910	1911–1930	1931–1950	1951–1970
Austria-Hungary	71	294	1551	479	11	77
Belgium	3	23	46	54	49	491
Denmark	8	121	124	116	138	339
Finland	0	26	218	140	10	103
France	63	185	104	36	5	1965
Germany	1450	1968	801	655	739	5282
Italy	32	1160	5195	3564	702	3737
Netherlands	36	69	52	54	79	771
Norway	134	272	286	149	16	160
Poland	0	0	0	634	164	0
Portugal	124	316	590	1397	177	923
Russia	0	346	1392	420	0	0
Spain	10	585	1882	1866	298	761
Sweden	139	430	529	193	31	216
Switzerland	21	121	72	81	65	121
U.K. and Ireland	2885	5108	5299	4738	1017	3185

Figure 1.42 European Migration, 1851–1970 (In Thousands)

The Impact of Modern Communications

Modern communications have brought people around the world in touch with one another as never before. Yet the tremendous variety of living standards, beliefs, and political systems continues to create tensions that could lead to disaster. It is important that as many people as possible learn to understand the forces at work in the world. Only in this way can sensible decisions be made and solutions be found to worldwide problems.

VOCABULARY

affluence	fossil fuels	OPEC
alluvial deposits	geologist	petrochemical
cartel	ghetto	industry
collage	Gross National	pie graph
commodity	Product per capita	polder
contaminate	(GNP per capita)	pull factor
dehydration	inflation	push factor
dense	inhospitable	refugee
deported	large scale	soil erosion
dike	literacy	sparse
eradicate	migration	terracing
exploitation	natural resources	urban
forced migration	nomadic herders	voluntary migration

RESEARCH QUESTIONS

To answer these questions, you will probably need to refer to library resources and other sources of information.

1. Investigate a recent earthquake or volcanic eruption. Use books, magazines, and newspapers for information on the topic.
   (a) Draw a simple map illustrating the location of the occurrence. Include the date.
   (b) Describe the strength of the earthquake or the type of eruption of the volcano.
   (c) Explain how it affected the land, natural objects, buildings, and people.
   (d) What efforts were made to rescue property and living things? How many lives were lost? What was the value of the property damaged or lost?
   (e) Describe any attempts to re-establish human activity in the area after the earthquake or volcanic eruption.

2. In question 11(b) in this chapter, you were asked to plot a pie graph to represent the following information. The proportions of various categories of land in hospitable areas:

	%
Cultivated land	49
Temperate grasslands and woodlands	20
Tropical grasslands	20
Areas of high urban concentration	8
Irrigated land	3

   (a) Devise two other, original methods of representing this information.
   (b) Plot this information. Each diagram should be fully labelled and have a suitable title.
   (c) Make a large pie diagram with an approximate diameter of 40 cm, using the data given above. In each sector (slice) of your diagram, make a collage of pictures representing that kind of land.

3. Answer the following questions on the oceans of the world. The subject catalogue in your library will give you information under the headings "Oceans", "Exploration", and "Mapping the Ocean". Magazines and periodicals will also provide important facts.
   (a) Why do people explore the oceans?
   (b) What techniques and equipment are used to explore the oceans?
   (c) Where has ocean research been conducted?

(d) What types of information have been found?

(e) In what ways are the oceans and their floors being used today? Give specific examples.

(f) What potential is there for use of the oceans in the future?

4. Research one of the following diseases: yellow fever, sleeping sickness, malaria.

(a) Draw a map showing the distribution of that disease in the world today.

(b) Describe the symptoms of the disease. Describe any treatment available, including any side effects.

(c) Explain how the disease spreads.

(d) Describe attempts being made to combat the disease. Comment on their degree of success or failure.

5. How is your life affected by products from, events in, or forces from other areas of the world? Focus your research on the following areas of concern.

(a) What are the countries of origin or manufacture of your personal items such as clothing, appliances, books, magazines, household objects, canned food? Design a chart to display your findings.

(b) What events that have taken place in other countries in the last week (as recorded in newspapers or magazines) could affect your personal life?

(c) What transportation routes link your local area to other countries of the world?

6. On a sheet of bristol board, create a collage based on the theme "Contrasts in the World Today". Use pictures from newspapers, magazines, and flyers. You might choose, for example, a picture showing a very rich lifestyle and one depicting a very poor lifestyle and place them side by side. Label your pictures appropriately.

SECTION II | Economic Geography

The Origins of Human Economic Activity

Introduction

Cultures of the world are rooted in prehistory. Early human activity laid the groundwork for much of what is done today and for the cultures of today.

Only educated guesses can be made about what really happened before written records were kept. In spite of the lack of records, it is known that major discoveries were made by early men and women. The development of fire or seed agriculture may not seem significant today, especially considering that now people have walked on the moon. Yet it would have been impossible for humans to walk on the moon if fire had not been discovered. Those early developments were revolutionary: they changed the course of human history.

From Hunting and Gathering to Agriculture

Only in relatively recent times have most people been able to obtain food conveniently. One stage in very early human history is referred to as the Stone Age (approximately one million years ago), when life was sustained through **hunting and gathering**. People, in their family or tribal groups, wandered across the landscape in search of food. The men would hunt wild animals such as boars (wild pigs), deer, bison, and wild sheep. They would use spears, sharpened sticks, clubs and, later, bows and arrows, to kill their prey. The women and children searched for edible berries, roots, and leaves.

Using simple digging sticks, they also hunted snakes, larvae, and grubs for their meals. This hunting-and-gathering way of life has been referred to as a **hand-to-mouth existence.** Today hunting-and-gathering peoples are found, for the most part, in very marginal areas in which food production through plant and animal domestication is not easily achieved. An important feature of the hunting-and-gathering way of life is that food and other resources are thinly spread in unpredictable arrays across the landscape. Everyone has to work in order for the group to survive, but even with co-operation the task of securing food is not easy. Hunting and gathering, therefore, cannot support large numbers of people.

Without more advanced **technology** for producing food, human life would still be dependent on hunting and gathering, with all its limitations. The term "technology" refers to devices developed from knowledge, skills, or resources, and used for some practical purpose.

1. (a) **If you were stranded in the middle of a forest with no food and no modern tools, what would you choose to eat?**
   (b) **From your answer to (a), what conclusions can you draw about the progress our society has made in food production?**
   (c) **In approximately 150 words, explain whether or not you would like to live in a hunting-and-gathering society.**

Domestication of Plants

Farming was a significant development in human history. There are no written records concerning this advance. Whether by design or by accident, or by a combination of both, the cultivation of seed and root crops—plant farming—evolved. People may have noticed that plants grew up where fruits and vegetables had been discarded. They may then have understood that seeds and roots could be planted to produce crops. This development probably occurred in many parts of the world at approximately the same period in human history.

Plant farming in its basic form involves the deliberate setting out of roots or seeds in the soil. The resulting plants are grown under human care. This process is also called the **domestication of plants.**

One example of plant domestication is **root agriculture,** a major development in food production. It involves the planting of fleshy roots or tubers, such as the potato, in the ground to grow and produce full-sized plants with more tubers. Root agriculture is thought to have first occurred with the cultivation of the cassava and taro in Southeast Asia, in or near present-day Vietnam.

Figure 2.1
A Potato with
Eyes and Roots

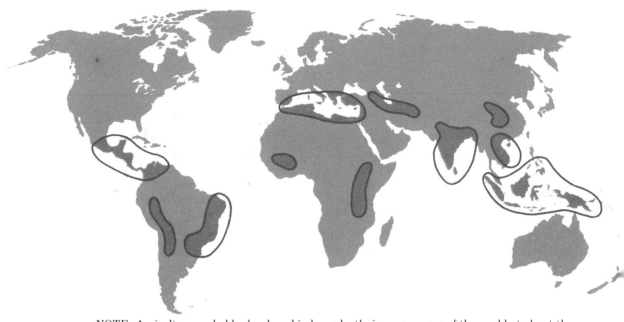

NOTE: Agriculture probably developed independently in many areas of the world at about the same time.

**Figure 2.2
Regions of the
World Where
Agriculture
Probably
Originated**

Seed agriculture is another example of plant domestication. It involves the planting of seeds to produce a crop.

Both root and seed agriculture allowed a tribe to tend and harvest a crop rather than to continually search for wild plants for food. In the early stages, both types of agriculture were likely occurring at the same time as hunting and gathering. As this early agriculture was able to produce more food, some tribes did less hunting and gathering. They then learned how to store the surplus produce that was grown.

Agriculture developed in a number of different regions around the world. Many of the foods that you eat every day had their origins in the regions marked on the map in Figure 2.2. Corn, for example, originated in Central America, and then spread through North America to Europe, Africa, and the rest of the world. The banana had its origins in Southeast Asia and spread through the tropical regions. At first the spread of crops was slow, but as methods of transportation improved, crops spread quickly to different regions of the world.

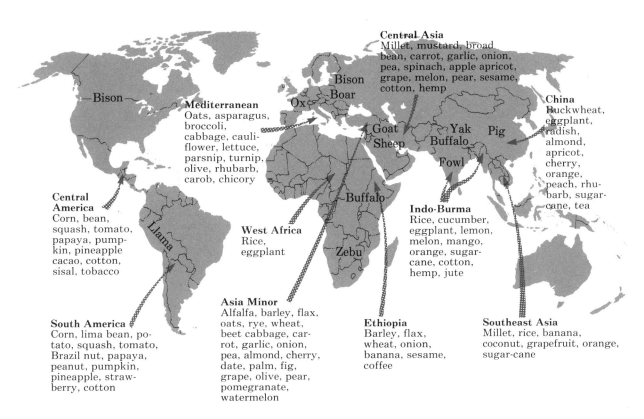

Bison

Mediterranean
Oats, asparagus, broccoli, cabbage, cauliflower, lettuce, parsnip, turnip, olive, rhubarb, carob, chicory

Ox

Boar

Bison

Central Asia
Millet, mustard, broad bean, carrot, garlic, onion, pea, spinach, apple apricot, grape, melon, pear, sesame, cotton, hemp

China
Buckwheat, eggplant, radish, almond, apricot, cherry, orange, peach, rhubarb, sugar-cane, tea

Goat
Sheep

Yak
Buffalo

Pig

Fowl

Central America
Corn, bean, squash, tomato, papaya, pumpkin, pineapple cacao, cotton, sisal, tobacco

Llama

West Africa
Rice, eggplant

Buffalo

Zebu

Indo-Burma
Rice, cucumber, eggplant, lemon, melon, mango, orange, sugarcane, cotton, hemp, jute

South America
Corn, lima bean, potato, squash, tomato, Brazil nut, papaya, peanut, pumpkin, pineapple, strawberry, cotton

Asia Minor
Alfalfa, barley, flax, oats, rye, wheat, beet cabbage, carrot, garlic, onion, pea, almond, cherry, date, palm, fig, grape, olive, pear, pomegranate, watermelon

Ethiopia
Barley, flax, wheat, onion, banana, sesame, coffee

Southeast Asia
Millet, rice, banana, coconut, grapefruit, orange, sugar-cane

**Figure 2.3
Regions of Origin
of Important
Crops and
Animals**

2. (a) List the various foods that you ate yesterday. Be specific.
   (b) Opposite each type of food eaten, record (where possible) the region of the world in which it originated. Use Figure 2.3 as your guide.

3. (a) Which regions of the world appear to have contributed the most to our diets?
   (b) Using an atlas and Figure 2.3, describe the climate and landscape of each major centre of agriculture.
   (c) Did any crops originate in Canada?

4. (a) In an atlas, turn to a map of South America. The potato originated in the Andes Mountains in Peru, Ecuador, and Bolivia. Discuss the obstacles to the spread of this crop to North America and Europe.
   (b) Who do you think would take a food like the potato from one region to another? Why would they take the potato at all?

As people began to grow field crops, they attempted to increase
the **yield**, or the amount of food grown, on a set piece of land.
One method of increasing a crop yield was **irrigation**, or the artificial watering of plants. (See Figure 2.4.) In drier areas of the world,
irrigation often meant the difference between the success or failure
of a crop. In turn, this determined whether or not people in the area
had enough food to survive.

Over the years farmers selected the strongest plants and **cross-
bred** them to produce more desirable crops. The new crops were
often healthier, more disease-resistant, and produced a higher yield.
With the increase in crop yields came an increase in population
because there was more food available. Figure 2.5 shows the results
of cross-breeding corn to produce a larger and healthier cob.

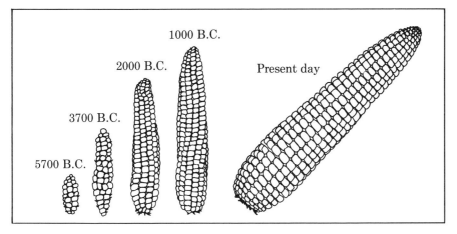

Figure 2.5 The Change of the Corn Cob over Time from Its Probable Origin in Mexico

5. What might have given an early farmer the idea of irrigating crops to increase yields?

6. Describe how irrigation is carried out on some farms in Canada.

7. (a) Under what circumstances is irrigation impractical? Give reasons for your answer.
   (b) In what environments is irrigation of little use? Briefly explain your answer.

With the domestication of plants, people did not have to be continually on the move and could settle down in one place. No longer needing to follow the animal herds or wander in search of fruit and seeds, they could confine their activities to a much smaller area. Eventually, as agriculture became more and more productive, people were able to settle in one location for a number of years and follow a **sedentary lifestyle**. A sedentary lifestyle means that people do not travel to a great extent in order to obtain food.

Domestication of Animals

During the hunting-and-gathering period, people did not rely on animal power to help in their day-to-day life. They had not reached the stage of **domestication of animals**, or taming them for their own use. Later, however, domestic animals became very important.

One of the first animals to be domesticated was the dog. As a camp follower, the dog likely lived on food scraps discarded by wandering tribes. People would leave their garbage or unused food in a pile called a **midden**. At night or when no one was nearby, the dogs would probably raid a midden and eat what food they could. The dog became a domestic animal that was closely dependent on human activity.

Other animals such as sheep, goats, cattle, and horses also were subject to human influence. For these animals, domestication meant a regular food supply and some human protection from their enemies. Domesticated animals provided those early people with a ready, portable food supply, and with animal skins.

Through the years, domestic animals were cross-bred to improve size, quantity of meat or milk, quality of coat or hide, or other characteristics. Wild cattle, for example, bear little resemblance to modern dairy cattle. Cross-breeding is principally responsible for this change. The improvement in milk production in Canada between 1930 and 1980 (see Figure 2.6) was also partly the result of cross-breeding cattle, for the specific purpose of making them become better milk producers.

Figure 2.6 Improvement in Milk Production in Ontario, 1930–80

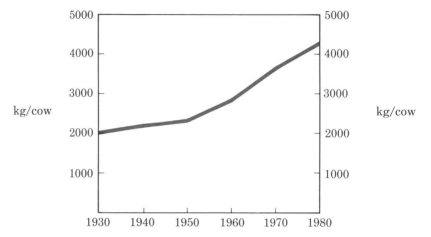

By controlling the breeding of various domestic animals, people have been able to assure themselves of a fairly reliable food supply. In turn, this steady food supply has encouraged other developments such as the settlement of villages and towns. Linked with other changes, animal domestication has led to the development of our modern civilization.

Improvements in Agricultural Techniques

Once people in many parts of the world had begun to grow crops, innovations were introduced to improve crop yield and quality. Better techniques were also developed for storing, transporting, and marketing agricultural products.

Let us examine some of the improvements that allowed great changes in farming to take place. Each of the tools in Figure 2.7 was used to plough or turn over the soil. The foot plough gave way

NAME OF TOOL	APPEARANCE		HOW IT WORKS
Digging stick	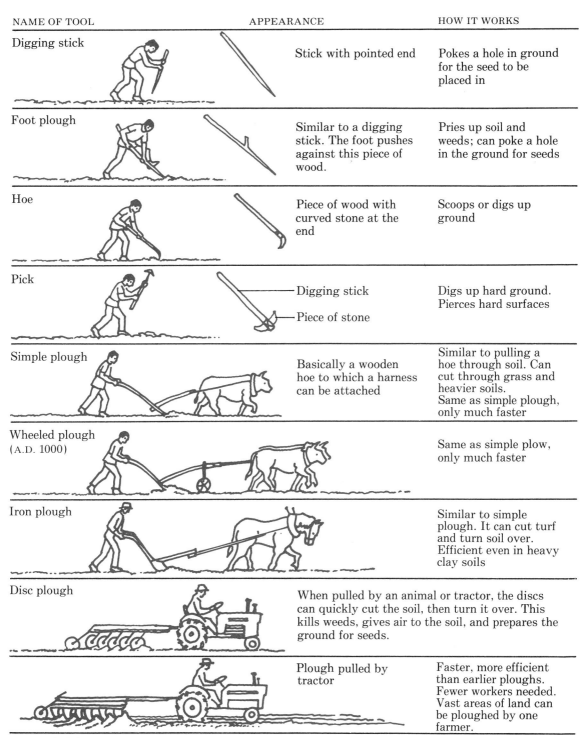	Stick with pointed end	Pokes a hole in ground for the seed to be placed in
Foot plough		Similar to a digging stick. The foot pushes against this piece of wood.	Pries up soil and weeds; can poke a hole in the ground for seeds
Hoe		Piece of wood with curved stone at the end	Scoops or digs up ground
Pick		Digging stick Piece of stone	Digs up hard ground. Pierces hard surfaces
Simple plough		Basically a wooden hoe to which a harness can be attached	Similar to pulling a hoe through soil. Can cut through grass and heavier soils. Same as simple plough, only much faster
Wheeled plough (A.D. 1000)			Same as simple plow, only much faster
Iron plough			Similar to simple plough. It can cut turf and turn soil over. Efficient even in heavy clay soils
Disc plough		When pulled by an animal or tractor, the discs can quickly cut the soil, then turn it over. This kills weeds, gives air to the soil, and prepares the ground for seeds.	
		Plough pulled by tractor	Faster, more efficient than earlier ploughs. Fewer workers needed. Vast areas of land can be ploughed by one farmer.

Figure 2.7 Changes in Agricultural Equipment

Figure 2.8
(a) Men Using a Foot Plough in Peru
(b) A Foot Plough

a

b

to simple animal-powered ploughs, which saved many hours of hard labour and prepared the soil well. The iron plough (see Figure 2.9), introduced into Europe in the 1600s, brought about a revolution in agriculture. Because iron is much stronger than wood, these ploughs could cut heavy soils that had not been farmed before. Gradually, farmers were able to do their ploughing more quickly and with less effort. Improved ploughing methods, as each new type of plough was developed, resulted in increased food production.

Figure 2.9 An Iron Plough

8. (a) **Name two great advantages the iron plough had over previous ploughs.**
   (b) **How could the iron plough help to raise the standard of living of Europeans in the 1600s?**
   (c) **In what three ways could the iron plough help bring about a "revolution" in farming?**

9. (a) **Make a list of common garden tools.**
   (b) **Beside each tool, write the name of the tool from Figure 2.7 that is most like it or that has the same basic use.**

Early Urban Centres

With the domestication of plants and animals, major changes began to occur in human activity. People started to construct more permanent homes, which were often grouped together to form small villages. These built-up areas are described as **urban**. Village life had significant advantages over life on the move.

New farming techniques brought increases in food production and, eventually, a **food surplus**. The surplus allowed some people to devote their energy to activities other than farming or searching for food. Craftsmen, for instance, could spend their time producing items such as jewellery, religious artifacts, pottery, and wood carvings.

Such societies usually had a political-religious leader, sometimes called a **priest-king**. Food and other supplies would be brought to such a leader for redistribution throughout the settlement. The early schools and writings were probably located in or near the home of the leader. The community, by this time, would have grown to the size of a small town.

10. (a) **What power or control might a leader have over those in the town and on the farms?**

(b) What might these leaders develop to exert their power? Explain.

11. Explain how the production of a food surplus led to a major change in the course of human history.

12. (a) Suggest reasons why a village would continue growing.
(b) What might limit its growth?

Early Technological Developments

Most of the highly industrialized areas of the world were once inhabited by people with a Stone Age technology. Slowly, ideas developed and spread from one area to another. The level of technology rose more quickly in some places than in others, depending upon certain major breakthroughs. These included the use and control of fire, the ability to communicate, and the development of the wheel.

Fire

Fire occurs naturally as a result of lightning strikes and volcanic eruptions. But in the early Stone Age, people learned how to create fire and control it for their own use.

Fire enabled early peoples to cook much of the meat they had obtained from hunting. This also eliminated many of the diseases related to the consumption of raw meat.

Modern industry to a great extent depends upon the controlled use of fire. An important burning process is the combustion of coal to produce electricity. Another is the burning of gasoline to power the engines of modern cars.

13. (a) In what ways would each of the following activities be affected by the lack of the controlled use of fire or sparks?
    • flying an airplane
    • making steel
    • heating and lighting your school
(b) List three activities that do not rely in any way on the burning process.

14. If you were isolated for many years in a remote Canadian forest without matches or other "modern" methods of producing fire,
(a) how would you start a fire?
(b) in what ways would fire be vital to your survival?

The Ability to Communicate

We learn much from other people's knowledge and experience. Before the development of writing, information was passed on by word of mouth.

Writing developed as a way to record the sale of property. The first people to transform words and ideas into signs on clay tablets were the Sumerians, who lived 5000 years ago in Mesopotamia (present-day Iraq). Writing also enabled the Sumerians to record significant events and the beliefs of their priests and philosophers. Examples of ancient hieroglyphs, and of the development of a modern alphabet from ancient ones, are shown in Figure 2.10.

In Germany in the mid-1500s, a major development occurred in the world of communication—the invention of the printing press

Hieroglyphs (a system of writing composed of pictures)
These are some interpretations of writing from early Egypt:

⚲ = live   ∫ = be healthy   👁 = eye   = to build

Alphabets
Latin   ⋖ ⊟ ⋊ ○ ۹   Modern European   *E H K O R*
Greek   ⅀ H Ƙ ◇ Ʀ

**Figure 2.10
Writing: Ancient and Modern**

(see Figure 2.11). Although printing had been developed in Asia hundreds of years before, it was probably not known to the inventors of European printing. For the first time in European history, multiple copies of books could be produced by machine in far less time than that required to hand-letter the books. Knowledge spread more quickly and more widely than ever before.

**Figure 2.11
An Early
Printing Works**

Today, printed material, radio, television, telephones, tapes, teletype machines, computers, and satellites spread information quickly to millions of people.

15. List and discuss five ways in which you would be affected if human beings did not have the skill of writing.

16. (a) If you were able to choose, what information would you like to have recorded about your life and possessions?
    (b) With the help of your teacher, parents, and friends, list the type of information that is already recorded about you.
    (c) As you grow older, what kind of information will be added?

17. (a) Explain how education today is dependent upon written material. Comment on the importance of being able to explain your ideas in writing.
    (b) How will the use of written material in education change in coming years? Explain your answer fully.

The Development of the Wheel

The lever, the pulley, and the wheel are all based on the same principle (see Figure 2.12).

The lever and pulley are important in helping to lift objects. In the early explorations of the Americas, for example, pulleys on sailing ships were used to raise and lower the sails. When wheels were first invented about 5000 years ago in Sumer, they were used in war chariots, giving the Sumerians marked superiority in battle. By the year A.D. 700, the wheel was adapted for use in water-powered mills. This was as major a change as the changes that occurred during the Industrial Revolution, centuries later.

18. Examine this list of frequently used objects.
    • a pair of scissors
    • a car jack
    • a wood screw
    (a) For each object, state whether it works on the principle of the lever, the pulley, or the wheel.
    (b) Explain how each object operates.

19. Choose any appliance that you are familiar with that has moving parts, such as a food mixer or blender, a stereo, or a can opener. Explain how it uses the lever, pulley, and/or wheel.

20. Imagine that we lived in a world without wheels. How would your life change as a result? Give at least six examples of change.

The lever, the pulley, and the wheel are all based on the same principle—namely, a small force can be used to move a larger load if the force is applied through a longer distance than that involved in moving the load directly.

Figure 2.12 How the Lever, the Pulley, and the Wheel Function

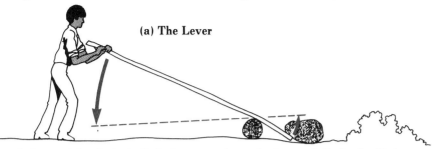

(a) The Lever

Push down with relatively little force on a long plank...and the load will rise a short distance.

(b) The Pulley

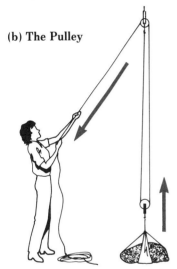

Pull 2 m on the rope...and the load will rise 1 m.

(c) The Wheel

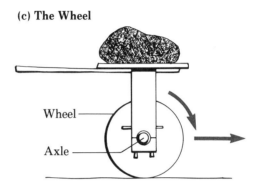

Wheel

Axle

By turning the wheel through a long distance, one turns the axle through a shorter distance, thereby moving a heavier load than would be possible if the force were applied directly to the axle.

Primitive Technology Today

Few people in the world today still use primitive, Stone Age technology. The Amazonian Indians and the Pygmies of Zaire are examples of peoples still using this technology. The Tasaday people, described in Chapter 1, are another example. The Tasadays live in a small group and obtain food by gathering it from the stream and the forest. Their shelter is a cave, their clothing is made from leaves, and they make only the simplest of tools.

Within the Australian Aborigine population there is still a small group who live as their ancestors did, although many Aborigines have adapted by choice or by necessity to the culture now prevalent in Australia. The Aborigines who follow their ancestral way of life

Figure 2.13
Australian Nom-
adic Aborigines
Living As Their
Stone Age
Ancestors Did

live in hot grassland and desert areas, and sleep in the open or build temporary lean-tos of grass, bark, leaves, and small trees. They use digging sticks, stone-cutting tools, and wooden spears when hunting for small animals. (See Figure 2.13.) The women gather berries, seeds, roots, nuts, grubs, and honey to add to the meat. They lead a **nomadic** existence, wandering in search of food, within a given territory and at specific times of the year.

Anthropologists claim that there are probably no areas of the world in which people live completely isolated from modern technology. When a group of people such as the nomadic Aborigines are exposed to modern technology, they usually experience **culture shock.** Their traditions and ways of life are suddenly challenged and often collapse. The Australian government has attempted to help these Aborigines, but major problems still remain. In some situations, modern technology was introduced too quickly. In others, government programs did not help to solve the problems faced by the nomadic Aborigines. Figure 2.14 shows the impact of change on the way of life of the nomadic Aborigines.

Figure 2.14
Advantages and
Disadvantages of
Modern Change
for the Nomadic
Aborigines

ADVANTAGES

—secure and varied food
  supply
—comfortable living
  accommodations
—material goods, such as
  televisions

DISADVANTAGES

—lack of independence
—unemployment
—way of life challenged and
  sometimes destroyed
—different values of old and
  new generations

21. **Why do you think so few groups in the world still use Stone Age technology?**

22. (a) **Suggest five examples of modern technology that would appeal to a nomadic Aborigine.**
    (b) **Explain the appeal of each of the five examples from (a) and the impact it would have on that individual and his or her family.**

23. (a) **Examine Figure 2.15 and then rank the continents from highest to lowest "value added per worker".**
    (b) **Using an atlas, suggest the physical problems that exist in the countries with the lowest levels of modern technology.**
    (c) **Using an atlas, suggest other factors that also relate to the problems and benefits of modern technology.**

**Figure 2.15
Worker Productivity around the World**

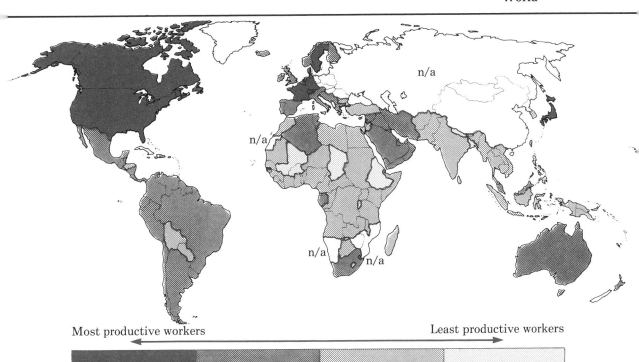

Most productive workers

Least productive workers

NOTES: Worker productivity depends largely on the level of technology in use. The divisions on this map are based on "value added per worker".

In some oil-producing countries, value added per worker may not reflect the level of technology.

The label "n/a" indicates areas for which figures are not available.

The Impact of Early Technology

The early technology discussed in this chapter can be regarded as the first major phase of human technological development. The second major phase of development first took place in Europe in the form of the Industrial Revolution. The effect of the Industrial Revolution was eventually felt around the world, spreading to countries such as the United States and Japan, as we shall see in the next chapter.

VOCABULARY

cross-breeding	hand-to-mouth	priest-king
culture shock	existence	root agriculture
domestication of	hunting and	sedentary lifestyle
animals	gathering	seed agriculture
domestication of	irrigation	technology
plants	midden	urban
food surplus	nomadic	yield
	plant farming	

RESEARCH QUESTIONS

To answer these questions, you will probably need to refer to library resources and other sources of information.

1. Using your library resources, identify three groups of people, past or present, who used or use Stone Age technology. For each group discuss the following:
   (a) the location of their homes
   (b) their specific tools and weapons
   (c) their homes, clothes, and food
   (d) changes they have experienced as a result of the impact of modern technology
   (e) prospects for the future

2. The progress of knowledge and technology in the world was interrupted by the destruction of the ancient library of Alexandria in A.D. 47, according to some sources.
   (a) List the famous scholars who used the Alexandrian Library.
   (b) Choose four of these scholars and describe the most important contribution that each made.
   (c) What led to the destruction of the library?
   (d) Imagine that the library had not been destroyed. In what ways might your life be different? Give three examples.

The Economic Development of the United Kingdom, the United States, and Japan

Introduction

Technological advances continued slowly in Western Europe throughout the Middle Ages, the Renaissance, and into the mid-seventeenth century. Beginning in the early eighteenth century, however, developments in technology (inventions and discoveries) began to have a greater effect on society. Figure 3.1 illustrates the impact of these technological changes since that time. The Western world was not to see such rapid technological change again until the beginning of the twentieth century.

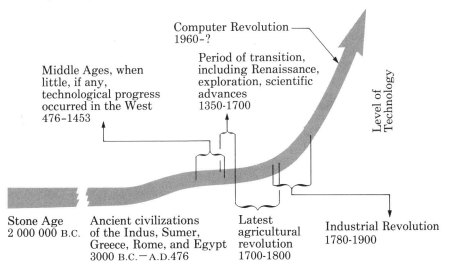

Computer Revolution — 1960-?

Period of transition, including Renaissance, exploration, scientific advances 1350-1700

Middle Ages, when little, if any, technological progress occurred in the West 476–1453

Level of Technology

Stone Age 2 000 000 B.C.

Ancient civilizations of the Indus, Sumer, Greece, Rome, and Egypt 3000 B.C.–A.D.476

Latest agricultural revolution 1700-1800

Industrial Revolution 1780-1900

Time

Figure 3.1 Changes in the Level of Technology from Prehistoric to Modern Times

One hundred years ago, Europe was considered to be the centre of the industrialized world. (**Industrialization** involves the widespread use of machines to perform work for people.) Industrial technology later spread to other areas of the world, particularly to North America. Japan, in turn, has become industrialized in the last 40 years. The Japanese have improved on much of the technology that originated in Europe and North America.

The Industrial Revolution in the United Kingdom

In Western Europe after 1700 new technology was introduced in both agriculture and industry. Many of these changes first took place in the United Kingdom as it is known today, but then called "Great Britain" because of its large empire of colonies (India, Jamaica, and Singapore, among others). A number of factors help to explain its industrial leadership between 1800 and 1900:

- *a more democratic system of government,* which allowed people freedom of choice. As in all societies today, however, this freedom was restricted by the need for individuals to earn enough money to live on.
- *a strong work ethic,* which valued and encouraged productive work.
- *the capitalist system,* by which those who invested wisely would receive a return on their money. If, for example, a businessperson invested money in a company that turned a profit, he or she could keep that profit. This fact was a key **incentive** (encouragement) to those in business to advance technology.
- *the presence of certain natural resources* in the United Kingdom, such as coal and iron ore. The availability of these resources was critical for many industries, such as steel manufacturing, which was vital in the construction of railroads and machinery.
- *a secure banking and financial system,* which could supply the money to be invested in roads, railways, schools, and factories.
- *a huge empire,* from which the U.K. could receive raw materials. The British Empire reached its peak in about 1900. Figure 3.2 shows the extent of the empire at that time.

1. (a) What impact would the U.K.'s industrial policy have on the growth of industry in its colonies?
   (b) What might the colonies do to change the impact?
   (c) What would be the U.K.'s reaction to the changes suggested in (b)? Explain your answer.

NOTE: Many of the smaller parts of the empire, such as islands, are not shown.

Figure 3.2 The British Empire in 1900

Agricultural Change

Scientific improvements in agriculture resulted in important changes to the British economic system. These improvements meant more food was produced by fewer people. Wealthy landowners, for example, started to use improved agricultural methods in the second half of the 1700s. They built fences, walls, and hedges around fields to carefully control their use. Many marshes were drained for farming, and fertilizers were used. A four-year **rotation** of crops was introduced to enrich the soil and reduce plant diseases.

Figure 3.3 Three Systems of Rotation

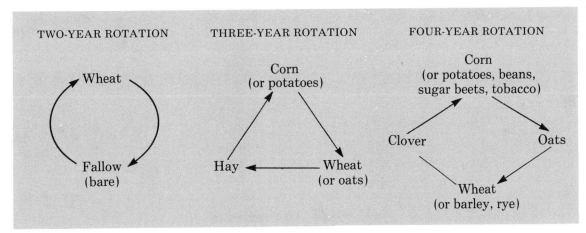

TWO-YEAR ROTATION

Wheat
Fallow (bare)

THREE-YEAR ROTATION

Corn (or potatoes)
Hay
Wheat (or oats)

FOUR-YEAR ROTATION

Corn (or potatoes, beans, sugar beets, tobacco)
Clover
Oats
Wheat (or barley, rye)

New kinds of farm equipment, designed to improve output, were also introduced. Jethro Tull's seed drill (c. 1701) enabled seeds to be planted quickly at the correct spacing and depth. As a result, crop yields increased.

Many small farmers who did not adopt this new technology were forced out of business. In addition, many farm labourers lost their jobs and were replaced by machines. These people and their families were forced to move to the cities to find work. This process is called **urbanization.**

As people from the countryside poured into the cities and towns, they took industrial jobs. Unable to produce their own food and goods, the new wage labourers created a demand for the manufactured goods of the new factories in the United Kingdom. The influx of former farm labourers into the towns also meant that the population of many towns grew. In Northern England for instance, cities doubled in population between 1800 and 1830.

The wealthy landowners reinvested their profits in industry and transportation. Very little of the money earned from industry was paid to the workers, who generally received minimal wages. This created hardships for workers but built up industry.

The British Empire

The British Empire was crucial to the growth of British industry. Not only did the U.K. bring back raw materials from its vast empire, it also sold its goods to these markets in return. Goods that were relatively inexpensive such as tea or furs were imported into the U.K. and then taxed by the government. Although these imported goods then became expensive, the government benefited from the revenue. Manufactured goods which were shipped from the U.K. to the colonies were relatively expensive. A number of private companies invested their profits in the development of roads and railways in India, North America, Australia, and Africa. Some of the profits returned to the U.K., paying for approximately one-third of the imports of raw materials and food to the U.K.

With the development of the steamship, the U.K.'s merchant ships were able to travel even more around the world. By 1914, 80% of its grain was imported, largely on those steamships.

The Development of Industry in the Cities

The industry that spearheaded the U.K.'s industrialization and economic take-off was **textile** (cloth) manufacturing. The statistics in Figure 3.4 indicate how new machinery affected the amount of cotton used in textile manufacture.

DATE	VALUE (In Thousands of Pounds)
1760	0
1780	211
1800	1 848
1820	4 934
1840	19 500

2. (a) Using the statistics in Figure 3.4, construct a bar graph to show the growth of imports of cotton by the U.K. from 1760 to 1840.

(b) What other developments would have to occur in the U.K. for the country to be able to accommodate the increase in imported cotton?

3. If you were a farmer in the U.K. in the early 1800s and you had to leave your farm for the city, what four major disruptive changes would occur in your life?

The increased output of the textile industry resulted from the invention of a variety of new machines designed to speed up production. The introduction of water power and then steam power allowed more and heavier work to be done more quickly than before. Later, sewing machines were introduced to allow large-scale production of affordable clothing. One sewing machine could do the work of several people, and usually more accurately.

Figure 3.5
Machines
Developed for
the Textile
Industry

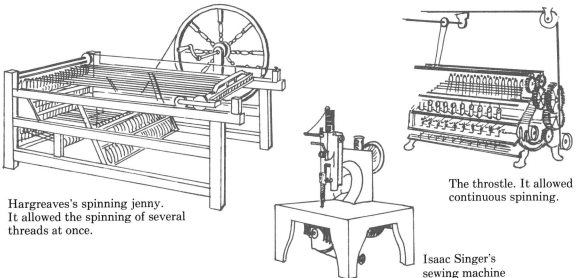

Hargreaves's spinning jenny. It allowed the spinning of several threads at once.

Isaac Singer's sewing machine

The throstle. It allowed continuous spinning.

Figure 3.6 New Technology and Its Impact on the United Kingdom

The textile industry was not the only industry to be affected by the introduction of new technology. Transportation, mining, steel manufacturing, and agriculture were also greatly changed. Figure 3.6 outlines some of these changes.

	INVENTION/DEVELOPMENT	INVENTOR/DEVELOPER	DATE	IMPORTANCE
AGRICULTURE	Seed drill and hoe	Jethro Tull	1701; 1709-15	Improved yields resulted. Fewer people were required in farming, so more were available for factory work.
	Threshing machine	Andrew Meikle	1784	
	Reaping machine	Daniel Bell	1828	
	Artificial fertilizer	John Bennet Lawes	1842	
FACTORIES	Flying shuttle	John Kay	1733	These machines greatly increased the speed and scale of production. Products could be sold in the colonies for big profits. Many machines were powered by water or steam.
	Spinning jenny	James Hargreaves	1764	
	Spinning frame	Richard Arkwright	1769	
	Spinning mule	Samuel Crompton	1779	
	Power loom	Edmund Cartwright	1785-87	
	Bessemer steel process	Henry Bessemer	1855	Stronger steel products, better ships.
MINES	Pumps and machinery for coal mines	Thomas Savery	1698	More coal could be recovered from greater depths. This was vital for industrial development, especially for the steel industry and, later, the coal-gas industry.
TRANSPORTATION	Transatlantic steamboat	Isambard Kingdom Brunel	1838	Large steamboats made worldwide transportation faster and more reliable.
	Steam railway locomotive	Richard Trevithick	1803	Fast, inexpensive transportation of materials and people contributed to the progress of industry.
	Railways	George Stephenson	1822	

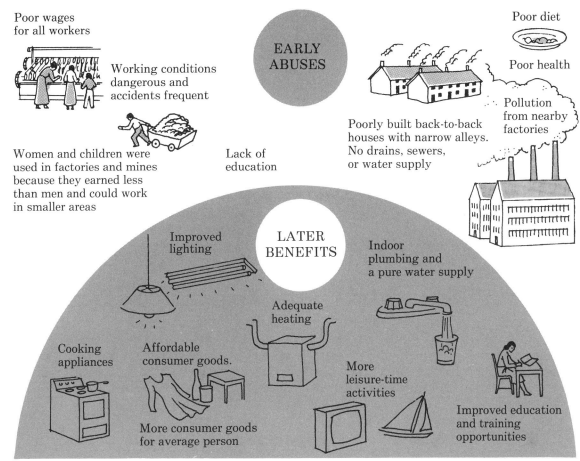

EARLY ABUSES

Poor wages for all workers

Working conditions dangerous and accidents frequent

Women and children were used in factories and mines because they earned less than men and could work in smaller areas

Lack of education

Poor diet

Poor health

Pollution from nearby factories

Poorly built back-to-back houses with narrow alleys. No drains, sewers, or water supply

LATER BENEFITS

Improved lighting

Indoor plumbing and a pure water supply

Adequate heating

Cooking appliances

Affordable consumer goods.

More leisure-time activities

More consumer goods for average person

Improved education and training opportunities

Figure 3.7 Results of the Industrial Revolution in the United Kingdom and Many Other Countries

In the early years of the Industrial Revolution, the drastic changes that occurred in living and working conditions had many negative effects on those who worked in the factories. The advances in industry, however, had a positive side, as shown in Figure 3.7.

That many of the factory workers and their families suffered squalid living conditions, nevertheless, can be seen from the following paragraph adapted from the novel *Mary Barton,* written in 1848 by Elizabeth C. Gaskell.

Any visitor to the cellar where this family lived had to go down one step to enter. "It was very dark inside" and most of the window panes were broken and stuffed with cloth. As a result there was a "dusky light that pervaded the place even at mid-day... [the] smell was so fetid as almost to knock...two men down. Quickly recovering themselves," these men began to make their way through the darkness, only "to see three or four little children rolling on the wet, brick floor through which the stagnant, filthy moisture" from the nearby street had seeped. There was no fire in the grimy black fireplace.

4. (a) Referring to a dictionary, determine and write down the meaning of each of the following words:

    dusky   pervade   fetid   stagnant

   (b) Rewrite the passage, using your own words to describe the scene given.

5. Elizabeth C. Gaskell wrote many books concerning the lives and problems of workers during the Industrial Revolution in England. Write your own story of 300 to 500 words to describe living and working conditions at that time. Include information from the paragraph above and Figure 3.7. The story may be written as if you were actually living or visiting in England at that time.

To combat the poor working conditions in British factories, workers set up **co-operatives** and **trade unions**. (Co-operatives are organizations owned by a group of people who share in the profit. A co-operative might operate a store, for example, and sell goods to members at reasonable prices and then split any profits. Trade unions are organizations of workers that negotiate with the employer to improve wages and working conditions.)

The benefits of the Industrial Revolution clearly were not enjoyed by all levels of society. The wealth from industry was concentrated because the upper classes controlled most of the items that industry needed to produce goods. Figure 3.8 illustrates this situation.

Figure 3.8 Control of Four Factors of Production in the Industrial Revolution in the United Kingdom

LAND		LABOUR		CAPITAL (money)		RESOURCES (e.g., cotton, timber, and coal)	
Needed to produce raw materials such as wool and flax.	Owned and controlled by upper class.	Large amounts of cheap labour used in industry.	Labourers had to work cheaply because there was no other way for them to earn a living.	Large amounts needed to buy new technology (i.e. machinery).	Controlled by upper class, who had invested it and received profits.	Greater amounts needed because resources were being used more quickly.	Largely controlled by the upper classes.

NOTE: Factors of production are those items needed for industry to produce its goods.

6. (a) Why was the control of the factors of production important in the Industrial Revolution?

(b) Compare the control of the factors of production in the U.K. at that time and in Canada today. How have Canadians built and improved upon British technology?

The workers in the United Kingdom used trade unions to gain increased rights as well as access to more of the money produced by industry. One method was the **strike**. (A strike is a work stoppage used by workers to force the employer to improve certain conditions, such as wages or working conditions.)

7. Imagine that you are in the position of a leader of factory or mine workers during the Industrial Revolution. Write a document addressed to your employer that makes at least three demands for improvements in wages and/or working conditions. In this document, explain to your employers the way in which you intend to back your demand for these improvements.

8. Many workers in Canada today do not have the legal right to strike. Give your opinion about whether or not members of the following occupations should have the right to strike. In each case, include arguments for and against strikes.

doctors   teachers   nurses
bank clerks   dairy farmers   workers in a cigarette factory
truck drivers   postal workers   newspaper reporters

Although the United Kingdom may have led the world in the process of industrialization, changes were taking place in many other countries of the world. Figure 3.9 shows some of these changes.

9. Using the data in Figure 3.9, answer the following questions:
   (a) Which country, in your opinion, was the most advanced industrialized European nation in 1850, and which was the least advanced?
   (b) Explain what information you used to reach a conclusion in (a).

10. (a) Which European country appears to have made the most spectacular progress in industrialization between 1850 and 1910?
    (b) Explain how you reached this conclusion.

11. In approximately 100 words, compare industrial development in the United States with that in the United Kingdom. Include statistics in your answer.

COUNTRY	DATE	POPULATION	% OF PEOPLE IN CITIES OF MORE THAN 100 000	NUMBER OF CITIES OF MORE THAN 500 000	LENGTH OF RAILROAD PER MILLION PEOPLE (In kilometres)	PIG IRON PRODUCTION (In thousands of tonnes)	SHIP TONNES IN PORTS (In thousands)
United Kingdom	1850	27 700 000	20 or more	3	384	3 500	12 000
	1910	45 800 000	20 or more	7	848	10 200	138 909
France	1850	35 800 000	6–10	1	83	650	4 200
	1910	39 600 000	11–20	3	1264	4 000	61 362
Germany	1850	34 300 000	5 or less	0	170	600	1 300
	1910	64 900 000	20 or less	8	960	13 100	49 460
Spain	1850	15 674 000	5 or less	0	0	27	1 300
	1910	19 200 000	6–10	1	704	370	41 403
United States	1850	23 000 000	6–10	1	848	1 000	8 500
	1910	92 000 000	20 or more	8	4352	27 700	64 750

Figure 3.9 The Industrialization of the United Kingdom, France, Germany, Spain, and the United States, 1850–1910

Technology that was developed in the U.K. has been exported to many countries, including Canada and the U.S. The steam engine, for example, made possible easier travel and communication between the U.K. and other countries. In this way, the U.K.'s influence came to be felt in many parts of the world. Canada, for instance, has acquired the economic system of free enterprise, the English language, and the parliamentary form of government.

The Decline of the United Kingdom

When World War I began in 1914, the United Kingdom was the most powerful among the nations of the world. Since that time, however, it has declined in a number of ways. The British navy, for example, has shrunk to only a fraction of the size it was early in this century. Many British factories are old-fashioned and have not been modernized in over 25 years. Consequently, the U.K.'s industries often cannot compete with those of the United States or Japan. In the early 1980s, the U.K.'s economy was actually shrinking—producing less each year than it had the year before. Most aspects of British life have been affected by the decline of the nation as a world power.

Many reasons have been given to explain the U.K.'s decline. One factor is the loss of its empire. The British Empire at its height, extended to most regions of the world and included about one-quarter of the world's population, but today most of the former colonies are independent and no longer under British rule. As the empire dissolved, so did much of the U.K.'s economic power, which was based on the empire's raw materials and markets.

The two world wars were also costly. Much money was invested in armaments rather than in building a nation. When the wars ended, the U.K. was deeply in debt.

Another factor in the decline of the U.K. concerns its government. At the beginning of the twentieth century, the U.K. began to develop a large **bureaucracy** (a work force employed by the government to run its programs). The bureaucracy grew in tandem with government programs such as welfare and social assistance. Unfortunately, after some time, the country could no longer afford the costs of these government programs.

In addition, personal taxes had to be increased to support the growing government operations, and this reduced the incentive to work. By the 1970s, many Britons had lost the desire to work at rebuilding their country's economy, and some unions were demanding higher wages for less work; thus, British **productivity** fell. (Productivity refers to the value or number of goods one worker produces in a certain period of time.) This lower productivity resulted in British goods being expensive in their own country, as well as often being too expensive to sell to other nations.

Competition from countries such as Japan, the U.S., and West Germany has also accelerated the U.K.'s decline. These countries have tended to introduce new technology at a fast rate, which, though initially very expensive, has dramatically increased the productivity of their industries.

12. **Write a 200-word essay to explain the decline of the U.K.**

13. **What five suggestions could you make that might help the U.K. improve its economy?**

Industrial Development in the United States

Since the 1600s when the United States was first settled by Europeans, it has risen to become a wealthy, powerful industrial nation. Consider the impact of the industrialization of the United States on your life; few aspects of Canadian life have been unaffected.

From McDonald's hamburgers and Coca-Cola to the IBM computer or the situation comedy on television, the United States influences the world. Americans have developed a distinctive "American way", which has helped to mould the thinking of hun-

Figure 3.10 Coca-Cola: A World-wide Phenomenon

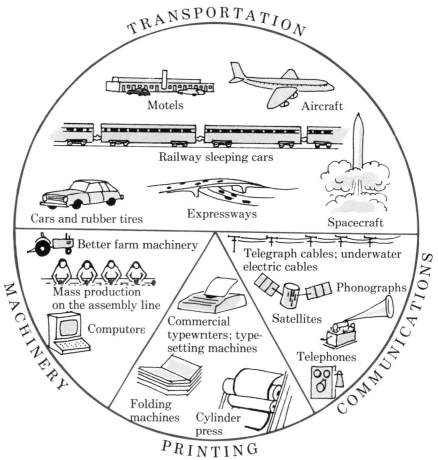

Figure 3.11 Some Developments in Which the United States was Initially Involved

TRANSPORTATION

Motels

Aircraft

Railway sleeping cars

Cars and rubber tires

Expressways

Spacecraft

MACHINERY

Better farm machinery

Mass production on the assembly line

Computers

Commercial typewriters; type-setting machines

Folding machines

Cylinder press

PRINTING

Telegraph cables; underwater electric cables

Phonographs

Satellites

Telephones

COMMUNICATIONS

dreds of millions of people during the second half of the twentieth century. Much of this influence can be traced back to the industrial and economic power of the United States.

14. **Write three-quarters of a page to outline how different your life might have been without the impact of the United States.**

The American Dream

Many of the early settlers who arrived in what is now the United States were escaping from various problems in Europe. The Puritan and Quaker groups, for example, arrived in New England in the 1600s to set up a society free from religious persecution. Along with the other settlers, the Puritans and Quakers worked hard to avoid establishing social classes similar to those in Europe. They stressed freedom for the individual—freedom to speak, worship, and determine one's own future. It should be noted that they were not entirely successful in putting these high ideals into practise.

For many, the U.S. became a land of opportunity, a place where "the poor boy could become rich". The "American Dream" focussed on the belief that "my only limitation is me". With a vast territory that stretched farther and farther west, the U.S. provided the physical space where people with daring could succeed. Ideas that were not risked in Europe were tried in the United States. Great resources in timber, minerals, and farmland provided the basis for the United States eventually to become the world's most powerful nation.

15. (a) **Describe, in two or three sentences, the American Dream.**
    (b) **Why would the American Dream have so much appeal to the average person?**
    (c) **What would motivate people to work hard in the U.S.?**
    (d) **How does your outlook for the future compare with the American Dream? Explain.**

16. **Think about the various American-made movies you have seen. Select two that you feel reflect at least some parts of the American Dream. Briefly describe each movie and how it reflects the American Dream.**

Historical Background

For about 200 years, until 1800, the United States was largely a pioneering country. Life was centred on farming and **cottage industry**, which is small-scale manufacturing in private homes. The U.S. remained very dependent on Europe. Most Americans still

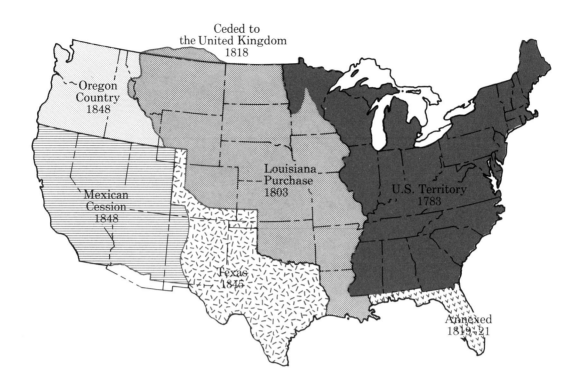

Figure 3.12 The Physical Growth of the United States in the 1800s

lived along the northeast coast, in and around cities such as Boston, New York, and Philadelphia. Most commerce, which involved shipping raw materials from the U.S. to Europe, was carried out in these centres. Agricultural goods such as wheat and cotton also went by ship across the Atlantic Ocean to waiting European markets.

In the early 1800s, events began to take place that changed the course of American history and eventually that of the world. One was the opening up of the American West. As the land along the Atlantic seaboard became more crowded, settlers began to cross the Appalachian Mountains and to farm the fertile soils of the Midwest. States such as Ohio, Missouri, and, later, Oklahoma were opened up for settlement. Figure 3.12 illustrates the westerly growth in the western United States during the nineteenth century.

The opening up of the western United States was very important for a number of reasons. First, hundreds of thousands of immigrants were drawn into the country to settle the new land, bringing with them new skills, ideas, and energy. As settlers spread west, the amount of food produced in the U.S. increased dramatically.

At the same time, settlers began to exploit raw materials such as minerals and timber in great quantities. These items were then shipped to the Atlantic coast, where they were either used in manufacturing or exported to Europe.

17. (a) **What qualities would a pioneer need in order to cross the Appalachians and set up a new farm in the Midwest?**
    (b) **What specific hardships would those early settlers have faced?**
    (c) **Consider your answers to (a) and (b). What relationship is there between these answers and the American Dream?**

The building of the railways also changed the course of American history. As they were extended from the Atlantic Ocean to the interior of the country, the railways became very important to the development of land and resources. With the technology of the steam engine, imported from the U.K., the railways could quickly bring raw materials out of and send manufactured goods into the interior. In addition, the railways brought more settlers to the West. Eventually, the railways spanned the continent to join the Atlantic and Pacific oceans. So quickly did the railways grow that it is estimated that 10% of the total wealth of the United States was invested in railways by 1910.

Railways opened the West for farming as never before. Between 1860 and 1910, two hundred million hectares were opened up for agriculture in the American West—an area almost as large as Western Europe. Technologically advanced farm machinery allowed a small number of farmers to work huge tracts of land. Fertilizers, irrigation of crops, and scientific farming each contributed to farming success in the United States. A bountiful food supply was essential for the growth of the country.

American railways proved to be very important in other ways. The more goods they transported, the more industry grew on the east coast. New York City, for example, grew quickly in the mid-1800s, and is one of the four largest cities of the world today.

Two industries were of importance in the American economy during the 1800s. Based largely on cotton, the textile industry was the first large-scale industry in the United States to be carried out in factories. The second industry was steel manufacturing, which provided a steady supply of steel for the building of American railways. The steel industry, in turn, relied on many other industries such as coal and iron mining, for the supply of mining raw materials.

The opening of the West thus led to a great economic development that helped to change the course of American history through industrialization. A thumbnail sketch of the life of Andrew Carnegie, which follows, illustrates the impact of certain people on the growth of the United States.

18. (a) Compare the U.K.'s sources of raw material with those of the U.S.
    (b) How did the differences you discovered in (a) affect the long-term growth of the two countries?

19. Explain the importance of the railway in the development of the U.S. Write about 100 words.

20. What specific characteristics of the textile and steel industries were significant in the growth of the U.S. economy?

CASE STUDY

Andrew Carnegie

Figure 3.13
Andrew Carnegie
1835-1919

Few people in the history of the United States illustrate the American Dream in action as well as Andrew Carnegie. Born in 1835 in Dunfermline, Scotland, Carnegie was familiar with poverty from the time of his birth; his father was a poor handloom weaver. The economic depression in the U.K. in 1848 forced the Carnegie family to leave for the United States—the land of opportunity. The trip across the ocean took much of the family's money.

After his family settled near Pittsburgh, Pennsylvania, Carnegie began work there at $1.20 per week. In 1850, he became a messenger boy in a telegraph office in Pittsburgh. Soon he started work on railroads, and then began to invest in local iron industries. His extraordinary talent to invest wisely and gamble on new technology quickly paid off. By 1868, his income was $50 000 per year.

As the American railways pushed to the West, the demand for steel increased greatly. The Carnegie Steel Company, which Andrew Carnegie built, introduced much new technology that could produce steel more efficiently and at a lower cost than before. The sale of steel to the railways helped Carnegie Steel to amass great wealth. Some of this was reinvested, in turn, to develop new technology. In 1900, he sold the Carnegie Steel Company for $250 million.

Andrew Carnegie probably did more than any other person to bring world leadership in the steel industry to the United States. He was also one of the early philanthropists, giving away millions of dollars to universities, libraries, and numerous charities. On the darker side, there were many thousands of people who worked for the Carnegie Steel Company for very low wages. Working conditions in the steel plants were dangerous, and injuries were common. Air and water pollution from the steel plants seriously affected Pittsburgh and its suburbs as well as other cities. Nearby were open-pit mines, which supplied coal for the steel mills. As the coal was mined, forests were chopped down and mountain sides excavated. Some of these scars on the land remain today. Industrial progress was made at great cost to workers and to the environment.

21. List four advantages and four disadvantages of the development of an industry such as the one of which Carnegie Steel was a part.

22. What do you feel people like Carnegie owe to American society in return for the wealth they have gained? Think of the responsibility they might have to people such as the citizens of Pittsburgh, their employees, and students.

23. Explain why you think that Andrew Carnegie was an example of the American Dream in action.

The Rise of the United States in the Twentieth Century

By 1900, the United States was experiencing very rapid economic growth, which can be traced to the following factors:

- the country's abundant natural resources such as agricultural land, minerals, and timber
- the strong work ethic among the American people
- rapid population growth, which provided a large labour force to work in industry and a huge market for manufactured goods
- the application of results of technological research to industry
- the free enterprise system, which allowed industrialists to make and to keep profits from their investments
- the democratic system of government, which gave individuals a certain freedom to develop their talents

24. (a) Compare the factors that led to the rise of economic growth in the United States and the United Kingdom.
    (b) Which factors were the same for the two countries?

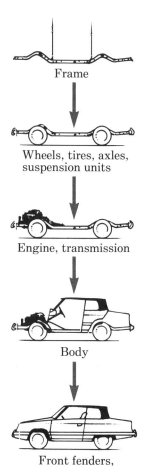

Frame

Wheels, tires, axles, suspension units

Engine, transmission

Body

Front fenders, hood, grille

Figure 3.14 The Assembly Line
Parts are added as the car moves along the assembly line. The same styles of parts are used on many thousands of cars without change.

(c) Of the factors common to the U.K. and the U.S., which one could be considered the most important? Explain your answer.

(d) To what extent did the economic growth of the U.S. follow the same pattern as that of the U.K.?

(e) Which factor in the gowth of the U.S. shows most clearly the difference between that country and the U.K.? Explain your answer fully.

New developments in the early twentieth century further advanced the United States' industrial progress. One of these developments was **scientific management** of the workplace, including innovations such as the **assembly line**. Henry Ford was among the first men to use the assembly line in a factory for large-scale production. The concept behind the assembly line is illustrated in Figure 3.14.

With the assembly line, the **mass production** of automobiles was possible. In 1913, for example, the Ford Motor Company was producing 1000 cars per day. By using the same number of workers to build an increased number of cars, Henry Ford increased production and lowered the cost per car. As prices declined, more and more people could afford cars. In 1914, there were 1 258 062 motor vehicles registered in the United States. By 1929, the number had skyrocketed to 26 501 443—one car for every five Americans. At that time the United States produced 83% of all cars in the world.

With the development of the automobile industry came the growth of related businesses such as oil companies, service stations, auto-parts manufacturers, and tire companies. Government services

Figure 3.15 Model T Fords on an Assembly Line

Figure 3.16 Some of the Unemploy- ed during the Great Depression

such as road building and parking facilities grew in relation to this industrial surge.

25. (a) List three items in your classroom or home that were probably built on an assembly line. Explain the reasons for your choice.
   (b) Consider an item of clothing such as a lace-up shoe. Assume that it is to be manufactured on an assembly line. How might the shoe appear as it starts on the assembly line, and what would be added as it moves along the line?
   (c) After someone has worked on an assembly line for a long time, what problems would he or she probably face? Explain your answer.

26. Henry Ford has been referred to as a genius of American business. Explain how this might be true.

The 1920s were years of economic boom in the United States. Businesses were growing quickly, and the country's prosperity (or wealth) was increasing at a high rate. There were, however, some serious problems in the American economy. People were encouraged to invest in growing businesses, and made commitments to make other investments, expecting great returns from the first ones. Sometimes those returns did not come in, and people found themselves in debt. Eventually, this happened on such a large scale that people could not pay their debts and it became obvious that many stocks were not worth as much as had originally been thought. Finally, in October 1929, the price of all stocks dropped rapidly, and the stock market "crashed". The entire American economy immediately entered a serious decline.

From the crash of the stock market in the fall of 1929 until the onset of World War II, most of the world experienced the **Great Depression**. During this period, economic activity was at a very low level as fewer people had the money or confidence to invest in businesses, and unemployment was extremely high. In the U.S. in 1933, more than 13 million people were without jobs out of a total labour force of about 52 million. Many banks and businesses went bankrupt. There was widespread poverty and much suffering. Despite the Depression, the American economy recovered during World War II and, by the 1950s, the United States had become the world's most powerful nation.

Multinational Corporations

After World War II, a number of companies emerged that had branches in many countries. Because their operations cross national boundaries, they are called **multinational corporations**. Multinationals encourage the worldwide spread of technology, business, and management skills. These corporations were originally seen as a way of improving international trade and relations. Today, however, multinationals are sometimes viewed less favourably. Some Canadians are concerned that foreign corporations control so much of Canada's industry that the multinationals, rather than Canadians, benefit from the profits. Yet, more than a million Canadians are employed by multinational corporations.

People who advocate Canadian ownership of Canadian industry hold a nationalist view. **Nationalism** involves intense pride in one's country and an unwillingness to allow outside influences to control its industry and culture. For these reasons, the activities of multinationals have been restricted in a number of countries.

27. (a) Of the multinational corporations listed below, whose products or services have you or your family used in the last six months?

General Motors	Eastman Kodak
McDonald's (hamburgers)	E.I. duPont de Nemours
Exxon (Esso)	(nylon, chemicals, film, etc.)
Sears	IBM
Procter & Gamble	Boeing

    (b) List four major effects on Canada and your life that would result if the foreign-based multinationals pulled out of Canada.

28. What do you think a company such as Exxon should do for Canada so that Canadians would benefit as much as possible from its business operations? Include reference to such items as investments and the training of employees.

The Economic Power of the United States

The United States has become economically and politically involved with many countries.

It buys raw materials from many other countries and these nations benefit from the money they receive. The United States, however, thus leaves itself vulnerable, as the supply lines of some of these raw materials could be easily cut. Botswana, Zimbabwe, Zaire, or Zambia, for example, could experience a revolution, which could cut off supplies to the U.S. Also ships carrying these materials could be attacked by unfriendly nations. This type of threat has resulted in the U.S. expanding the areas patrolled by its navy and air force.

29. **Does the United States have the right to invade another country to defend the sources of its raw materials? Explain the reasoning for your answer, as well as any conditions you might apply.**

The United States has reached a point in its development where its economic growth has slowed. Other countries such as Japan and West Germany have begun to challenge its economic leadership.

Figure 3.17 World Sources of Vital Commodities for the United States

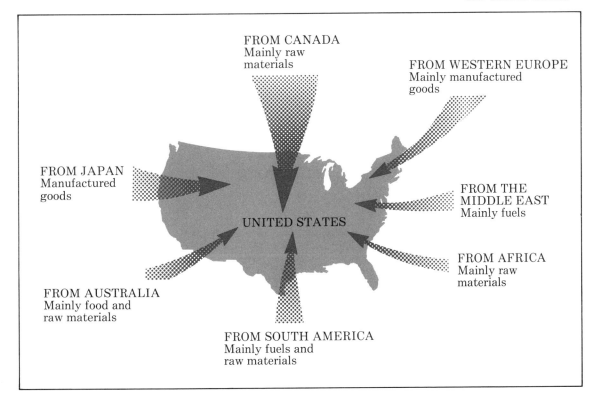

FROM CANADA
Mainly raw materials

FROM WESTERN EUROPE
Mainly manufactured goods

FROM JAPAN
Manufactured goods

FROM THE MIDDLE EAST
Mainly fuels

UNITED STATES

FROM AFRICA
Mainly raw materials

FROM AUSTRALIA
Mainly food and raw materials

FROM SOUTH AMERICA
Mainly fuels and raw materials

American industries such as automobile and steel manufacturing are facing serious problems. Thousands of workers have been laid off and many factories have been faced with the need to modernize quickly. The U.S., like the U.K., faces the challenge of introducing new technology into its economy.

One important factor in the economic slowdown of the U.S. is the breakdown of the American Dream. It has become clear that for many, the American Dream will only be a dream. Minority groups such as blacks and Hispanic Americans have begun to fight against their exclusion from the benefits that their society has to offer. They have seen that the possibility of "making it" is available only to the more fortunate. Most major cities have neighbourhoods where the residents are poor and the crime rates are high. Many families are breaking up, unable to cope with the changes of modern society. The human toll related to these factors is enormous.

Today, however, the economy of the United States is still the most powerful in the world.

30. Examine Figure 3.18. What might result in the United States from such differences continuing over a long period of time?

Figure 3.18
Contrasts in the United States
(a) Biltmore House, North Carolina
(b) An Older Neighbourhood in Buffalo

a

b

31. As American society has become more complex, government has imposed restrictions on individual freedom. These restrictions have contributed to the decline in the belief in the American Dream. What restrictions on individual freedom do you think are necessary in Canada or the United States today? Explain how these restrictions benefit the country as a whole.

32. Write a short essay entitled "Change Is the Only Constant in North American Life Today."

Japan: A Modern Industrial Miracle

Japan is one of the fastest growing countries of the modern world. Since World War II, Japan has risen from defeat to become the second-greatest industrial power in the non-communist world. Only the United States produces more than Japan.

In order to understand, "economic miracle" it is important to try to visualize the country's state in 1945. Two industrial cities—Hiroshima and Nagasaki—had been devastated by atomic bombs. (See Figure 3.19.) The central portion of the capital city of Tokyo had been fire-bombed and lay largely in ruins.

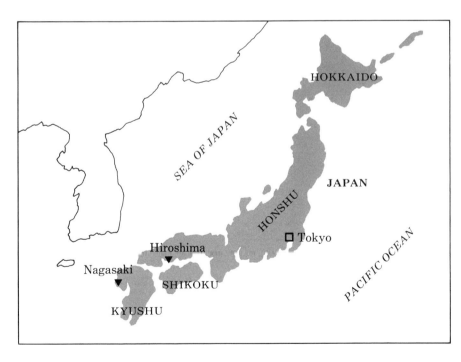

Figure 3.19
Location of Nagasaki and Hiroshima, the Cities Devastated by Atomic Bombs in 1945

**Figure 3.20
Japanese
Industrial
Problems and
Their Solutions**

The Japanese economy was disorganized and war-torn, its work force decimated by the loss of hundreds of thousands of soldiers and civilians. Yet, despite its many problems, Japan succeeded in building a modern industrial economy, as is shown in Figure 3.20.

PROBLEMS FOR THE DEVELOPMENT OF INDUSTRY IN JAPAN	JAPANESE ANSWERS TO THESE PROBLEMS
• Japan is a long distance from the Western industrialized world (e.g., Canada, the United States). This makes trading difficult.	• Japan has developed a huge merchant-marine fleet for importing and exporting materials.
• Japan is composed of four main islands and 4000 small ones, making communications difficult. Parts of the country are mountainous.	• Modern ship, rail, road, and air communications enable people and freight to move about quickly. Tunnels have been constructed to join islands and overcome mountain obstacles.
• Japan has few suitable sites for industry.	• Japan has concentrated its industry on small areas of flat land. The Japanese use their land wisely. Land is being reclaimed from marshes and shallow areas of the sea to form sites for industry.
• Japan has few raw materials and cannot provide enough food for its population.	• By developing its industry and increasing its exports, Japan is able to pay for imported raw materials and food. Japan has also developed a highly efficient farming industry.
• Energy is a major expense.	• Hydro-electric and nuclear power are highly developed. Conservation of energy is encouraged in transportation, industry and housing.
• Japan faces competition from well-established industrial nations.	• Japan has been able to produce many items efficiently and sell them at a lower cost than its competitors. A high level of technology and a strong work ethic contribute to Japan's competitiveness. Large investments by foreign countries, especially by the U.S., have been made in Japanese industry.

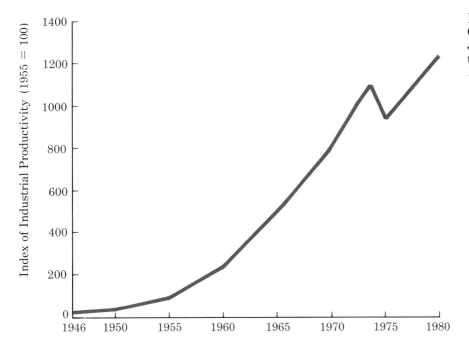

Figure 3.21
Growth of
Japanese Indus-
trial Productivity,
1946–80

The statistics in Figure 3.21 indicate the extent of Japan's economic recovery after World War II.

33. Examine Figure 3.21.
    (a) When was the period of greatest economic growth in Japan?
    (b) In the mid-1970s, the world suffered a serious oil supply shortage. How did this affect Japan? Explain your reasoning and suggest the reasons for the impact.

34. Using Figure 3.22 as a guide, answer these questions.
    (a) What item is the principal Japanese import?
    (b) Which import category is the second most important?
    (c) List the materials that Japan imports in raw form. What percentage of its imports do they account for?
    (d) What is the single most important item being exported from Japan?
    (e) Which of the imports would be used in making the item in (d)?
    (f) Between the time raw materials are imported and the finished goods are exported, various factors add to the cost of a product. What are these factors?

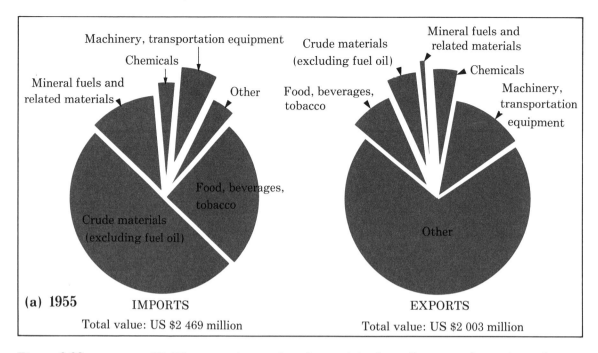

(a) 1955   IMPORTS
Total value: US $2 469 million

EXPORTS
Total value: US $2 003 million

Figure 3.22
Japanese Imports
and Exports
(a) 1955
(b) 1981

35. **The two pie graphs above, (a), show Japanese imports and exports in 1955, while the two below, (b), present the corresponding information for 1981. Describe how the percentages of imports and exports changed between 1955 and 1981.**

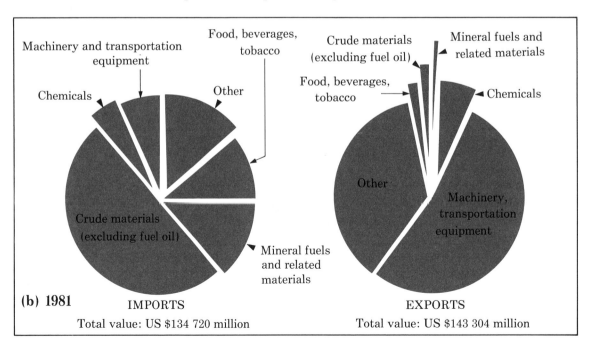

(b) 1981   IMPORTS
Total value: US $134 720 million

EXPORTS
Total value: US $143 304 million

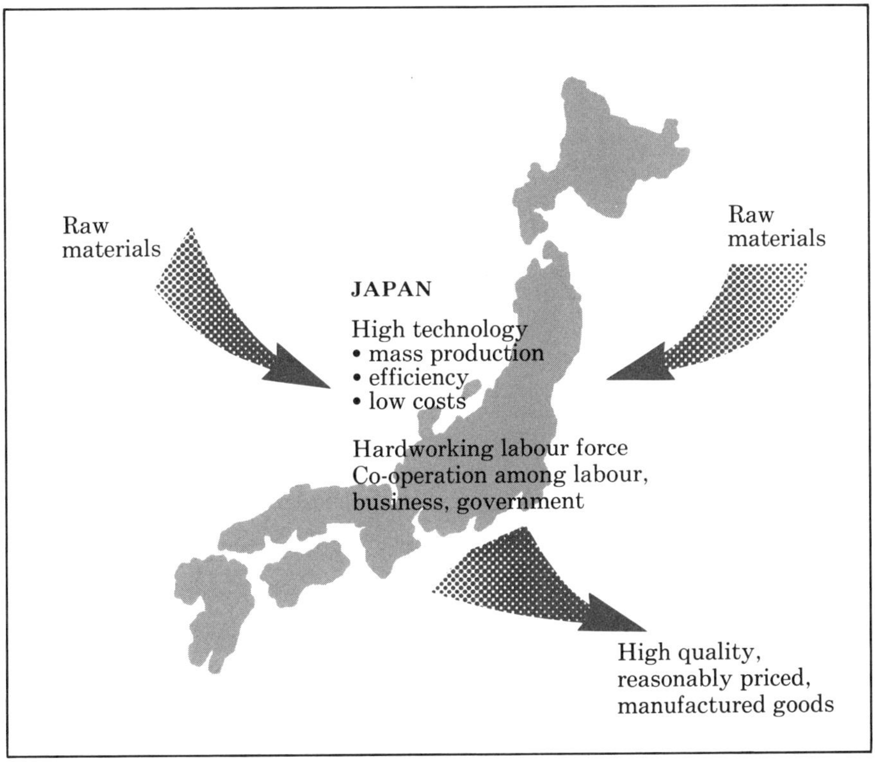

Figure 3.23
Japan's Industrial
Strategy

Figure contents:

Raw materials

Raw materials

JAPAN

High technology
- mass production
- efficiency
- low costs

Hardworking labour force
Co-operation among labour,
business, government

High quality,
reasonably priced,
manufactured goods

Rise in Productivity and the Standard of Living

Japan has overcome many obstacles in developing its economy.
Its central strategy for industry is illustrated in Figure 3.23.

Japan has a highly educated and hard-working population that
is determined to win foreign markets. The country has concentrated
on light industries for the export markets because such industries
combine the skill of Japanese workers with few raw materials. Cal-
culators, radios, watches, and cameras are typical products from
Japanese light industries.

36. (a) **Compare the industrial strategies of the United States and
Japan. What are some specific ways in which the strategies
differ?**

   (b) **What does your answer to (a) indicate about the differences
between the two countries?**

Matsushita Electric is one company that clearly illustrates
the extraordinary growth of Japanese industry. As Matsushita
Electric grew, so did Japan.

Matsushita Electric

Figure 3.24 Konosuke Matsushita

The life of Konosuke Matsushita in his early years was very different from that of Andrew Carnegie. In fact, the Japanese society in which Matsushita developed his electronics empire contrasts sharply with society in the United States.

In 1918, Matsushita began peddling his new adaptor sockets for light bulbs in Osaka, Japan. His investment of $50 represented every cent he could raise. Together with his wife and brother-in-law, he assembled the sockets in his small home. They did not sell well, however, and the business failed.

Shortly afterward, however, Matsushita developed a new, superior product that was better than any other socket on the market. A trickle of orders turned into a flood, and the Matsushita electronics empire was born. Central to the success of Matsushita Electric was the inventiveness of its founder and its workers. New ideas led to the development of products known by the brand names Panasonic, National, Quasar, and Technics. In 1980, the world-wide sales of Matsushita Electric were close to $14 thousand million in 130 countries, and there were 128 000 employees. Japan is now the world leader in electronic products, thanks to Matsushita and other similar companies.

Figure 3.25 Range of Products Made by Matsushita Electric

Training programs for
managers and workers

Recreation at a health resort

Employees encouraged to
make suggestions to
improve products

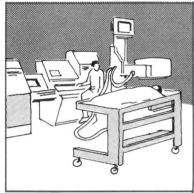

Health care in a
well-equipped hospital

Rehabilitation for injured
or ill employees

Sports teams

**Figure 3.26
Employee Pro-
grams at Matsu-
shita Electric**

 Contributing to the success of this company, however, is a
responsible philosophy toward its employees and society. Matsushita
attempts to serve people in society by producing quality goods
at the lowest prices. Because the company uses the resources of
society—people, capital—Matsushita feels it must benefit society
in return. As a result of this philosophy, company programs put
emphasis on employee benefits, as illustrated in Figure 3.26.

 The employees who work in Matsushita's factories consider
themselves part of a family. The supervisors in the factories take
a personal interest in the workers. Employees are usually hired

for life by Matsushita; strikes are almost unknown. In turn, worker loyalty to the company is very strong. Employees give up much of their individual freedom to work for the company. Much of their lives, including recreation, revolves around Matsushita. They are dedicated to hard work for their company and their country.

Konosuke Matsushita built his company in a society that stresses the value of working together. The individual is valued primarily as a member of a group. Yet, Japan is a democracy in which each person has the basic freedoms.

37. **In a paragraph, describe the factors that led to the enormous success of Matsushita Electric.**

38. **Compare the United States in which Andrew Carnegie worked with Konosuke Matsushita's Japan. How are their values different? (See the case study on Andrew Carnegie in this chapter.)**

39. **In what two ways did Carnegie Steel and Matsushita Electric each contribute to the growth of their home countries?**

Business and Japanese Society

To understand Japan's economic power, you must examine its people and their character. The Japanese are very different from Europeans and North Americans in their attitude and outlook. Japanese society is highly ordered, with rigid social traditions. The family unit, for example, is strong; it is expected that sons and daughters will honour their parents and consult them on important matters. Loyalty is considered an important virtue, whether it be to one's family or friends. It is vital for the Japanese not to disgrace those they are close to. There is also a strong desire among the Japanese to be part of a group and to be loyal to that group. These characteristics combine with a strong work ethic to produce a very dedicated work force in Japan.

This spirit is extended to the way in which business, labour, and government co-operate. "Japan Incorporated" is a term that refers to this co-operation among these three groups. The goal is to allow Japan's economy to strengthen and to grow at a high rate. Constant discussion between the government and the corporations allows this to take place. It is believed that what is good for Japanese corporations is also beneficial for the government and labour. In addition, Japanese banks have been eager to lend money to help the economy to grow, and this has helped to strengthen the country.

40. (a) From the point of view of an American, the Japanese have given up some of their personal freedoms to achieve economic success. What personal freedoms do they appear to have given up?
  (b) What lessons might the Americans or British learn from the Japanese?
  (c) Almost all people who live in Japan are from a similar culture and race. How does this compare with the racial and cultural mix of the U.K. and of the U.S.? What importance might this factor have in these various economies?

Robots

In many Japanese industries robots are widely used. Of the 58 000 industrial robots in the world in 1981, 80% were in Japan. One worker in the Nissan Motors plant near Tokyo watches over the activities of 15 mighty robots. (Robots are also used by some Canadian industries, as shown in Figure 3.27.)

The key to the development of robots and computers is the microchip, (see Figure 3.28). Although very tiny, these chips can store thousands of pieces of information, and can be used to give directions to computers. Robots, which contain computers with these microchips, can duplicate some activities of the human brain and muscles. Besides their use in manufacturing, robots have been

Figure 3.27
Robots Assembling Cars

**Figure 3.28
A Microchip. A paper clip shows the relative size of a microchip.**

developed to check medical drugs and tablets, select fruit, and determine the freshness of fish.

Robots are now being developed to explore the ocean floor, rescue fire victims, diagnose difficult medical cases, clean up spills at nuclear reactors, and serve the blind as replacements for seeing-eye dogs.

41. Consider each of the following groups. For each group, outline the positive and negative aspects of using robots to make a product.
    (a) factory workers   (c) people who use the product
    (b) factory owners   (d) government

42. It has been noted that Japan's success has depended to a large extent on wise factory managers. Agree or disagree with this statement and give reasons to back up your opinion.

43. (a) Examine figures 3.29 and 3.30. Describe briefly what each indicates.
    (b) In what ways does Figure 3.29 support what has been said about Japan, the U.S., and the U.K. in this chapter?
    (c) What is the relationship between figures 3.29 and 3.30?

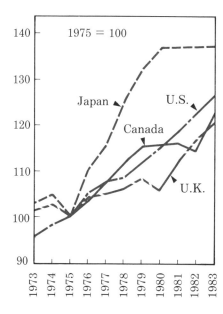

Figure 3.29 Comparative Productivity Output per Person-Hour in Manufacturing, 1973-83

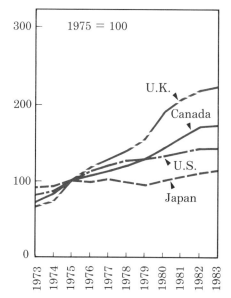

Figure 3.30 Comparative Wage Costs per Unit in Manufacturing, 1973-83

Japan's Prospects

The prospects for Japan appear very bright. The problems of infla-tion, unemployment, and sagging productivity have not affected this nation very much. While many countries such as Canada, the U.S., and the U.K. have suffered serious economic problems, Japan appears to have escaped most of them.

In spite of its industrial success, there are several areas of concern for Japan. One of these concerns is its trading situation. Because Japan imports most of its raw materials, it is very sensitive to any disruption in the flow of these materials. At the same time, Japan has been accused of flooding certain countries with its manufactured goods. Canadian manufacturers, for example, have been seriously hurt by Japanese imports. It should also be pointed out that Japan permits few imports of manufactured goods. This situation could lead to future difficulties in trading with countries around the world.

Japan also faces concerns about the quality of life of its people. Air and water pollution, and overcrowding, are examples of problems confronted by the Japanese. They must continue to work hard to maintain a strong economy while improving their quality of life.

44. Copy the following table into your notebook and fill in the ap-propriate answers to compare the United Kingdom, the United States, and Japan. Refer to an atlas.

BASIS OF COMPARISON	THE UNITED KINDOM	THE UNITED STATES	JAPAN
The time period of its greatest economic rise			
Six factors that explain its economic success			
New technology introduced or developed by the country			
Advantages or disadvantages presented by its location and geography			
Three factors it has in common with the other two countries			
Outlook for the future			

SAMPLE ONLY

45. Using your own words, write 250 words to explain the major conclusions that you can draw from comparing these three countries. Be sure to outline the factors that were important for each country in achieving economic success.

> **VOCABULARY**
>
> | | | |
> |---|---|---|
> | assembly line | industrialization | scientific |
> | bureaucracy | mass production | management |
> | co-operative | multinational | strike |
> | cottage industry | corporation | textile |
> | Great Depression | nationalism | trade union |
> | incentive | productivity | urbanization |

RESEARCH QUESTIONS

To answer these questions, you will probably need to refer to library resources and other sources of information.

1. Research the British Empire and then write a five-page report, including maps. In your research concentrate on the following:
   (a) the first territories included in the empire and pertinent dates. Refer to early trading within the empire.
   (b) the importance of the British navy.
   (c) three people who were active in building the empire (e.g., Cecil Rhodes). Describe their activities and why they were important to the empire.
   (d) the territories included in the empire in 1800, 1900, and 1950. Refer to a map.
   (e) the British Commonwealth and its role today.

2. Research the life of Cornelius Vanderbilt, a wealthy industrialist of the United States in the mid-1800s. Determine the following about him:
   (a) where he was born
   (b) how he started out in business
   (c) the business that he built up
   (d) how he built his vast industrial empire
   (e) his accomplishments

3. After you have completed the research on Cornelius Vanderbilt for question 2,
   (a) write three-quarters of a page comparing him with Andrew Carnegie. In what ways are they similar and different?

(b) write one-third of a page comparing Vanderbilt and Matsushita. Stress similarities as well as differences.

4. Was Vanderbilt's contribution to American society generally positive or negative? Explain your answer.

5. Visit a local electronics store and record the following:
   (a) the products that were produced in Japan
   (b) your general impression of the quality of these products
   (c) the various functions of these products
   (d) the differences in price between Japanese products and those made elsewhere

   Do the results of your survey appear to show that the industrial strategy of Japan has been followed (see Figure 3.23)?

Economic Systems of the World

Introduction

Different countries of the world produce varying amounts of wealth for their inhabitants, depending on the strength of their individual economies. Some countries, such as the United States, Canada, Japan, and France, generate enormous wealth for many of their citizens and are often referred to as "developed nations". Other countries, such as Bangladesh, Mozambique, Bolivia, and Indonesia, produce much less wealth for their populations and are referred to as "lesser developed nations".

The economic systems of the world may also be considered as being divided into three smaller economic systems or "worlds". From this viewpoint, the **First World** includes the wealthiest industrial countries such as Canada, the United States, the United Kingdom, France, and Australia. In general, First World countries are liberal-democratic, with parliamentary forms of government, and are based on private ownership of companies.

The **Second World** includes countries that are Communist, such as the Soviet Union, Poland, Czechoslovakia, and China. These countries are characterized by a one-party system of government and state ownership of most aspects of the economy.

Most people in the world live in the **Third World**, which is composed mainly of poorer countries such as India, Zaire, Peru, and the Philippines, most of which need time and technology to develop their economies fully. Yet, there is considerable variety within the Third World. Saudi Arabia, for example, has great wealth based on its oil revenues and provides free medical care for its citizens.

By contrast, the African country of Burundi is so poor that many of its people die from lack of medical care and food.

There are many conflicts among the three worlds as well as within each world. The First and Third worlds, for example, are in conflict over how wealth should be distributed more evenly between them. The Third World desires a share of the wealth that it sees in the First World. The First World countries want to maintain or even increase their wealth. The First and Second worlds are in a struggle for political and military supremacy, as you will see in this chapter.

1. (a) Using an atlas, list 22 countries that are part of the First World. Give a short explanation for each choice.
   (b) What other factors can you add to the description of the First World given in the text?

2. (a) Identify 20 countries that are part of the Third World. Use the GNP per capita information listed in an atlas.
   (b) Discuss six major differences that exist among the Third World countries that you have chosen.

The Superpowers

In the 1980s, there are two nations that have a great deal of power and wealth, so great that they are often referred to as **superpowers**. These countries are the United States of America and the Union of

Soviet Socialist Republics (U.S.S.R., or Soviet Union). Few people in the world live outside the influence of either superpower.

The U.S. and the U.S.S.R. are in conflict with each other, conflict that has led to many problems. During the 1950s and 1960s, this superpower conflict was so great that it was called a **Cold War**. The war was "cold" because it did not involve actual fighting between the two powers. The continued build-up of nuclear weapons by both superpowers has led to a renewal of the Cold War.

You have already studied the background and the rise to power of the United States. Equally important is the recent history of the U.S.S.R.

The Rise of the U.S.S.R.
True Communism

Communism, a political philosophy, is derived from the writings of Karl Marx, who lived from 1818 to 1883. In the world around him, Marx noticed many problems that disturbed him deeply. He saw, for example, that in most countries of Europe, a relatively small, wealthy group controlled the economy. This group, which he called the **bourgeoisie**, economically dominated the rest of the population. The bourgeoisie was the middle class, which did not rule the countries of Europe politically, but had economic importance.

According to Marx, the basic conflicts in society were between the bourgeoisie on the one hand and the **peasants** (poor farmers) and workers (or **proletariat**) on the other. The peasants and workers were not paid adequately and thus remained poor—they were **exploited** by the bourgeoisie.

Marx suggested a solution. A revolution by the peasants and workers would overthrow the bourgeoisie-oriented rulers and place control in the hands of the workers and peasants. In this new society, everything would be shared. "From each according to his [or her] abilities, to each according to his [or her] needs" would be the new philosophy of society. Each person would give to others according to how much he or she earned. In turn, each person would receive whatever he or she needed to live. No longer would peasants or workers be exploited, and every one would be considered equal.

The Origins of the U.S.S.R.'s System

In the late 1800s and early 1900s, Russia, now a republic of the U.S.S.R., was much like the world described by Marx. A few people controlled the wealth and had the power; this left a huge gap between the very rich and the very poor. The Czar (emperor) had enormous power, ruling over millions of peasants and workers (Figure 4.1).

Figure 4.1
Contrasts in
Russia
(a) One of the
    Czar's Palaces
(b) A Peasant's
    Home

a

b

During the early years of the twentieth century, there was increasing pressure for change to improve the quality of life of the poor illiterate masses. The Czarist regime, however, was unwilling to change the system. The only alternative was revolution. In 1917, that is what took place. The Russian Revolution of that year overthrew the ruling class and led to the establishment of the world's first Communist state.

3. The Communism based on Karl Marx's writings has been criticized as being impractical and unrealistic. Discuss this criticism, giving reasons for your position.

4. Judging by the Russian experience, what conditions in the world today might lead to a similar revolution elsewhere?

The U.S.S.R. Today

The U.S.S.R. today is far from the perfect Communist society envisioned by Marx. In fact, a small group of Communist leaders rule the country and there is little individual freedom. The U.S.S.R. can be considered a **police state** as the army and police are used to put down opposition to the leaders. Some criticism is allowed— of traffic laws or food shortages—but anyone who criticizes the political system risks being jailed.

The cornerstone of the economy of the U.S.S.R. is planning. They plan how they want their economy to grow as well as what types of factories they will build. These plans are set down in reports called **Five-Year Plans**, which look ahead to what it is hoped the economy can produce over a period of five years.

The plans and goals for the economy come largely from the capital city of Moscow. It is here that planners put together the Five-Year Plans for the Soviet economy. Although the planning sounds promising in theory, it does not always work in practice. Most of the Five-Year Plans since 1970 have predicted outputs that are too high: Soviet factories and farms have not met these predictions (Figure 4.2).

Figure 4.2 Grain Production According to Five-Year Plans

| | WHEAT, BARLEY, OATS, ETC. (In tonnes) | |
	1975 (End of Ninth Five-Year Plan)	1980 (End of Tenth Five-Year Plan)
Planned production	215 000 000	230 000 000
Amount actually produced	140 000 000	181 000 000

Great progress has been made, however, in the economy of the U.S.S.R. since 1917. People no longer starve, and almost everyone has comfortable living accommodation. Yet, between 1917 and 1953, the amount of grain produced per person remained about the same. What has happened is that food is distributed among the population more fairly today than in 1917.

Problems in the U.S.S.R.

Despite significant progress, there are a number of areas in which major problems still exist in the U.S.S.R. today. Agriculture is one.

Problems exist in the production, storage, transportation, and distribution of agricultural products. As a result, much food is wasted or allowed to rot before people can buy it. Also, because

Soviet agriculture does not grow enough staple food for its population, significant quantities must be imported. Even then there are major food shortages throughout the U.S.S.R. Many people spend hours every week lining up to buy the food that is available, as shortages are frequent.

The government owns all farmland but allows farmers to work small plots of land and keep the profits. The results are shown here.

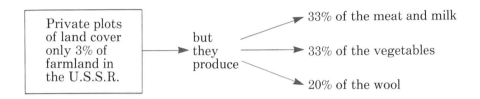

Private plots of land cover only 3% of farmland in the U.S.S.R. but they produce → 33% of the meat and milk → 33% of the vegetables → 20% of the wool

5. (a) **Why do you think private plots of land produce so much of the food in the U.S.S.R.?**
   (b) **What weaknesses does this indicate about the economic system of the U.S.S.R.?**

In the U.S.S.R., a wide variety of consumer goods is produced, including such items as clothing, radios, and televisions. Some of these goods are of high quality and are exported. Other **consumer goods**, of lower quality, are sold to Soviet citizens through state-run stores.

Other consumer goods are available on the **black market**. (Illegal buying and selling of products is referred to as a black market.) American cigarettes, Levi's jeans, and radios are among goods sold illegally at great profit on the black market. People who have other jobs work part time selling black-market goods.

Although the Soviet Union is, in theory, a worker's state, Communist party officials, like many owners and managers of corporations in the First World, acquire much of the wealth in the country. The average wage of $250 per month in 1983 did not satisfy many workers.

Crime and alcoholism are among the social problems of the U.S.S.R. Poorly run factories and production that is far below what is planned reflect these and other problems.

6. **In approximately 100 words, describe some aspects of life in the U.S.S.R. that are different from some in your life.**

7. **Discuss two differences between Marxist Communism and the Communism of the U.S.S.R.**

The United States and the U.S.S.R.

In Chapter 3, the economic system of the United States was discussed. Before reading on, briefly review that chapter, and examine the comparison of the U.S. and the U.S.S.R. economies presented in Figure 4.3.

8. (a) Which characteristic do you think is the most important point of contrast between the systems of the U.S. and of the U.S.S.R.? Explain your reasoning.
   (b) Why do you think the Soviet government attempts to control life in the U.S.S.R. so closely?

Figure 4.3 Comparison of the Economies of the U.S. and the U.S.S.R.

BASIS OF COMPARISON	U.S.	U.S.S.R.
Freedom	—All the basic freedoms	—Limited religious freedom —Limited freedom of speech or the press —No free voting in the democratic sense
Ownership of farms, factories	—Most are owned by individuals or groups of people —Many decisions made by individuals	—The state owns almost all farms and factories —All major decisions are made by government or its representatives
Competition	—Competition between companies or producers to make new products	—Very little competition
Role of government	—To regulate (set laws for) certain areas of life —To protect individuals and property —To allow people to find "truth" themselves	—To control all major aspects of life —To tell people what "truth" is
Important factors in economy	—"The customer is always right" —Stress on consumer goods	—Government as planner is "always right"

Other Economic Systems

The economies of the countries of the world can be marked on a scale or continuum to show how each is run. Such a continuum is shown in Figure 4.4

Figure 4.4 Economies around the World

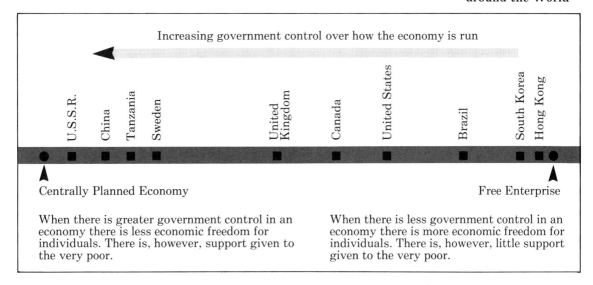

Increasing government control over how the economy is run

U.S.S.R.　China　Tanzania　Sweden　United Kingdom　Canada　United States　Brazil　South Korea　Hong Kong

Centrally Planned Economy

Free Enterprise

When there is greater government control in an economy there is less economic freedom for individuals. There is, however, support given to the very poor.

When there is less government control in an economy there is more economic freedom for individuals. There is, however, little support given to the very poor.

CASE STUDY

Tanzania

The system of government in Tanzania represents one of the boldest experiments in socialism in the world. In order to ensure that the country's wealth is distributed as equitably as possible, the government controls the planning of the economy. At the same time, however, the country has attempted to protect democratic ideals and freedoms.

The government of Tanzania took control of many companies in the country about ten years after independence from the U.K. in 1961. No one was allowed to own a farm individually. All farmers were to live in villages and work on **co-operative** farms.

Since the 1970s, a number of social programs have been introduced in an attempt to improve the quality of life in Tanzania. The quality of education has not improved, for example, nor has the overall standard of health in the country, despite massive social programs. The economy has suffered and is near collapse. Tanzania is still one of the poorest countries in the world (Figure 4.6) and, in fact, is becoming poorer.

Figure 4.5 The Location of Tanzania

A number of reasons can be suggested to explain Tanzania's problems. One factor involves government control of industry. In 1967, the government set up 330 state companies to run the economy. These companies have proved to be poorly run and a great deal of money has been wasted. Many have gone bankrupt. By 1980, about half of the remaining companies were losing money.

Tanzania also set very high taxes for the wealthy of the country. Faced with this and the government takeover of their businesses, most of the wealthy and educated people have left Tanzania. The people left behind, in many cases, do not have the training necessary to run the economy.

Many of the projects set up by the government of Tanzania were not practical. One project, built with Canadian aid, was a modern bakery in the largest city, Dar-es-Salaam. Equipped with modern machinery, this bakery could produce bread very cheaply using only a small number of workers. The result was that hundreds of small bakers in the city lost their livelihood because they could not compete.

9. (a) **Would this bakery have been valuable if built in Canada? Explain.**
   (b) **Why do you think this bakery was a poor choice for Tanzania?**
   (c) **Why would Tanzania have decided to build such a bakery? Suggest three reasons.**

10. **Government control of the economy appears to have worked more effectively in the U.S.S.R. than in Tanzania. Suggest four reasons to explain why this has been the case.**

Figure 4.6 Poor Housing in Tanzania

In Tanzania today few farms or companies are privately owned. In principle, this means that the profits from any work that is done is shared by the people as a whole. In practice, this means that the government retains the profit generated by the economy. As a result there is very little incentive to work hard, as the profits will not come back to the person who works hard.

Tanzania has also had problems such as drought, disease, and armed conflict with Uganda, which have harmed its progress. The statistics in Figure 4.7 illustrate how Tanzania compares with Canada.

	TANZANIA	CANADA
Population	20 500 000	24 343 181
Population density (average)	21.7 people/km² (12% urban)	2.4 people/km² (80.1% urban)
Population-growth rate (shows how quickly a population grows)	3.06%/a (very high)	1.15%/a (low)
Infant-mortality rate (the number of infants who die soon after birth)	120/1000 live births	12/1000 live births
Life expectancy (the number of years, on average, a person will live)	Male, 49 years Female, 52 years	Male, 69 years Female, 76 years
Number of doctors	0.61/10 000 population	17.76/10 000 population
Illiteracy rate (the percentage of the population that cannot read or write)	87%	under 1%
GNP per person (the value of all goods and services produced per person per year, on average)	$274	$11,450
Radios	17.2/1000 population	865/1000 population
Televisions	Found only in Zanzibar, not on mainland of Tanzania	348/1000 population
Telephones	29/1000 population	856/1000 population

Figure 4.7 Statistics on Tanzania and Canada, 1981

11. Select three statistics from Figure 4.7. For each statistic, draw a bar graph to compare Tanzania with Canada. Give the graph a suitable title.

12. Write about 75 words comparing life in Tanzania with life in Canada.

13. Might there be a relationship between the population growth rate and the infant mortality rate? If so, explain what that relationship might be.

Sweden

SWEDEN

EUROPE

Figure 4.8 The Location of Sweden

Sweden reflects a number of the goals and ideals of Tanzania. Despite similar goals, however, life for the average Swede is very different from that of most Tanzanians.

Population	8 800 000
Population density	19.5 people/km^2
Population growth rate	0.2%/a
Infant mortality rate	8/1000 live births
Life expectancy	75 years
Number of doctors	16/10 000 population
Illiteracy rate	Under 1%
GNP per person	$8766
Radios	368/1000 population
Televisions	363/1000 population
Telephones	771/1000 population

Figure 4.9 Statistics on Sweden, 1981

14. Examine the statistics for Sweden in Figure 4.9 and those for Tanzania in Figure 4.7. Select five statistics that show the contrast between the two countries. Briefly explain what each statistic reveals about each country. (Include the Illiteracy Rate as one of your statistics.)

Sweden is recognized as an outstanding example of a **welfare state**. Such a state is a country in which the government programs ensure that everyone has his or her basic needs met. The government operates the welfare state through programs such as medical and hospital care, urban planning (Figure 4.10), public housing for the poor, leave from jobs for new fathers and mothers, open prisons (in some cases), guaranteed room in an old-age home for the elderly,

Figure 4.10
A Housing Development in
Sweden

and equality for men and women, by law. Swedish society is very organized—the average Swede is a member of five organizations or unions.

The Swedes are generally very proud of what their country offers. Not everyone, however, could live happily in Sweden. In order to have such a planned society, there are costs to the individual, such as

- very high taxes
- restrictive laws on most aspects of life (e.g., restrictions on how parents may discipline their children)

15. Would you enjoy living in Sweden? Compare the benefits and costs before making your decision.

16. It would appear that people in Sweden have all the basic material things in life. The standard of living in Sweden is among the highest in the world. The suicide and divorce rates in Sweden, however, are very high. Might there be a relationship between the suicide and divorce rates and the welfare state system there? Explain your answer?

Most industry in Sweden is privately owned. There are, however, many government restrictions on business. Small businesses, for example, must pay very high taxes.

In recent years, there have been a number of proposals to change the ownership of industries in Sweden. The idea is to turn over control and ownership of factories to the workers. In this way, there would be no wealthy class to control the economy. This change would bring Sweden much closer to true equality for all.

17. **What dangers can you see arising if this proposed ownership policy is brought about?**

As was noted earlier, Sweden and Tanzania share some of the same attitudes toward their economy. In Sweden, however, the economy is quite healthy and can afford to support a welfare state. In Tanzania, the economy is in such trouble that it can barely operate, and a welfare state is out of the question. Sweden's history reveals that its economy has developed over hundreds of years. Even 200 years ago Swedish industry was introducing new technology. The Swedes have also had a strong work ethic to support their economy. Tanzania has many problems to overcome before its economy will be able to develop in a way similar to that of Sweden.

CASE STUDY

Hong Kong

Figure 4.11 The Location of Hong Kong

Located along the southern coast of China, Hong Kong has an area of only 1000 km². With almost no natural resources, Hong Kong must buy even its water. Most of the land is mountainous or wasteland, and with a population of 5 150 000, Hong Kong is one of the most crowded areas in the world. Many of the inhabitants of Hong Kong escaped as refugees from Communist China. Figure 4.12 illustrates the crowded and dirty conditions in which the poor live.

Despite its obvious problems, Hong Kong has a relatively high standard of living, as shown by the statistics in Figure 4.13.

Many of the people of Hong Kong have a very strong work ethic and are willing to work for low wages. Their hard work has meant that manufactured goods can be produced at lower cost in Hong Kong than elsewhere in the world. Hong Kong's basic economic plan is illustrated in Figure 4.14.

Figure 4.12
Crowded Condi-
tions in Hong
Kong

Population	5 150 000
Population density	5150 people/km^2
Population-growth rate	1.89%/a
Infant-mortality rate	13.4/1000 live births
Life expectancy	Male, 68 years
	Female, 74 years
Number of doctors	8.74/10 000 population
Illiteracy rate	15%
GNP per person	$4200

Figure 4.13
Statistics on
Hong Kong, 1981

| FROM OTHER COUNTRIES Raw materials (e.g., oil, cotton, silk, glass) | | HONG KONG Refining and manufacturing | | TO OTHER COUNTRIES Finished products (e.g., digital watches, calculators, toys, radios, clothes) |

Figure 4.14 Hong
Kong's Economic
Plan

18. Look at the description of Hong Kong's finished products in Figure 4.14. Why do you think Hong Kong produces these types of goods?

19. (a) In what ways are the economic policies and the industrial strategies of Hong Kong and Japan similar (see Chapter 3 for details of Japan's industrial development)?

    (b) Compare the results of the economic policies in Japan with those in Hong Kong. Explain any differences you find.

The availability of inexpensive labour, a strong work ethic, and extensive trading links help to explain why Hong Kong is bursting with economic activity. Being so close to large markets, Hong Kong can usually sell its products quickly. Many businesses in Hong Kong also have investments around the world.

20. (a) **How has the government's basic economic plan affected the economy of Hong Kong?**
    (b) **Who suffers most under the Hong Kong system?**
    (c) **Who benefits most economically in Hong Kong? Give reasons for your answer.**

21. (a) **Imagine that you are a Swede who arrived in Hong Kong just two days ago. List five thoughts that would likely come into your mind.**
    (b) **Write one-third of a page to describe how someone from Tanzania might react to Hong Kong.**

Hong Kong is still a British colony, although its territory is owned by mainland (Communist) China. The U.K. holds a lease on the land until 1997. The governments of the United Kingdom and Communist China have reached preliminary agreements that will allow the colony to be transferred to Communist rule before the end of this century. However, it is impossible to predict exactly what life will be like in Hong Kong when Communist China takes control.

CASE STUDY

Brazil

Brazil, a former Portuguese colony, is the largest country in South America. With an area of 8 512 000 km², Brazil is almost as large as Canada (9 976 000 km²).

Brazil has an auto industry that is among the world's top five. Its engineering industry produces diesel locomotives, satellites, and televisions. Brazil is the world's leading coffee producer. In the last 20 years, Brazil has had one of the world's fastest-growing economies.

Brazil also contains the largest tropical rain forest in the world, and has enormous undeveloped resources—the world's largest reserves of high-grade iron ore, bauxite (for aluminum), tin, uranium, and diamonds. Huge deposits of gold as well as some of the world's greatest stands of timber are found in the Amazon basin.

Figure 4.15 The Location of Brazil

a

b

Figure 4.16 Brazil:
A Country of
Contrasts
(a) São Paulo:
Possibly the
World's Fastest-
growing City
(b) The Amazon
Rain Forest

There is, however, a darker side to Brazil's economy. Over 35 000 000 people live in dire poverty. In the city of Vitória, for example, 300 000 of the total 721 000 inhabitants live in shantytowns. Among the poor, most have never visited a doctor or dentist, and many children die before the age of two.

22. **Brazil has been called a country of contrasts (Figure 4.16). Describe three major contrasts within Brazil.**

Poor government management of Brazil's economy has led to very high rates of inflation. For example, the inflation rate in 1982 was 106%. Statistical information on Brazil is shown in Figure 4.17.

Figure 4.17
Statistics on
Brazil, 1981

Population	130 000 000
Population density	15.2 people/km² (65% urban)
Population-growth rate	2.83%/a (high)
Infant-mortality rate	82.7/1000 live births
Life expectancy	Male, 61 years Female, 67 years
Number of doctors	6/10 000 population
Illiteracy rate	14%
GNP per person	$2200
Radios	380/1000 population
Televisions	150/1000 population
Telephones	51/1000 population

23. Construct a table similar to the one in Figure 4.18. Complete the first four columns from the information given in the text. Complete the column on Canada from your general knowledge.

Figure 4.18 Comparison of Five Countries

BASIS OF COMPARISON	TANZANIA	SWEDEN	HONG KONG	BRAZIL	CANADA
Government role in economy					
General standard of living (high, medium, or low)					
Personal freedoms		SAMPLE ONLY			
Geographic location					
Level of medical care					
Government programs for the poor					

24. (a) In which of the four countries—Tanzania, Sweden, Hong Kong, Brazil—would you least like to live? Explain.
    (b) In which of these four countries would you most like to live? Give reasons for your answer.

25. From the study of Tanzania, Sweden, Hong Kong, and Brazil, what factors would you say contribute to prosperity in a country?

The Problems of Debt

Most of the poorer countries of the world have borrowed a great deal of money. The programs that have been established with this money are designed to increase the standard of living of those nations. Unfortunately, many Third World countries have borrowed so much money that they cannot meet their debt payments.

These debts include money owed to private banks, such as the Royal Bank of Canada. Other debts are owed to the **World Bank**.

The World Bank was set up to lend money to countries that could not borrow from private banks. Projects for which the World Bank lends money include dams, railways, and factories in the Third World. Canada, the United States, and other First World countries provide money to the World Bank for such loans.

Most of the nations that have large debts belong to the Second and Third worlds (Figure 4.19).

COUNTRY	DEBT (US$ THOUSAND MILLIONS)	THE DEBT AS A PERCENTAGE OF ALL EXPORTS FROM THE COUNTRY IN ONE YEAR
Brazil	$ 87	117
Mexico	80	126
Argentina	43	153
South Korea	36	49
Venezuela	28	101
Israel	27	126
Poland	26	94
U.S.S.R.	23	25
Egypt	19	46
Yugoslavia	19	41
Philippines	17	79
East Germany	14	83
Peru	12	79
Romania	10	61

Figure 4.19 Countries with Large Debts, 1983

NOTES: Some of the money borrowed has been wasted on poorly designed projects. In these cases, money must be repaid even though the projects have collapsed.

The higher the percentage in the last column, the more difficult the repayment of the loan.

26. (a) **What would happen to the world's economy if some countries gave up trying to pay off their debts?**
    (b) **How would the problem discussed in (a) affect you? (Think of jobs, loans to businesses, etc.)**

The countries looked at cannot, of course, be considered in isolation. Each country is linked to others by trade and the exchange of money and information. When there is a frost in southern Brazil, for example, the cost of coffee goes up in Canada. Most baseballs now used in the United States are made in Haiti, where labour costs are 20% of those in the U.S. Therefore, Americans have begun to save money when they buy baseballs.

Major Economic Organizations

The European Economic Community (EEC)

In 1957, a group of six European nations signed the Treaty of Rome. Agreed on by West Germany, France, Italy, Belgium (where the EEC headquarters are located, see Figure 4.20), the Netherlands, and Luxembourg, the treaty established the **European Economic Community** (also known as the **European Common Market** or simply the Common Market).

The Common Market was created to bring about a united European economy. To this end, the member countries set the following goals:

- to work co-operatively
- to build a strong, prosperous Western Europe
- to prevent Communism from taking over Western Europe
- to remove tariffs from goods traded among EEC countries, and to apply common tariffs to goods from non-EEC countries
- to develop a common agricultural policy

In general, these goals have been achieved. Today there are ten members of the European Economic Community. The ten include the original six, as well as Greece, the United Kingdom, Denmark, and the Republic of Ireland (Eire). Spain, Portugal, and Turkey have expressed interest in joining as well.

27. **Use an atlas for help in answering with this question.**
    (a) **On a map of Europe, label the countries that belong to the EEC. Colour those countries red.**

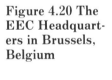

Figure 4.20 The EEC Headquarters in Brussels, Belgium

(b) On the same map, label those countries that have shown interest in joining the EEC. Shade in those countries in blue.

(c) What is the total population of the EEC?

(d) What advantages does the location of the EEC provide for trading with the rest of the world?

(e) Examine the thematic maps in an atlas, such as those that deal with industry, GNP per capita, agriculture, production of raw materials, and trading links with the rest of the world. How does the EEC compare with the following areas?

- North America
- Eastern Europe
- Africa
- Asia

Despite the achievements of the EEC, many people today believe that it has failed. In 1972, at a meeting in Paris, the leaders of the Common Market countries agreed on greater goals. The new Common Market was to have united policies on energy, industry, science, taxes, and economics. There was even discussion of EEC countries forming a political union. These goals, however, are as far away today as they were in 1972. Many people feel that the Common Market has begun to depart from the goal of unity. In addition, economic growth has slowed greatly in Common Market countries.

It is not surprising that the EEC countries hesitate to join in a political union. They must think seriously before linking themselves politically. This is because of differences in their current systems of government, past enmities (during World War II, for instance,) and other major socio-political reasons. In general, the countries of the EEC want to keep many of their unique traditions and ways of life.

28. Consider the positive and negative aspects of a political union for the countries of the EEC. Overall, would such a union be beneficial? Include your own ideas and attitudes in your answer.

COMECON

The Council for Mutual Economic Assistance (COMECON) is a treaty organization that, like the EEC, has attempted to bring about economic co-operation. **COMECON** is dominated by the U.S.S.R., which provides aid to the other members. In return for this aid, these countries are expected to follow instructions from the U.S.S.R. For certain countries, such as Poland and Czechoslovakia, the U.S.S.R. has used its army to make sure they follow its policies. Cuba has sent its soldiers to Africa to support the policies of the U.S.S.R. In return, Cuba receives about $3 million each day from the U.S.S.R. COMECON also involves trade agreements.

The members of COMECON are

Bulgaria	Hungary	U.S.S.R.
Cuba	Mongolia	Vietnam
Czechoslovakia	Poland	Associate member: Yugoslavia
East Germany	Romania	

29. **Use an atlas for help in answering this question.**
    (a) **On a map of the world, label the countries that belong to COMECON. Colour them red.**
    (b) **Label Yugoslavia and colour it yellow.**
    (c) **For each country in COMECON, list the GNP per person. How do these countries compare with those of the EEC with respect to wealth?**
    (d) **In what ways is COMECON different from the EEC? Explain.**

OPEC

Unlike COMECON and the EEC, **OPEC** (Organization of Petroleum Exporting Countries) is an organization of countries (see Figure 4.21) set up to control the production and pricing of a vital commodity — oil. OPEC has proved to be an important force in the world economy. Composed of the major oil-exporting countries outside of the Communist world, OPEC was formed in 1960 to increase the price of oil. At the time of its formation, OPEC was selling its oil for US $1.80 per barrel. By 1982, the price had jumped to US $34.00 per barrel, although it did decrease to US $28 per barrel in 1984 (Figure 4.22).

30. **Use an atlas for help in answering this question.**
    (a) **Determine the distance (by tanker route) from Saudi Arabia to each of the following countries: West Germany, Canada, and Japan.**
    (b) **What dangers are involved in transporting oil those distances by tanker?**
    (c) **Examine the GNP per capita for these OPEC members: Saudi Arabia, Venezuela, Libya, and Iran. How do their GNP per capita figures compare with those of the countries around them that do not belong to OPEC?**
    (d) **What effect has the production of oil had on the four OPEC countries listed in (c)?**

The price of a barrel of oil was very low during the 1950s and 1960s. This cheap energy allowed the economies of Canada, the United States, and other countries in the First World to grow quickly. The automobile, for example, gained popularity among consumers during those years, as the gasoline refined from oil was inexpensive.

The entire picture of oil supply in the world began to change in the early 1970s. Libya began to increase the price for its oil, cutting off supplies to any oil company that would not pay the higher price. Gradually the oil companies did pay. One by one, other OPEC members boosted their oil prices. Figure 4.22 shows the increases in oil prices from 1971 to 1983.

Figure 4.21
Members of
OPEC

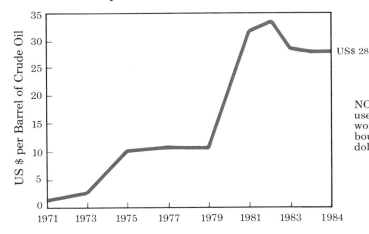

US$ 28

Figure 4.22
Changes in the
Price of OPEC Oil,
1971–84

NOTE: US dollars are used here because on world markets oil is bought and sold in US dollars.

31. (a) List the years shown in Figure 4.22, along with the price of a barrel of oil for each year.
    (b) In which year did the price increase most? Give some reasons why the price of oil was set so high in that particular year.

32. As the price of oil increases, so do the prices of other items that use or are produced from oil. As prices go up, people can afford to buy less. How are each of the following people affected by the oil-price increases?
    (a) a truck driver
    (b) an airline employee
    (c) a gasoline-station owner
    (d) an employee of a company that sells plastic packaging

33. As you have noticed, the price of OPEC oil declined somewhat in 1983. What might explain that decline? (How have Canadians reacted to higher oil prices?)

During the oil-price increases of 1973 and 1974, the members of OPEC brought in money more quickly than they had expected. The transfer of money from the oil-buying countries to OPEC was the largest, fastest transfer of wealth in the history of the world. If money had continued to move to OPEC members at that rate, OPEC would have had all the money in the world by the year 2000.

34. (a) Examine Figure 4.23. What resulted from the rapid increase in oil prices by OPEC?
    (b) Why would the members of OPEC be disturbed by the figures in Figure 4.23? Explain.

Figure 4.23
OPEC's Oil
Production,
1973–84
Millions of Barrels
per Day

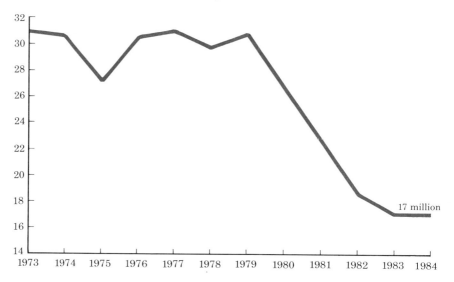

Although the oil crises of the 1970s hurt our economy, Canadians have learned valuable lessons. One is that it is important to conserve energy and use it wisely. Also, Canada has been forced to search out other sources of energy. If the price of oil had not risen so high, Canadians would not have looked for other energy sources as soon.

35. (a) Re-examine Figure 4.23. If the price of OPEC oil goes up again, how will the increase affect Canadians and their use of energy?
    (b) What happens when OPEC oil prices go down?

36. Could a group of countries form an organization similar to OPEC to control the price of chocolate? Explain.

Other Economic Agreements

The EEC is potentially one of the most workable economic agreements; yet, as you have seen, it is having problems. Other trade agreements have fallen apart. The Latin American Free Trade Association, for example, has broken up largely because the countries involved were not willing to co-operate with one another.

The Caribbean Community (**Caricom**) is an economic organization that is designed to promote trade between countries in the Caribbean area. It has experienced very limited success and still faces many problems.

While many large economic organizations such as the EEC and COMECON have been formed in recent years, there has also been a movement toward smaller units. More and more small countries are being formed, despite the economic problems that such small nations face. Some new countries are tiny, consisting of only a few islands in some cases. These small countries seem somehow out of place in our modern world.

37. Why would some people wish to create small countries?

38. What problems do you think these new countries might face in the future?

The Rise of Large Cities

One development that accompanies the economic progress of a country is the rapid growth of large urban centres. These large cities are the centres of economic activity as well as of social and political change. The large cities of the world are growing in population as

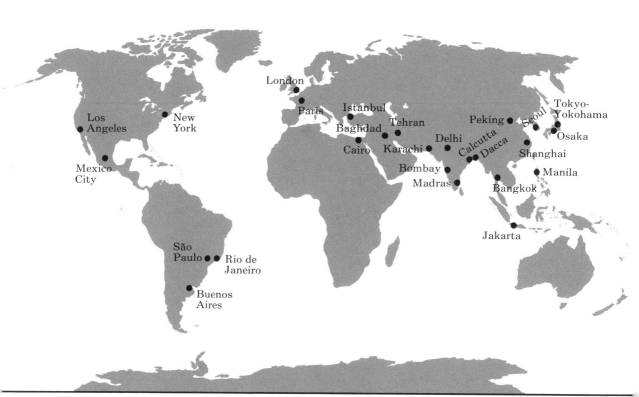

Figure 4.24 Cities That Will Contain Ten Million or More Inhabitants by the Year 2000

well as in size. In 1950, for example, only two cities in the world—New York and London—had populations of over ten million. It is estimated that by the year 2000 there will be 26 cities with ten million or more inhabitants. In addition, there will be many other cities with between five and ten million people.

These cities started to grow from a single centre but have joined with other cities to form a **megalopolis**, which is a very large city. The Tokyo-Yokohama area is a megalopolis of enormous size. Recently, the population of Tokyo-Yokohama has been growing more quickly than that of Japan as a whole. There are more people in the Tokyo area than in all of Portugal, for example.

39. In an atlas, examine a map of Tokyo-Yokohama and discuss the following topics:
    (a) its general location in Japan
    (b) the specific site, including the size of built-up areas
    (c) human and physical factors that have affected the pattern of growth of Tokyo-Yokohama
    (d) smaller cities that have been engulfed by its urban growth

(e) possible future directions of growth (explain)

(f) problems the area could face

40. Identify two other megalopolises in the world.

    (a) Describe their size, location, and approximate population.

    (b) Explain the possible reasons for their growth.

    (c) Suggest future directions of growth.

41. (a) Explain what appears to be the relationship between the location of the world's largest cities and

    • the oceans

    • a country's areas of dense population

    • major transportation routes

    • productive farmland

    • major mineral deposits

    (b) Write about 150 words explaining in general the reasons for the location of the world's largest cities.

It is estimated that by the year 2000, over half of the world's population will live in cities of significant size. Figure 4.25 illustrates the worldwide movement to the cities since 1800.

YEAR	1800	1850	1900	1950	2000
Percentage of world population living in urban areas (over 20 000)	2.4	4.3	9.2	20.9	50.5
Percentage of world population living in rural areas	97.6	95.7	90.8	79.1	49.5

Figure 4.25
Changes in the World's Urban and Rural Populations

42. Construct a bar graph and label it "Growth of Urban Population in the World". Use information from Figure 4.25 to complete the graph.

43. Draw another bar graph labelled "Changes in the Rural Population in the World". Use information from Figure 4.25 to complete the graph.

44. Describe three ways in which life might change for someone who moves to the city from a rural area. Refer to items such as jobs.

45. (a) Obtain a base map for South America and one for Australia. Mark and label the major cities, using an atlas as a guide.

(b) Describe the location of the cities, and suggest four general reasons for their location.

(c) What problems have been avoided by the fact that the cities are located where they are? Explain your answer fully.

The **site** of a city refers to the actual physical qualities of the area the city occupies. Perhaps it occupies a site on a flat coastal plain or a narrow strip of land in a valley. The **situation** of a city is far more important. It refers to the general position of a city relative to such things as other cities and countries, transportation routes, natural resources, and good farmland.

46. Describe the site and situation of two cities near you.

47. (a) Select four cities from any place in the world and describe their sites and situations.

(b) Which city has the most desirable situation? Explain.

Urban Hierarchy

There is a wide variety in the size of settlements around the world. The smallest settlement in North America is usually a hamlet containing fewer than 100 people. A hamlet would provide perhaps seven or eight services for its inhabitants as well as for the rural people who live nearby. You might find a gas station or a coffee shop in a hamlet; for a post office or a grocery store you would probably have to travel to a village.

A village would have a population of about 800 and provide perhaps 60 services. A town of 2800 people would provide more services still, including some that would not be found in a village. A town could have a doctor, a dentist, or a furniture store—greater specialization of services than in a village. As settlements increase in size to that of a city or perhaps a megalopolis, the number and specialization of services also increases. This order of settlements is called a **hierarchy**.

48. (a) What five services would you find in a city that you would likely not find in a town or village?

(b) Give the reasons for this.

As you have seen, settlements provide a variety of services. Some settlements may provide one service or economic activity that dominates the others.

a

b

c

49. (a) Describe what appears to be the chief economic activity for each city in Figure 4.26.
    (b) Why might your conclusions in (a) be inaccurate?

Many cities have an important main function as well as a variety of other functions. New York City, for example, is an important port city, but is also a major banking, manufacturing, and retail centre. New York City is thus a **multifunctional** city.

50. (a) Using an atlas, select two Canadian cities that are multi-functional. List the main activities of each.
    (b) Over a number of years, what advantages would a multifunctional city have over one that had only one main function?

Figure 4.26 Cities with Dominant Economic Activities
(a) Corfu, Greece
(b) Ramsgate, England
(c) Atlantic City, U.S.A.

Figure 4.27 Urban Deterioration in Buffalo, New York

Urban Problems

The growth of cities around the world is not without its accompanying problems. Many cities are overcrowded, noisy, dirty, and lack some of the basic necessities of life for a large proportion of their population.

As the urban environment disintegrates, people experience greater difficulty in coping with life. Under conditions of poor housing and little privacy, people experience high levels of stress and anxiety. Social problems such as family breakup, crime, drug abuse, and violence develop. Overcrowding can also lead to a breakdown in mental and physical health. Other problems such as traffic jams, pollution, and increasing living costs add to the stresses of life in the world's large cities.

51. **What problems are you aware of in cities in your area? Describe the nature of each problem.**

A SIMULATION GAME

Imaville

Imagine that you are the mayor of a rapidly growing city of a million people called Imaville in South America. Your city has a wide range of urban problems that are typical of other large South American cities. These problems include the following:

- desperately poor areas on the outskirts of the city that are home to 80 000 people
- clean water supply for only 150 000 people
- many water-borne diseases such as typhoid and dysentery from polluted city wells
- high unemployment, especially among young people
- massive traffic jams on narrow streets
- some corruption among government workers who fail to carry out needed social programs
- a large oil refinery that employs 4000 people but also produces a chemical fog that hangs over your city
- lack of educational facilities—only a quarter of your city's children go to school
- 100 textile co-operatives that are in great need of money to expand
- a small tourist industry centred on a group of hotels on a nearby beach that needs new access roads

Your job is to suggest four well-designed projects to help tackle the problems of Imaville. Because your resources are limited, you must select your projects carefully to ensure that they have the greatest impact. Give reasons to support your projects; include the specific problems that you are confronting. Explain why you did not deal with the other problems.

Why People Move to Cities

Despite all their problems, cities around the world continue to grow. São Paulo, Brazil, for example, is growing at the rate of over 1000 people every day.

One reason for the growth of cities is the promise of a better life. People hope that cities will provide them with better jobs, more income, and improved housing. In addition, cities are the centres of entertainment, shopping, education, mass media, medical facilities, and government. Change and new technology is introduced first in the cities. In some cases, the hopes people have of improving their lives in the city become a reality; in many instances they do not. Although cities could probably help some people improve their lives, cities cannot cope with the millions who have flooded in during the last 40 years.

Cities also offer hope for women, and for people belonging to racial or religious minorities. Within the economy of a city, these people are likely to have more freedom and a greater chance to improve their lives. Cities often have a more liberal, open society than do other areas of a country.

People also move to cities for social reasons. A woman might come with her family to join her husband who moved there to work. Friends and relatives provide an important attraction for those outside the city. Recent immigrants to a country will likely settle in cities where others of similar background live.

Young people may also go to the city, seeing no future for themselves in rural areas, including farms. Life on the farm often involves hard work for little pay. Droughts, floods, or simply low incomes can make life on the farm very difficult, if not unbearable.

Although the growth trend of urban centres in much of the Third World appears to be strong, in the First World it is slowing. In the United States, for example, many cities have stopped growing in the 1980s.

52. (a) If you live in a city, what are your impressions of life in a rural area? Would you like to live there? Explain.

(b) If you live in a rural area, what are your impressions of life in the city? Would you like to live there? Explain.

53. What programs would you suggest for the Brazilian government to deal with or possibly limit the great number of immigrants entering São Paulo?

VOCABULARY

black market	European Economic	police state
bourgeoisie	Community (EEC)	proletariat
Caricom	exploit	Second World
Cold War	First World	site
COMECON	Five-Year Plan	situation
consumer goods	hierarchy	socialism
co-operative	megalopolis	superpower
European Common	multifunctional	Third World
Market	OPEC	welfare state
	peasant	World Bank

RESEARCH QUESTIONS

To answer these questions, you will probably need to refer to library resources and other sources of information.

1. Use your library and its encyclopedias as well as other books for this question.
   (a) Research the U.S.S.R. under these headings:
   • Geographic size and location
   • Main crops and where they are grown
   • Climate
   • Problems in agriculture
   (b) Using the headings above, write two pages to discuss agriculture in the U.S.S.R.

2. Select three of the following countries for research:

Singapore	India	Australia
Mexico	Pakistan	Bolivia
China	Taiwan	Nigeria

For each country that you have selected,
(a) place it at the appropriate point on the scale in Figure 4.4. Give reasons for your decision.

(b) record the basic statistics, as is done in the text for Brazil
(c) describe the general standard of living
(d) outline the problems it faces from an economic point of view

3. (a) What is the International Monetary Fund (IMF)?
   (b) When and why was it set up?
   (c) What importance does it have for the economy of the world today?

4. Discuss the major programs and policies set up by the EEC. What importance do these policies have for the countries in the EEC, and for countries outside it? Your answer should be about 300 words in length.

5. Select one of the following cities for study:

Cairo, Egypt
Calcutta, India
Manila, the Philippines
Buenos Aires, Argentina

For the city you selected, research the following items:
(a) site and situation
(b) principal industries
(c) population and rate of growth
(d) problems
(e) attempted solutions to problems
(f) future prospects

Industry in Canada Today

The Sectors of Industry

Canada ranks among the top ten industrial nations in the value of its Gross National Product.

Industry can be divided into three main groups: primary, secondary, tertiary. These groups are illustrated in Figure 5.1.

Figure 5.1 The Three Industrial Sectors

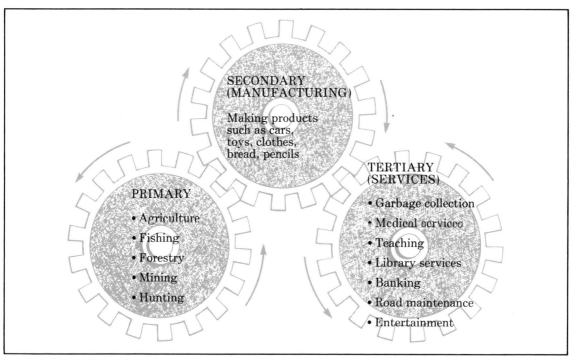

SECONDARY (MANUFACTURING)

Making products such as cars, toys, clothes, bread, pencils

PRIMARY

• Agriculture
• Fishing
• Forestry
• Mining
• Hunting

TERTIARY (SERVICES)

• Garbage collection
• Medical services
• Teaching
• Library services
• Banking
• Road maintenance
• Entertainment

1. **Primary industry** involves the extraction of raw materials from the land or water. Agriculture is included in this sector because it uses the land directly. The products of primary industries are often the raw materials of secondary industry.

2. **Secondary industry** is commonly referred to as **manufacturing**. In manufacturing, the raw materials provided by primary industries are processed or made into items that are often retailed, mostly in stores.

   Primary manufacturing, such as steelmaking, makes up the first stage in the processing of raw materials. **Secondary manufacturing** involves their further processing into more complex items, such as cars or appliances.

3. **Tertiary** (or service) **industries** are those that sell or provide a service to people. Tertiary industry often involves selling or using a product from a secondary industry.

1. (a) Below is a list of jobs. Copy the list into your notebook. Beside each item write P (primary), S (secondary), or T (tertiary), depending upon the sector in which it falls.

   Gas-pump attendant
   Steel-mill worker
   Professional hunter
   Fisherman
   Medical-research worker
   Construction worker
   Farm-equipment salesperson
   Logger
   Social worker
   Railway engineer

   (b) Write down the names and occupations of five employed people whom you know. Beside each, write down whether they work in primary, secondary, or tertiary industry.

   (c) What kind of permanent employment do you hope or expect to have? In which industrial sector does it fall?

2. (a) Using Figure 5.2, write about 100 words to describe the changes in employment between 1951 and 1982. Your description should mention
   • total employment in Canada
   • changes in the proportion of people employed in each industrial sector

Figure 5.2
Changes in the
Number of People
Employed in Each
Sector of Industry
in Canada,
1951-82

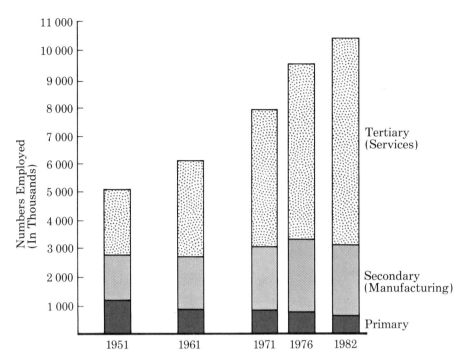

(b) Although the number of people employed in primary industries decreased between 1951 and 1982, productivity has
increased greatly. As you will remember, productivity refers
to the amount of work produced by one person.

What reason can you suggest to explain why the productivity of workers has increased so much in primary
industries? Give an example from an industry such as farming
to back up your answer.

3. (a) Figure 5.3 shows the percentage of the total work force
employed in each industrial sector in Canada from 1951 to
1981. Plot these statistics, using the same method as is illustrated in Figure 5.2.

Figure 5.3
Percentage of
Total Work Force
Employed in Each
Industrial Sector
in Canada,
1951–81

SECTOR	1951	1961	1971	1976	1981
Primary	23	14	9	7	6
Secondary	33	30	28	27	23
Tertiary	44	56	63	66	71

(b) Compare your graph with the one in Figure 5.2. What advantages and/or disadvantages are there in dealing with
• actual figures, as in Figure 5.2?
• percentages, as in your graph?

4. The tertiary sector may continue to expand in the future. Name three types of services that you think might become more important in the future. Give reasons for your answer.

5. Assume that you have saved enough money to start your own business in tertiary industry. Think of a small service business that you would enjoy running, such as a portrait photography studio, a window washing company, or a small restaurant. You might be able to start the business by running it out of your residence. Describe the business under these headings:
   (a) type of business
   (b) who would use your business/service
   (c) the advertising you would use
   (d) equipment necessary
   (e) probable hours of work during a week

Industrial Location

All types of industries have basic requirements that determine where they will be located. For example, as shown in Figure 5.4, Canada's primary industries are situated close to raw materials or, as in the case of agriculture, close to suitable farming areas. Manufacturing activities are concentrated in urban areas, which provide the labour requirements, **markets,** and transportation services.

Figure 5.4 The Location of Secondary and Tertiary Industries in Canada

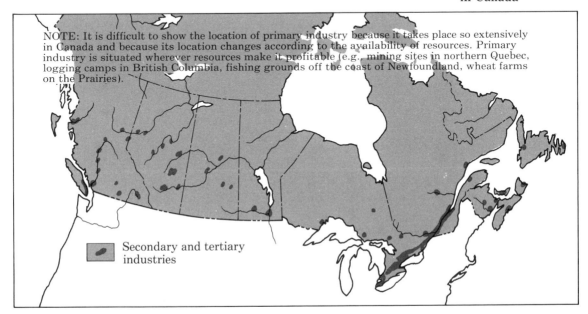

NOTE: It is difficult to show the location of primary industry because it takes place so extensively in Canada and because its location changes according to the availability of resources. Primary industry is situated wherever resources make it profitable (e.g., mining sites in northern Quebec, logging camps in British Columbia, fishing grounds off the coast of Newfoundland, wheat farms on the Prairies).

Secondary and tertiary industries

Deciding Where to Locate

When a company decides whether or not to proceed with the development of an industry in Canada, it is first interested in the amount of profit it will make. This is called the **profit motive**. The success of the venture depends to a great extent on choosing the best possible location, where costs will be kept to a minimum and the value of sales will be highest.

A S I M U L A T I O N   G A M E

Choosing the Best Site for a Steel Plant

Imagine that you are a consultant to the steel industry. A company has employed you to determine the suitability of six possible locations for their smelter and steel mills. Each of the six cities has a suitable labour force, an adequate supply of fresh water, and the necessary waste disposal facilities.

Figure 5.5 The Situation of Six Possible Steel Centres

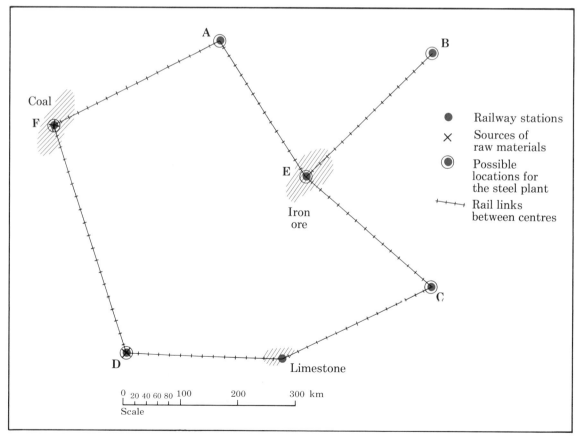

Once your evaluation has been made, the accessibility to markets will be considered. This, however, is not part of your assignment. You are concerned only with the costs of transporting raw materials to each of the possible locations. The six cities appear in Figure 5.5.

The following information is supplied to you. The cost of transporting one year's requirements of the three main raw materials to the steel plant would be

iron ore	$15 000/km
coal	$10 000/km
limestone	$ 2 000/km

6. (a) **Set up a table in your notebook similar to that in Figure 5.6. Fill in information by measuring distances between pairs of cities. To obtain the cost of transporting raw materials, multiply this distance by the appropriate cost per kilometre. The calculations for city C are done for you.**
  (b) **From your answers to question (a), rank the cities from 1 to 6, with 1 being the most suitable and 6 the least suitable.**

	A	B	C		D	E	F
Iron ore							
Distance (kilometres)			280				
Annual cost per kilometre ($)			(× 15 000)				
Cost ($)			4 200 000				
Coal							
Distance (kilometres)			870				
Annual cost per kilometre ($)			(× 10 000)				
Cost ($)			8 700 000				
Limestone							
Distance (kilometres)			280				
Annual cost per kilometre ($)			(× 2 000)				
Cost ($)			560 000				
Total annual cost ($)			13 460 000				

Figure 5.6 Cost Involved in Transporting Raw Materials

SAMPLE ONLY

After narrowing the search to several cities, an executive would make a much more detailed study of each place before selecting one. He or she would ask the additional questions shown in Figure 5.7.

Figure 5.7 Further Locational Considerations

Are there other firms in the area that would be of value?

Is there a good local market?

Are there local incentives for establishing a plant?

Is there a suitable, serviced site?

What facilities would attract valuable employees?

Are there suitable workers, and housing and facilities for them?

7. Study Figure 5.8. Name the city in which you would choose to locate a large factory. Give reasons for your choice. Explain why you rejected the other two cities.

Figure 5.8 Local Conditions in Three Cities

	CITY 1	CITY 2	CITY 3
Population	250 000	150 000	400 000
Facilities	Good	Limited	Varied, good
Serviced land available	Yes	Yes	Yes
Local incentives	20% reduction in land taxes	30% reduction in land taxes	None
Special facilities or features	Technical college, hotel, ski slopes	Safe, quiet, small city	University, hotels, golf course

Important Locational Factors

- availability of resources and the cost of transporting them
- availability of significant markets and the cost of transporting finished items to them
- suitability of the site. Is the site adequate and flat enough for the plant? Is it serviced with water, sewage disposal, and power? Is the cost of the site reasonable?
- availability of labour suitable for the industry. Are there facilities to attract labour to the area? Is there adequate housing, or will houses and services have to be provided by the company?
- sufficient **capital** (money) to build and equip the industry. Towns, cities, provinces, and even the federal government sometimes offer incentives to industries to encourage them to locate in certain places. Tax reductions, interest-free or low-interest loans, and even grants may be offered; these are significant pull factors in attracting industry to a particular place.

8. **Explain the benefits that result from offering incentives to industries to locate away from large industrial cities. Consider**
   (a) **the benefits to the people living in the community where the industry locates**
   (b) **the benefits to the larger city where it does not locate**

9. (a) **Discuss urban and rural centres that you would expect to use incentives, and why they would use them.**
   (b) **Where would industries choose to locate if no incentives were offered? Give reasons for your answer.**

10. **Calgary's industries are based primarily on the processing of raw materials from the areas near the city. Among its industries are**

    - **flour mills, which depend on wheat**
    - **meat packing, which depends on cattle farming**
    - **a distillery, which depends on grain**
    - **oil refineries, which depend on oil supplies**
    - **fertilizer manufacturing, which depends on chemicals from oil refining**
    - **railway equipment, which depends on steel from scrap metal**
    - **asphalt roofing, which depends on gravel and oil residues**

    (a) **Print the names of all of these industries, spread out on a sheet of paper. Draw arrows between those that have some connection to each other.**
    (b) **Choose any four industries and, one at a time, explain how each benefits from the presence of at least three of the other industries in Calgary.**

The Importance of Resources

To satisfy needs and desires for the products of manufacturing—houses, cars, clothing, and food—**resources** are required. Natural resources can be divided into two kinds. **Renewable resources**, such as forests and fish, replace or regenerate themselves. Minerals, on the other hand, took millions of years to form. In effect, once they are gone, they cannot be replaced. Thus they are called **non-renewable resources**.

**Figure 5.9
Our Natural
Resources**

Water

Minerals

Falling water

Wild animals

Forests

Fish

Soil

Human skills

People are a valuable renewable resource. Human skills, brainpower, and motivation help determine the future prospects of this planet.

11. **Set up a table with the following headings:**

Renewable Resource	Ways in Which It Can Be Destroyed	Ways in Which It Can Be Protected
	SAMPLE ONLY	

In the left-hand column, list five renewable resources that appear in Figure 5.9. Then fill in the remainder of the table.

Canada's resources are being used up at a high rate. Many are being exported to other, resource-hungry nations. Predictions about when the world's non-renewable resources will run out are given in Figure 5.10.

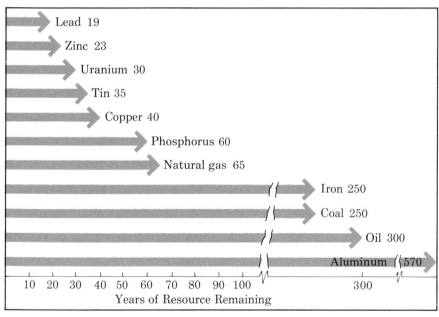

Figure 5.10 Estimated World Reserves of Some Nonrenewable Resources

Technology affords a more economical use of resources. New processes make it possible to

• discover more deposits
• use low-quality deposits that were previously unusable
• recognize the value of previously untapped resources
• improve methods of recovery and recycling
• substitute plentiful minerals for those that are in short supply

Many minerals exist in the form of nodules (which look rather like burned baked potatoes) on the floor of the oceans. Figure 5.11 compares estimated world reserves of certain minerals (calculated at the present rate of consumption) on the land and beneath the sea.

Figure 5.11 Land and Sea Reserves of Selected Minerals, 1981

MINERAL	LAND RESERVES (In Years)	OCEANIC RESERVES (In Years)
Manganese	100	400 000
Cobalt	100	200 000
Nickel	100	150 000
Copper	40	6 000
Bauxite	100	20 000

Figure 5.12 Some Environmental Problems Resulting from Our Increasing Demand on the Earth's Resources, and Their Solutions

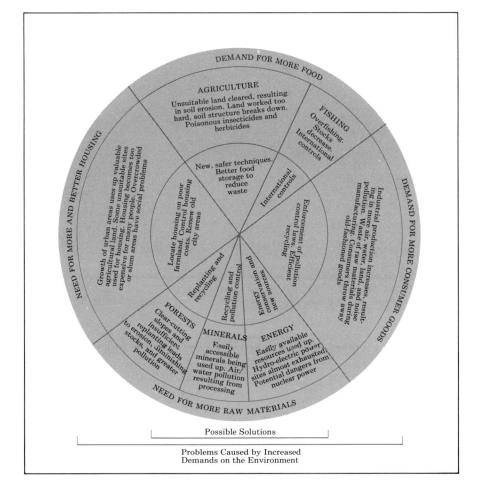

Nodule-collection technology is currently being developed by Japan, the U.S., and France. This kind of breakthrough will change the future of life on this planet.

Figure 5.12 provides a brief summary of the problems that people create as the standard of living rises. Mines and their waste, and extensive logging by the forestry industry scar the landscape. Precious soil is washing and blowing away. Canada loses six thousand million tonnes of topsoil annually, enough to reduce our crop production by the equivalent of half a million hectares of land each year. Waterways are often blocked by the soil lost due to logging and erosion, and to the debris produced by industries and sewage systems. This can result in increased flooding, which creates a great deal of damage. Air and water are being polluted by the chemicals used in agriculture, forestry, and industry.

Not only is the environment being poisoned, it is being buried in garbage. Large areas near our cities are used to bury the wastes collected. Good land is already being used for this purpose, and suitable sites for garbage dumps are running out. Recycling of waste will be part of the long-term answer.

Transportation Provides the Vital Link

In a country as large as Canada, transporting raw materials and finished products is a major component of industrial costs. The construction and maintenance of transportation links is costly, yet very important to our economy.

12. List each of the following resources in your notebook. Beside each, write the most likely method(s) of transportation used to move it in Canada.

coal   wheat
oil   iron ore
electricity   fresh water

13. Obtain maps of Canada that show
   • the distribution of primary and manufacturing industries
   • major transportation links
   • population distribution

   Locate three isolated cities in Canada that are involved in extracting raw materials (e.g., a mining or a pulp and paper industry). Describe the location of each city, the raw materials extracted in each, and the types of transportation used. Design a table similar to the one on the following page.

NAME OF CITY	LOCATION	TYPE OF RAW MATERIAL BEING EXTRACTED	TYPES OF TRANSPORTATION LINKS TO OUTSIDE CANADIAN CENTRES AND OTHER COUNTRIES
1			
2			
3			

SAMPLE ONLY

14. (a) Where are the greatest densities of highways in Canada? Choose three general areas.
   (b) Suggest reasons for high-density areas transport facilities.

Figure 5.13 shows where the manufactured goods produced by each region in Canada in 1981 were eventually sold.

Figure 5.13 Origin and Destination of Goods Manufactured in Canada, 1981 (In Percentages)

ORIGIN	DESTINATION						
	ATLANTIC PROVINCES	QUEBEC	ONTARIO	PRAIRIE PROVINCES	BRITISH COLUMBIA	OTHER COUNTRIES	UNALLOCATED AND REPAIR WORK
Atlantic provinces	41	9	7	1	1	34	7
Quebec	4	50	19	4	2	14	7
Ontario	3	11	51	6	3	20	6
Prairie provinces	1	6	7	63	8	9	6
British Columbia	1	1	3	8	39	38	10

15. Using Figure 5.13 as a guide, answer the following questions.
   (a) Examine the statistics for the region in which you live. Where are most goods sold that are manufactured in your region?
   (b) Is the pattern that you discovered in (a) true for other regions of Canada? Why or why not?

(c) When goods manufactured in your region are sold elsewhere in Canada, where are the most important markets? Why is this so?

(d) Which regions export over 15% of their products to other countries? How has the geographic location of these regions affected their international trade?

16. Why is trade between Canada's regions vital to our economy?

International Trade

Canada is very dependent on international trade, more so than are most other countries. Canada's exports of resources enable it to pay for its imports. Figure 5.14 shows the value of its imports and exports in 1981.

**Figure 5.14
Canada's Major
Imports and
Exports, 1981**

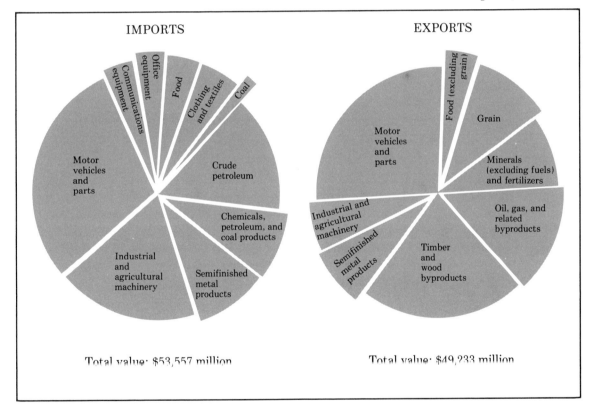

The countries with which Canada trades are called **trading partners**. Figure 5.15 shows the major trading partners and what percentage of Canada's imports and exports each of these countries accounted for in 1981.

Figure 5.15
Canada's Major
Trading Partners,
1981 (In
Percentages)

COUNTRY	IMPORTS	EXPORTS
United States	64	64
Japan	5	5
United Kingdom	3	4
West Germany	2	2
Venezuela	3	1
France	1	1
Italy	1	1
Other	21	22

17. Plot two pie graphs to illustrate the information in Figure 5.15. (See Chapter 1 for instructions on how to draw a pie graph.) Label and colour your graphs and give them appropriate titles.

18. (a) Most of Canada's international trade is with the United States. What reason can you suggest for this?
    (b) Canada also carries on much trade with the United Kingdom. Suggest four reasons for this. Refer to a world map in an atlas as well as to the discussion of the U.K. in Chapter 3.
    (c) Canada's exports to Japan consist chiefly of raw materials such as coal and wood, whereas our imports are mostly manufactured goods, such as stereos and cars. What are the long-term results of this pattern of trade?

19. Consider your answer to question 18.
    (a) What benefits would result from increasing our own manufacturing industries?
    (b) What problems would have to be overcome to develop these industries?

20. In many newly industrialized countries, such as South Korea, Taiwan, Mexico, and Brazil, manufactured goods can be produced at a much lower cost than in Canada.
    (a) Why?
    (b) Should Canada try to compete with these countries? Explain.
    (c) What can Canada do to deal with the problem? Develop your ideas fully.

The Organization of Industry

Canadian businesses vary greatly in size and structure. They fall into four main groups, as shown in Figure 5.16.

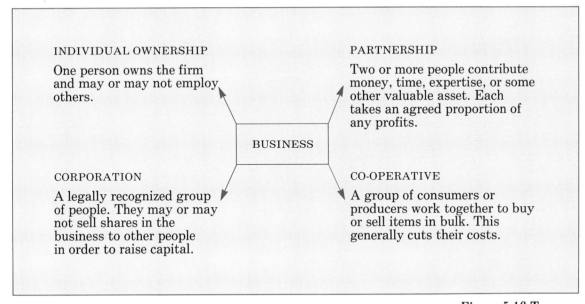

INDIVIDUAL OWNERSHIP

One person owns the firm and may or may not employ others.

PARTNERSHIP

Two or more people contribute money, time, expertise, or some other valuable asset. Each takes an agreed proportion of any profits.

BUSINESS

CORPORATION

A legally recognized group of people. They may or may not sell shares in the business to other people in order to raise capital.

CO-OPERATIVE

A group of consumers or producers work together to buy or sell items in bulk. This generally cuts their costs.

Figure 5.16 Types of Business Structures in Canada

21. Read each of the following descriptions. What type of business structure is involved in each?
    (a) Jane and Ahmed open a bookstore. They agree to share all costs and profits equally.
    (b) Bryan needs more capital to expand his photographic company. He sells 5000 shares to other people, who will receive a percentage of any profits.
    (c) Having inherited $20 000 from a relative, Riccio leaves school and opens his own motorcycle repair shop.
    (d) Ten wheat farmers together buy a grain elevator to cut the cost of grain storage.

22. (a) If you were to inherit $30 000, what kind of business would you set up? Explain the various items on which you would spend the money in setting up your business.
    (b) When you leave high school, college, or university, you might decide to start your own business. How could you raise $20 000 capital? What arrangements would you make with those who had lent the money?

23. Examine Figure 5.17. Describe how the relative importance of the various types of business structures in Canada has changed since 1946. Suggest some reasons for these changes.

Figure 5.17 Relative Importance of the Various Types of Business Structures in Canada, 1946-76

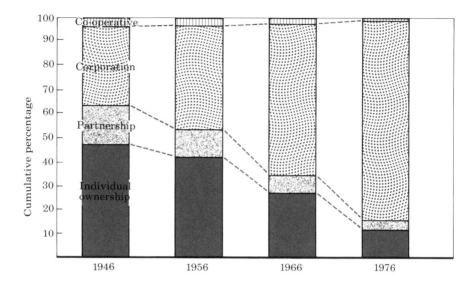

Some of the larger companies in Canada are part of multinational corporations, including oil companies, food processors, department stores, and book publishers. Most of the multinationals operating in Canada have head offices in the United States. As Figure 5.18 shows, there are advantages and disadvantages to this arrangement.

Some Canadian companies have branch plants in other countries. These include Massey-Ferguson, the Royal Bank, and Noranda Mines.

Figure 5.18 Some Advantages and Disadvantages of Having Multinational Branch Plants in Canada

ADVANTAGES	DISADVANTAGES
• They create jobs for Canadians.	• They often operate in the best interest of foreign owners.
• They may encourage associated economic growth.	• Profits from foreign countries are returned to the head office.
• They often introduce new technology.	• Little research and development takes place in Canada.
• They often invest large amounts of capital in Canada.	

Figure 5.19
A Massey-
Ferguson
Tractor Being
Used in Thailand

Labour-Management Relations

One in every three Canadian workers is a member of a trade union. The earliest-known trade union in Canada was the Printers Union in Quebec City in 1827. Today, the largest union in Canada is the Canadian Union of Public Employees (CUPE), with more than 200 000 members.

Strikes, the withdrawal of labour by a group of workers, are given a great amount of publicity, although 90% of all labour-management negotiations end in agreement. Workers consider the strike to be an important vehicle in attempting to protect their rights, and in winning important concessions from their employers.

Figure 5.20 Some
of the Results
of a Strike by
Grainhandlers in
Vancouver

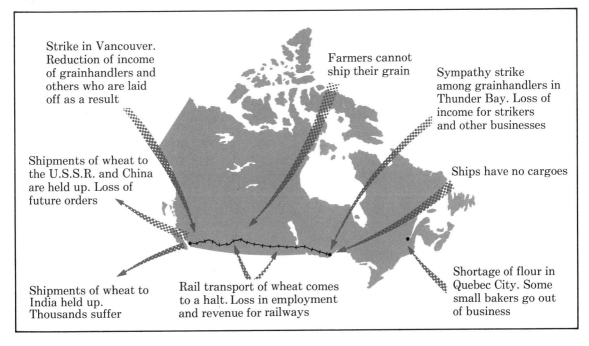

Strike in Vancouver. Reduction of income of grainhandlers and others who are laid off as a result

Farmers cannot ship their grain

Sympathy strike among grainhandlers in Thunder Bay. Loss of income for strikers and other businesses

Shipments of wheat to the U.S.S.R. and China are held up. Loss of future orders

Ships have no cargoes

Shipments of wheat to India held up. Thousands suffer

Rail transport of wheat comes to a halt. Loss in employment and revenue for railways

Shortage of flour in Quebec City. Some small bakers go out of business

Figure 5.20 illustrates how far-reaching the effects of a strike can be. Strikes are especially costly for workers and employers. To avoid strikes, some firms use a system that encourages workers to increase productivity and profits. Dofasco, a steel company in Hamilton, and the Sears chain of department stores give their long-term employees shares in their companies so that they are able to benefit from the profits. This system is called **profit sharing**.

As Figure 5.21 shows, unions work to secure many worthwhile benefits for their members. Union demands sometimes backfire however. One photographic firm had intended to make its Ontario plant one of its most important centres. Once the workers had established a union, however, the firm revised its plans, keeping the Canadian plant at a minimum size while expanding its non-unionized operations in New York.

24. (a) **In what ways have you or your family been affected directly or indirectly by strikes?**
    (b) **Would you prefer to work at a unionized or non-unionized job? Carefully explain your answer.**

**Figure 5.21
Trade Union
Activities**

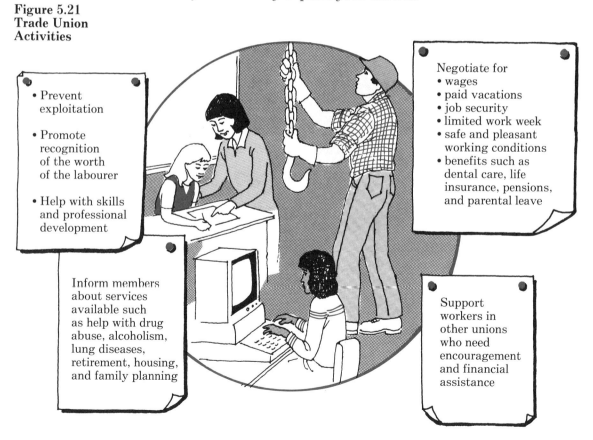

• Prevent exploitation

• Promote recognition of the worth of the labourer

• Help with skills and professional development

Inform members about services available such as help with drug abuse, alcoholism, lung diseases, retirement, housing, and family planning

Negotiate for
• wages
• paid vacations
• job security
• limited work week
• safe and pleasant working conditions
• benefits such as dental care, life insurance, pensions, and parental leave

Support workers in other unions who need encouragement and financial assistance

25. (a) List two advantages of the Dofasco and Sears system of
        employee relations
        • from the employer's point of view
        • from the employees' point of view
    (b) List as many reasons as you can think of why most firms
        do not use the Dofasco and Sears system.

26. Imagine that you are the president of a firm that has 400
    employees. Would you prefer to
    • have your workers involved when making decisions, and also
      sharing in the firm's profits, or
    • have them belonging to a union, or
    • have them non-unionized and excluded from profit sharing
      and decision making?

    Carefully explain why you made your choice and rejected the
    others.

Government Influence on Industry

Governments, whether federal, provincial, or municipal, have a
tremendous direct or indirect effect on industrial development.
Tariffs and import quotas, for example, are controlled by the federal
government. They may determine how well Canadian manufacturers and their products can compete with products from other
countries. The federal Department of Regional Economic Expansion
(DREE) was formed in 1969 to co-ordinate three programs. Each
one is designed to improve economic conditions in depressed areas.
The programs are

• the Prairie Farm Rehabilitation Administration (PFRA)
• the Agricultural and Rural Development Act (ARDA)
• the Fund for Rural Economic Development (FRED)

    Federal and provincial governments are also responsible for
setting up agreements for exporting Canadian products. The more
that Canada can export, the healthier its industries will be. Trade
fairs in foreign countries are one method of displaying Canadian
goods. Provincial and municipal governments attempt to attract
industries to certain areas. Their incentives to industry might
involve lower taxes or less expensive land.
    Environmental and safety controls enforced by federal and pro-
vincial laws usually increase industrial production costs. These
controls are designed to benefit workers and people living near
industries. In some cases, however, these laws are relaxed to lower

the costs of industry and save jobs. INCO, which owns a nickel-smelting operation in Sudbury, Ontario, is North America's greatest single source of sulphur dioxide, a major cause of acid rain. Strict laws to reduce this pollution have been relaxed to reduce the cost to INCO and to save jobs. In Alberta, sulphur is being emitted from natural-gas scrubbers. Little has been done by the government to impose controls on these sulphur emissions, which are known to be harmful to cattle.

The government finds itself in the centre of a conflict. On the one side are those whose health is affected by poor pollution control and those concerned about maintaining the supply of renewable resources. On the other side are the owners of industry. Strict pollution-control laws protect the environment, but they can discourage industry. This, in turn, may hurt the economy and result in lost jobs. Figure 5.22 illustrates the conflicting pressures exerted on government.

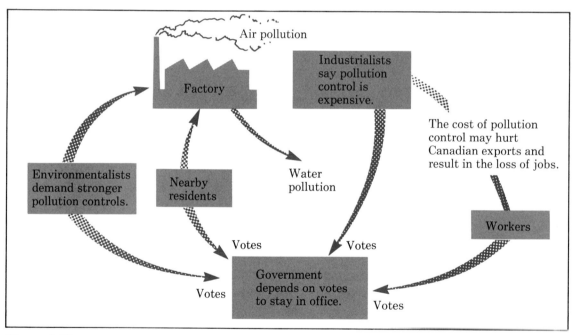

**Figure 5.22
The Conflicting
Pressures on
Government**

27. Consider the following situations, each of which involves pollution. Outline the interest groups that would be involved in each
situation and outline their viewpoints.
   (a) Gasoline and oil from a marina have created surface pollution
      on a fresh-water lake in a cottage area. A nearby town
      draws its drinking water from the lake.

(b) Some dyes are being emptied from a leather tannery into a small creek. The tannery is located on the edge of a small town in a dairy-farming area.

(c) A pulp-and-paper plant in a remote, forested area has been dumping toxic chemicals into a river.

(d) A slaughterhouse is the main employer in a small city. It produces smoke and a strong smell.

28. Which of the four situations in question 27 would be the most difficult to resolve? Explain.

The Effects of Industrialization and Increased Technology

Despite the improvements in our living standards, we hear of and read about crime, suicide, drug addiction, and mental and physical illnesses that are thought to relate to the modern way of life. These problems are not new, however. More than four hundred years ago, Sir Thomas More recognized many of these problems in England. In 1516, he described what he considered to be **Utopia**—the perfect place to live. More's Utopia had the following features:

- It was an island in the northern hemisphere where the temperatures were moderate, the winds gentle, and the grass was green.
- The laws were good and wholesome, and there was no need for lawyers.
- Everyone was employed but nobody was exploited or overworked.
- Work days were six hours long, and city workers and farmers changed places every two years so that no one ever became bored with work.
- There were plenty of recreational activities available.
- The cities were spaced well apart, each surrounded by successful farms.
- The city streets were wide, with large and airy houses, each with its own garden.
- There was religious freedom, free medical care, and a guarantee of peace, freedom, and security for all.

29. The word *Utopia* comes from the Greek words meaning "no place". Why do you think that Sir Thomas More created the word Utopia?

30. In the region of Canada in which you live, how close are people's lives to those in More's Utopia? Refer to each item in his ideal world.

31. **Select three Utopian concepts as outlined by Sir Thomas More. For each one, (a) explain why you think it does not exist, and (b) where you can, explain how it might be possible**

Many people feel isolated from others around them. This feeling is referred to as **alienation**. It is common in a **mass society**, which is an urbanized society with a dense population. Figure 5.23 presents some of the characteristics of a mass society. Others are represented by some students in schools and universities who question the value of years of study that may never lead to a satisfactory job, and some factory workers who find assembly-line jobs to be mindless, dreary, and dehumanizing.

Many activities in the lives of Canadians involve machines and computers rather than human contact. When most people shop, for example, they do not talk to the butcher or baker or shopkeeper. Instead, they shop in large, impersonal stores. Your school report card may be printed by computer rather than handwritten by your teacher. Very soon you will use computers to buy goods from stores and never have to leave your home to shop. Developments such as these isolate people more and more from those around them.

32. **If you could bring changes to society to make it more human, what would those changes be? Write a 200-word essay describing the improvements that you think would combat alienation in Canada today.**

Figure 5.23 Some Characteristics of a Mass Society

Mass communications make us aware of world problems. We feel unable to help.

Our lives may seem dull in comparison with the lives of others.

Advertising encourages us to buy goods that we often do not need and may not be able to afford.

We may become aware of our personal shortcomings (faults).

The Mobility of the Labour Force

Up to about four generations ago, a person would expect to work and die in the community in which he or she was born. Today it is common for people to work in places far away from their homes. Perhaps they travel each day, week, month, or even less frequently to rejoin their families. Those who have special training and skills may find that they need to move to other areas for employment. Manitoba newspapers often contain advertisements for specialists required in Alberta, for example.

In some regions of Canada certain industries are in decline, leaving some workers unemployed or **underemployed** (working at a job that requires less skill and ability than a person has). The auto industry in Windsor in the early 1980s, for example, laid off thousands of workers who then had to search elsewhere for jobs. Improved transportation makes it fairly easy for workers to move to areas where employment opportunities are better, either temporarily or permanently. Thus, in Calgary, there are many people from Newfoundland, but the majority of these people intend to return to Newfoundland when conditions there improve. Figure 5.24 shows the movements of Canadians between regions.

Figure 5.24
Movements of Canadians, 1982 (In Percentages)

ORIGINATING REGIONS	RECEIVING REGIONS					TOTAL LEAVING
	ATLANTIC PROVINCES	QUEBEC	ONTARIO	ALBERTA	WESTERN PROVINCES (Excluding Alberta)	
Newfoundland	4	<1	4	8	3	19
Atlantic provinces (excluding Newfoundland)	2	<1	2	8	2	15
Quebec	1	16	3	4	1	25
Ontario	1	1	10	11	5	28
Western provinces	<1	<1	1	5	6	13
Total arriving	9	17	21	36	17	100

33. Are you a member of a family that has moved within the last ten years for a reason related to a job, or do you know a person or family who has? Describe when the move took place and where the people moved from. Explain why the move took place.

34. (a) What would cause you to move from your home town to another area?
    (b) What disruption in family life would occur with such a move?

Economic Conditions in Canada

During the late 1970s and early 1980s, Canada experienced a fairly high rate of unemployment. As unemployment has risen, so has the cost of living. Inflation has also been a serious problem. In 1983, for example, most consumer goods cost three times as much as they did in 1963. Figure 5.25 shows how inflation has increased the **consumer price index** in Canada. The consumer price index (CPI) gives an indication of the cost of living. It is calculated by including the costs of housing, clothing, transportation, health and personal care, recreation, reading and education, tobacco, and alcohol. One year is chosen for comparison purposes. In Figure 5.25, the base year is 1949, with the CPI at 100.

Figure 5.25 The Consumer Price Index and a Sample Hourly Wage in Canada, 1900−1980

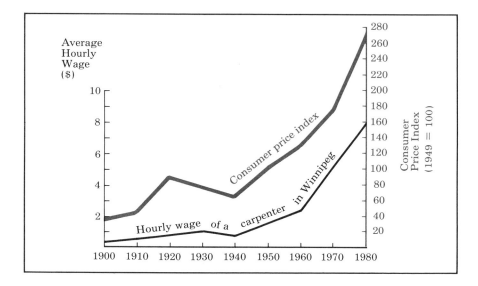

There are two main causes of inflation in Canada. One is external (the influence of the economy on the economies of other countries). The other is internal and results from Canadian economic activity. These factors are summarized in Figure 5.26.

The economies of many industrialized countries such as Canada have experienced high rates of inflation, a stagnant economy, and high levels of unemployment—often suffering all three problems at the same time. This situation is referred to as **stagflation**. As with other problems, stagflation is not a permanent condition of our economy.

Various programs to improve our economic situation have been suggested:

• provide jobs for more Canadians, and match the skills of Canadians to these jobs.

External Reasons

- Oil prices have gone up greatly from $2 a barrel in 1971 to $29 a barrel in 1983.
- Imported goods such as food have gone up in price.

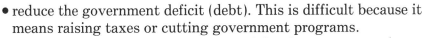

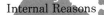

Internal Reasons

- Government allows more money into the economy than the economy can handle. Each dollar, therefore, can buy less.
- People want more and more. With more demand, prices are forced up.
- Wages are increased too quickly at times, thus forcing up prices of manufactured goods.
- Canadians and their governments live beyond their means by borrowing a great deal. Canadians buy goods on credit cards. The government spends more than it takes in in taxes, so it also borrows—for example, it borrows from the Canadian public by selling Canada Savings Bonds.

- reduce the government deficit (debt). This is difficult because it means raising taxes or cutting government programs.
- increase money spent on research and development to produce new products and technology that can be sold to other countries.
- develop high-technology industries such as telecommunications, aerospace, health sciences, and the manufacturing of computer products. This will allow the use of the highly educated work force and will result in products that can be sold throughout the world. These new products are produced by few other countries and are in great demand.
- depend less on foreign countries for oil, energy, and minerals, which are vital to our economy.
- search for new markets for technology and products, especially in the Third World.
- improve the productivity of Canadian industry. This will allow Canadian goods to sell at lower prices in other countries.

Figure 5.26 Factors Causing Inflation

35. (a) **Examine the above list of proposals for the Canadian economy. Although each proposal is important, select two that you feel are particularly significant and on which governments in Canada should concentrate. Give reasons for your selection.**

(b) Which of the proposals might work against some of the other proposals? Explain.

(c) Regardless of the programs that a government might set up, some Canadians would not be pleased. Explain what a government might do to try to reduce criticism of its programs.

Computers

We live in a time of "information explosion". The amount of information available is increasing very quickly. Figure 5.27 shows that every three to five years the amount of information available doubles. Computers enable the storage of this information and the retrieval of any part of it very quickly.

Figure 5.27 The Doubling Time of Information Available to Us

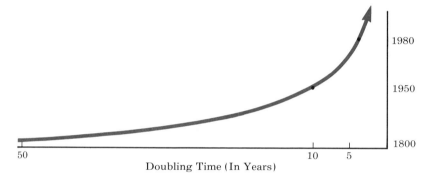

Doubling Time (In Years)

Simple arithmetic can be done by computers faster than by the average human brain, and the results are more reliable. One calculation can be accomplished in about one nanosecond, which is 0.000 000 001 s. The introduction of compact, inexpensive computers means that even small businesses can afford computers to keep track of inventories, payroll, taxation, and accounts.

Computer costs are declining as more and more computers are being built. This is an example of **economy of scale**. It is estimated that, in 1945, a person employed to do simple bookkeeping for a year could be replaced by a computer that would cost $1000 to operate. In 1950, that cost was reduced to $100. In 1955, this amount was further reduced to $10, and in 1975, to $0.01

Home computers are already common in many homes in the U.S., and are becoming increasingly common in Canada. The Telidon system (Figure 5.28), which was devised in 1978 in government laboratories in Ottawa, has been adopted across North America. This may lead to a tremendous growth in the electronics industry of Ontario. Telidon involves a small piece of equipment attached to a television set. When the correct numbers on the handset are pressed, the required information is displayed on the screen.

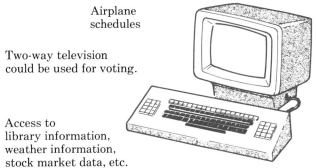

Airplane
schedules

Two-way television
could be used for voting.

Access to
library information,
weather information,
stock market data, etc.

Shopping
at
home

People in homes and
businesses can send
information to a
central computer.

**Figure 5.28
Capabilities of the
Telidon System**

36. Imagine that your family purchased a Telidon decoder to be
    attached to your television set. What information could a com-
    puter supply that would help you in each of the following?
    (a) organizing a family vacation
    (b) making grocery purchases
    (c) making business decisions
    (d) acquiring medical advice
    (e) doing school research assignments

SOMEHOW, I NEVER IMAGINED COMPUTER CRIME TO BE QUITE LIKE THIS!

37. Consider the information about computers given in this section. What skills may be important for Canadians seeking jobs in the next 25 years?

38. Review this chapter and select three themes or ideas that you feel are particularly important. Write a short essay that focusses on those themes and their importance for Canada.

VOCABULARY

alienation	non-renewable	secondary industry
capital	resources	secondary
consumer price	primary industry	manufacturing
index (CPI)	primary	stagflation
economy of scale	manufacturing	tertiary industry
manufacturing	profit motive	trading partners
markets	profit sharing	underemployed
mass society	renewable resources	Utopia
	resources	

RESEARCH QUESTIONS

To answer these questions, you will probably need to refer to library resources and other sources of information.

1. Select a major manufacturing industry in your area. Write a report that focusses on the following topics. Combine your own observations with an interview, if possible, with someone who works in the industry.
   (a) a description of the site of the industry relative to cities, physical features, and other major industries
   (b) major locational factors that apply to the industry
   (c) major markets for the products of the industry
   (d) future of the industry, including problems as well as opportunities for growth

2. Find out how much it costs to advertise in the following media:
   (a) a large-circulation newspaper, in its classified advertisements
   (b) the same newspaper, in its display advertisements (include a number of sizes)
   (c) a local radio station, for 30 s, at various times of the day
   (d) a local television station for 30 s
   - during the morning
   - between 19:00 and 21:00

• during a program that draws a large audience, such as the
     Grey Cup
What conclusions can you draw about the importance of advertising to Canadian industry?

3. The Great Lakes–St. Lawrence Seaway is an important route,
   permitting ocean-going vessels to reach Thunder Bay at the
   western end of Lake Superior.
   (a) Draw a map of the Great Lakes and the St. Lawrence River.
       Mark on your map the major Canadian and American cities
       located near them. Name each of the lakes and the
       St. Lawrence River.
   (b) Draw a profile of the seaway, showing where canals and
       locks have been used to bypass obstructions.
   (c) Using information from an atlas or other reference (the latest
       Canada Yearbook is a good source), list the kinds of products
       moved through the seaway system.
   (d) Imagine that the seaway had never been constructed. In
       what ways would this have affected
       • the development of industry in Ontario?
       • the level of activity at the ports of Halifax, Saint John,
         Quebec, Montreal, Thunder Bay, and Vancouver?
       • Canada-U.S. trade? Give specific examples wherever
         possible.

4. Search newspapers and magazines for articles about labour dis-
   putes in Canada. Collect these articles and paste them into a
   scrapbook. In each case
   (a) identify the firms involved and briefly describe their location,
       the number of employees, and the type of product or service
       provided by the firm
   (b) outline the matters that are in dispute and the state of
       negotiations
   (c) explain who is or who will be affected by a strike

5. The future development and prosperity of the Atlantic
   provinces, particularly of Newfoundland and, to a lesser extent,
   of Nova Scotia, may depend upon the location and exploitation
   of offshore oil and gas deposits.
   (a) Describe how oil and gas deposits are discovered beneath the
       sea. Include diagrams in your answer.
   (b) Using up-to-date information from newspapers, magazines,
       and government sources, produce a map that shows where
       resources have been found. Indicate the size of the deposits,
       where possible.

(c) Explain how offshore drilling rigs extract oil and natural gas from beneath the sea. Include diagrams.

(d) Describe how oil and gas are brought to shore and how they might be brought to shore in the future.

(e) Describe working and living conditions on board an offshore drilling rig.

(f) Would you like to work on an offshore drilling rig? Explain, giving the advantages and disadvantages of such an occupation.

(g) Explain why the Atlantic provinces would benefit from oil and gas discoveries. Include direct and indirect effects.

Transportation: The Essential Link in Our Economy

Introduction

North Americans live in a highly mobile society (one in which people travel a great deal). Transportation systems are designed to move both passengers and freight. Each commodity requires its own special conditions for transport. As a result, the transportation network in North America has become complex.

Freight Transport

The movement of freight is essential to the operation of Canada's economy. Raw materials, finished goods, and semifinished goods are on the move all the time to provide for the high standard of living that most Canadians enjoy.

Figure 6.1. shows several examples of **industrial linkage**, in which goods are moved from one industry to another. The shipment of steel from the steel mill to the engine-assembly factory is one example of industrial linkage.

If the industrial linkages are kept short, there is less likelihood of transportation problems developing. As a result, related industries often cluster together to keep transportation costs low and to avoid disruption.

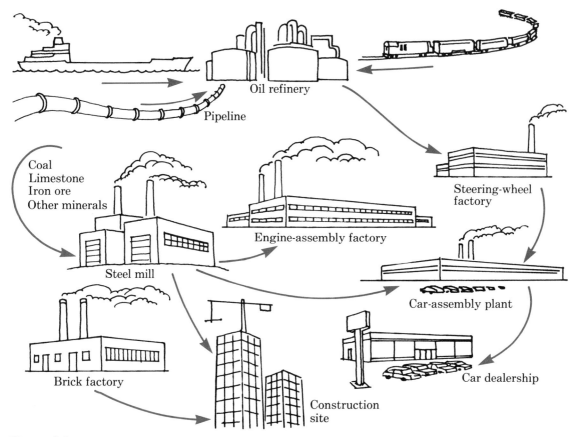

Coal
Limestone
Iron ore
Other minerals

Oil refinery

Pipeline

Steering-wheel
factory

Engine-assembly factory

Steel mill

Car-assembly plant

Brick factory

Construction
site

Car dealership

**Figure 6.1
Freight Transport
is Important to
the Canadian
Economy**

1. There are many industrial linkages missing in Figure 6.1. In some cases, the movement of raw materials to the factory has not been shown. Clay, for example, might be used at the brick factory. List 25 other items that would be shipped to any of the factories illustrated.

2. Using the information in Figure 6.1 and your answer to question 1, write about one-half of a page to show how the transport of freight is important to the economy.

In recent years, as the price of energy has gone up, factories have begun to share other items, such as heat. Factories that are located close to one another can easily share heat energy. This process is referred to as **co-generation**.

With co-generation, the wasted heat is used for a number of purposes, such as those illustrated in Figure 6.2. Of the energy that

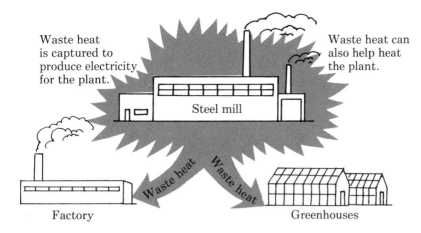

**Figure 6.2
Co-generation
Saves Energy**

Waste heat is captured to produce electricity for the plant.

Waste heat can also help heat the plant.

Steel mill

Waste heat

Waste heat

Factory

Greenhouses

utilities deliver to the user, about 40% goes to industry. Of this amount, close to 75% is used to produce high-temperature heat for food processing, steel making, and other manufacturing processes. For example, the steel plant produces high-temperature heat in its steel-making furnaces. Some of this heat is wasted. With co-generation, this waste heat is used to produce steam, which can in turn generate electricity. The remaining hot water can either heat the plant or supply heat for nearby factories.

Co-generation serves to reduce the transport cost of energy supplies such as coal.

3. **Suggest two types of buildings, other than those in Figure 6.2, that could use heat from a steel plant.**

4. **Write a letter to the president of a steel mill. In the letter, explain the advantages of co-generation and how you hope it can be introduced at the steel plant. Your letter should be about half a page long.**

Methods of Freight Transport

Different goods need to be transported using different methods. Fresh fruit, for example, often needs to be transported quickly from the farm to the store. There are four key modes (methods) of transporting freight in Canada today. Each has its advantages and disadvantages.

5. **(a) Copy Figure 6.3, on the following page, into your notes, including the few points given.**

Figure 6.3
Methods of Transporting Freight in Canada

MODE OF TRANSPORT	CHARACTERISTICS	ADDITIONAL CHARACTERISTICS
Trucks	—Travel time from Halifax to Vancouver approximately four days —Less costly than trains for short distances	
Trains	—Travel time from Halifax to Vancouver approximately 10–14 days —Less costly than trucks for long distances	
Airplanes	—Travel time from Halifax to Vancouver less than one day —Very expensive	
Ships	—Halifax to Vancouver trip would take several weeks —Inexpensive for large quantity of goods	

(b) Complete Figure 6.3 by adding in the blank column various characteristics for each mode of transport. Consider factors such as facilities needed for each mode of transport and restrictions on where each one can travel.

6. Select the most suitable mode(s) of transport for these goods. Give reasons for your answers.
   (a) eggs to be transported 2 km
   (b) furniture to be moved from a house in Winnipeg to one in Vancouver
   (c) a valuable shipment of diamonds to be rushed from Toronto to Halifax
   (d) 4000 t of wheat to be moved from Vancouver to Lima, Peru
   (e) an extra-wide combine harvester to be moved from Hamilton to Regina

Trains

Although railways have been very important in the historical development of Canada, they are of less significance today. Trains

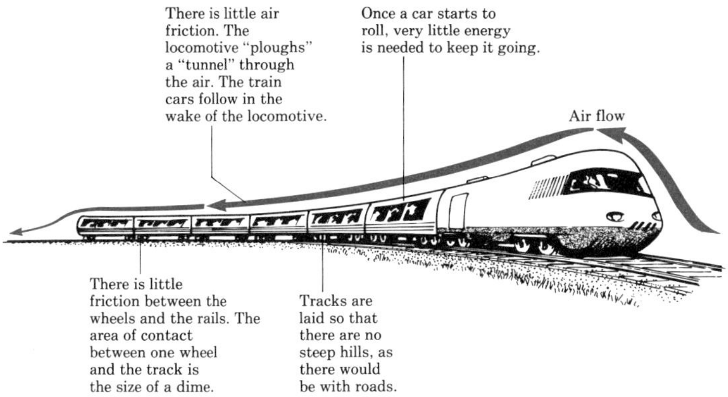

There is little air friction. The locomotive "ploughs" a "tunnel" through the air. The train cars follow in the wake of the locomotive.

Once a car starts to roll, very little energy is needed to keep it going.

Air flow

There is little friction between the wheels and the rails. The area of contact between one wheel and the track is the size of a dime.

Tracks are laid so that there are no steep hills, as there would be with roads.

**Figure 6.4
Trains Use Energy
Efficiently**

are, however, very efficient in their use of energy, as is shown in Figure 6.4

Railway companies, like other transportation companies, are always working on new technology to improve the movement of freight. One recent development is the computer-run **marshalling yard**. In these yards, freight cars are organized to form trains. Different types of cars enter the marshalling yard and are directed to the appropriate track so they can be connected with the correct train. The system for sorting the cars requires little labour and is enhanced by the use of computers.

7. **In your own words, describe what happens to a freight car as it moves through a marshalling yard (left to right in Figure 6.5).**

8. **Why should the freight in a railway car be well tied down?**

9. **What impact would the construction of a marshalling yard have on a nearby community?**

The CN Laser

The letters CN stand for Canadian National. In October 1982, the railway introduced the CN Laser, which is a **piggyback** method of freight transport. A piggyback system is one where trailers from trucks are carried on flat railcars, as is shown in Figure 6.6.

The CN Laser is more than a regular piggyback service. It travels overnight so that, for example, trailers loaded on at 21:00 in Toronto (Brampton) are in Montreal by 04:00 the next morning. With the Laser, there are two identical trains that run in opposite directions every night through the week.

The Toronto-Montreal corridor (route) is very heavily travelled. Over a million trailers move along the highways between Montreal and Toronto every year. This means that new methods of transport such as the Laser can be introduced fairly easily, due to high demand.

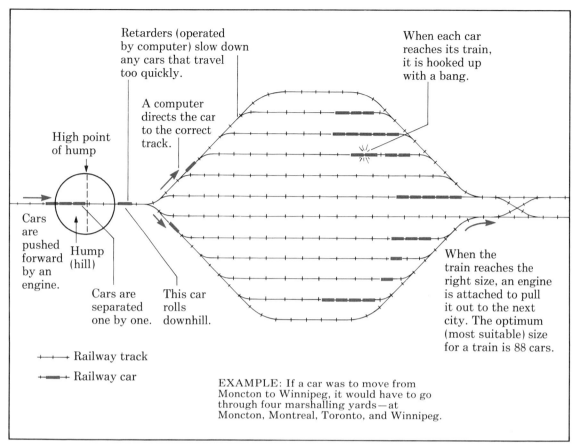

**Figure 6.5
A Computer-Run
Marshalling Yard**

The Laser offers a number of advantages over truck travel or regular freight trains:

- less traffic on highways
- less damage to highways and, consequently, fewer repairs
- less energy used
- almost as fast as truck transport
- fairly inexpensive
- trucks can take trailers to and from rail depots without unloading goods

10. **What two reactions might a trucker who drives the Toronto-Montreal route regularly have to the Laser?**

11. **Design a full-page advertisement for the CN Laser. In the advertisement, you want to point out the positive side to this method of transport. You might want to sketch a picture to help with your advertisement.**

Figure 6.6
A Piggyback

12. (a) In an atlas, turn to a map showing the major cities of North America. Select three other routes where a Laser service might be started. For each of the three routes look for
- two cities that are 600 km or less apart
- two cities, each with a population of at least 1 000 000
- an existing railway track between the cities (if shown on the map)

(b) Using the information on manufacturing listed in an atlas, list the types of products that might be moved along each of the three routes you selected in (a).

CASE STUDY

Moving Pipe to the Beaufort Sea

In certain situations, goods can be moved using a number of methods of transport. This was the case for the movement of 96 lengths of pipe from the Netherlands to an oil-drilling site in the Beaufort Sea. Dome Petroleum workers decided to build an artificial island in the Beaufort Sea and they needed this pipe for the job.

13. (a) Using an atlas, a ruler, and Figure 6.7, measure the distance that the pipe travelled.
(b) Why was the pipe not carried all the way to the Beaufort Sea by ship? (Check the atlas to help with the answer.)

(c) Why were barges chosen to transport the pipe from Hay River to the Beaufort Sea?

(d) From this movement of pipe, what two key conclusions can you draw about transporting freight in Canada?

Figure 6.7
How Ninety-six Lengths of Pipe Were Moved from the Netherlands to the Beaufort Sea

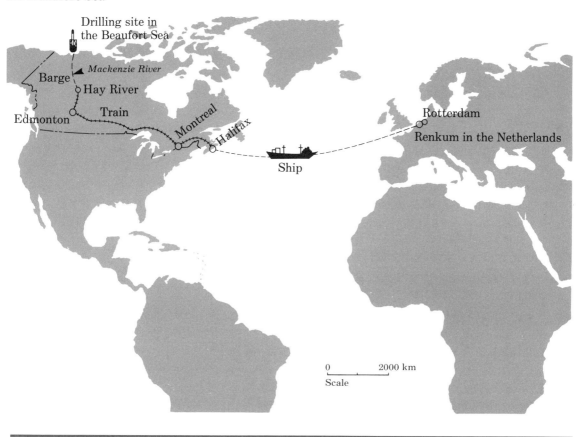

Break-of-Bulk Point

A **break-of-bulk point** is a location where freight is transferred from one mode of transport to another (Figure 6.8). The cities of St. John's, Halifax, Saint John, Montreal, Vancouver, Prince Rupert, and Churchill are examples of break-of-bulk points in Canada. In other parts of the world, New York, Rotterdam, Shanghai, and Lagos, Nigeria, are busy break-of-bulk points.

Figure 6.8 Break-of-Bulk Points
(a) Containers Being Lowered onto a Train
(b) Ship Being Loaded with Grain

Access to Isolated Areas

Isolated areas present particular problems for transportation and freight transport. Geographic conditions may make access to these areas difficult.

14. Examine Figure 6.9. Imagine that you have been hired as a transportation consultant, whose job it is to determine a route for an access road from the highway to the gold deposit.
   (a) Sketch a map similar to that in Figure 6.9.
   (b) Set out the most suitable route for a road into the gold deposit.
   (c) Outline the specific obstacles that you would have to deal with in reaching the site of the gold deposit.
   (d) Measure the length of the road and compare it with straight-line distance. What conclusion can you draw?

**Figure 6.9
Building an
Access Road
to Isolated
Resources**

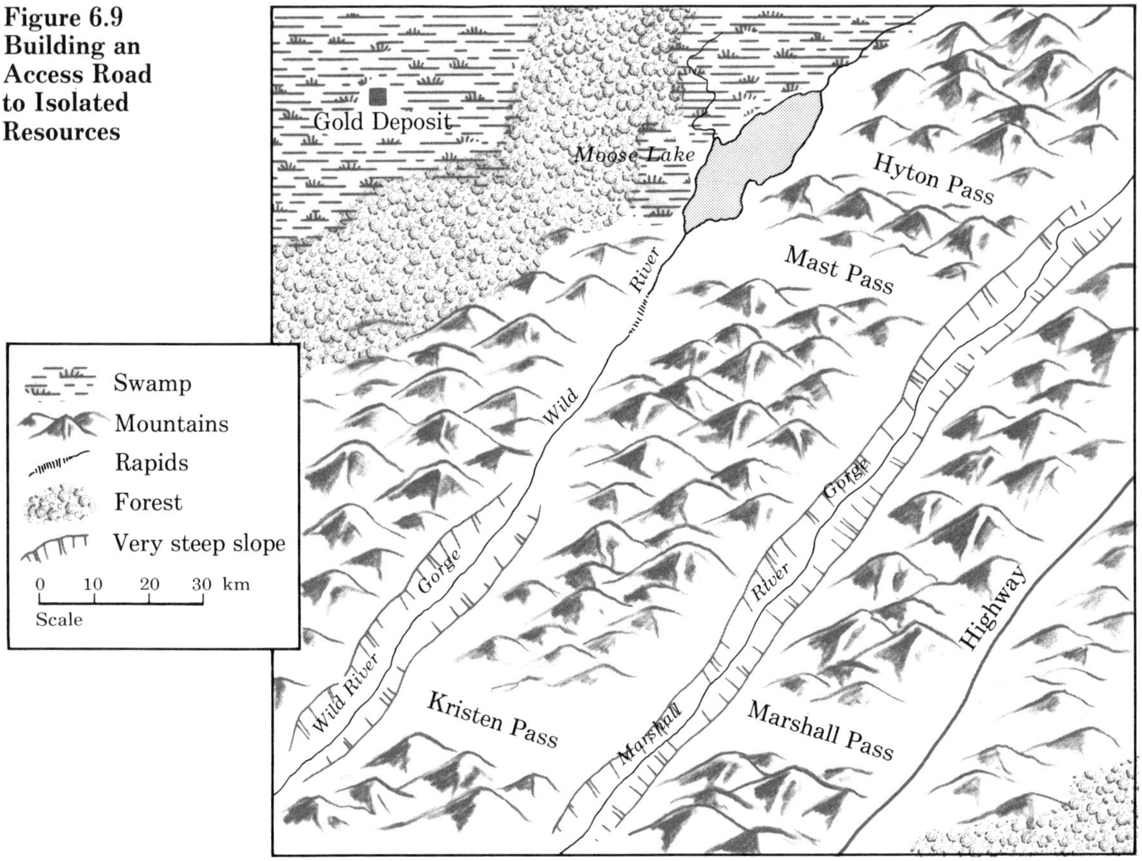

Legend:
- Swamp
- Mountains
- Rapids
- Forest
- Very steep slope

Scale
0 10 20 30 km

Map labels: Gold Deposit, Moose Lake, Hyton Pass, Mast Pass, Wild River, Gorge, River, Gorge, Highway, Wild River, Kristen Pass, Marshall, Marshall Pass

(e) After a town has been set up around the gold mine, what
facilities would need to be developed? Assume the population
of the town is 4000. Give reasons for your answers.

(f) What problems would there be in servicing the town from
the outside?

Freight Transport in Other Countries

Whenever freight is moved in a country, it is important to use the
most suitable method of transport. The modes of transport that a
country uses are influenced by a number of factors, including road
conditions, geographic factors, and the wealth of the people.

15. (a) Examine the photographs in Figure 6.10. What factors
have influenced the type of transport used in each case?

(b) In what ways is each mode of transport well suited for
areas of the Third World?

(c) What modes of transport in Figure 6.10 would not be suitable for the area in which you live? Explain why.

a

b

c

d

Figure 6.10 Modes of Freight Transport
(a) Donkey (Israel)
(b) A Hand-Pulled Cart (Corfu, Greece)
(c) A Man Carrying a Keg of Nails weighing 70 kg
(d) A Sailboat in Peru

(d) How does the energy consumption of these modes of transport compare with those used in Canada?

(e) What does your answer to (d) reveal about Canada's economy compared with those of Third World countries?

International Trade: A Global View

World Shipping Lanes

Shipping on the world's oceans is a very important link in international trade. Although many goods are transported over land by truck or train, the world's shipping lanes also carry great quantities of cargo, especially between continents.

16. (a) Obtain a base map of the world. Using the maps in an atlas, mark the world's major shipping lanes on the base map.

(b) Select 20 of the most important ports around the world. Place an asterisk on each port and label it.

17. (a) Where are the most important (by volume) shipping lanes in the world?
   (b) What does this reveal about the interrelated nature of the economies of the world?

18. (a) Examine the shipping lanes closely. Identify six major straits or canals used by ships.
   (b) What events might occur to prevent traffic from passing through one of these straits or canals?
   (c) What impact would the blocking of one of these routes have on international commerce?
   (d) What might major world powers, such as the United States, do to prevent the kinds of problems that you identified in (b)? What might be the results?

19. (a) In which regions of the world is there a significant volume of international trade moved over land?
   (b) Explain why these regions would use land routes so extensively.

The Role of Trade Agreements

GATT (General Agreement on Tariffs and Trade)

GATT is the framework that controls about 80% of the world's international trade. Most of the countries belonging to GATT are highly industrialized and their exports are mainly manufactured or semi-finished goods. Eighty-eight countries are members of GATT.

GATT came into operation on January 1, 1948. Its primary goal was to increase the volume of trade by reducing **tariffs**. (A tariff is a tax that a government applies to goods imported into the country.) As would be expected, the higher the tariff on goods imported into a country, the fewer the goods that actually do come in.

The prime purpose of a tariff is to protect a country's industries from less-expensive imported goods. If imported goods sell for less than those goods that are produced within a country, the country's citizens will buy the imports rather than domestic goods.

20. Explain the impact of the tariff illustrated in Figure 6.11 on
   (a) the Taiwanese manufacturer
   (b) the Canadian consumer
   (c) the Canadian manufacturer
   (d) the Canadian watchmakers

Figure 6.11 An
Example of the
Impact of Tariffs

(a) Without a Tariff

Watch from Taiwan:
selling price $100.00

Watch made in Canada:
selling price $110.00

(b) With a Tariff

Watch from Taiwan:
Selling price $100.00 plus
$16.70 tariff = $116.70

Watch made in Canada:
selling price $110.00

21. **What would be the result of leaving this tariff in place for
    many years? Consider these factors:**
    (a) efficiency of Canadian watch manufacturing
    (b) international relations
    (c) sales of Canadian goods to Taiwan

The maintenance of a great many tariffs on imported goods
into a country is referred to as **protectionism**. Tariffs are viewed as
a means of protecting the economy of a country. GATT was developed to help break down those tariff barriers and to allow a freer
flow of goods between countries. If there were no tariff barriers
between two or more countries, then there would be **free trade**.

22. **During a period of high unemployment and slow economic
    growth, which philosophy would a country probably support—
    free trade or protectionism? Explain your answer.**

23. **Many people are opposed to free trade. Explain why.**

There are other controls besides tariffs that countries use to
limit trade. Import restrictions limit the number and types of goods
that may be imported into a country. In the case of Japan, for
example, many restrictions apply to the import of goods.

The European Common Market countries and the United
States are dissatisfied with Japanese trading policies. Japan exports
thousands of millions of dollars worth of goods to these countries,
but allows very few goods from these countries back into Japan.
If these other countries seriously restricted the import of Japanese
goods, this would be called a **trade war**.

24. Imagine that a trade war is being waged against a country. Discuss the effects it would have on the country. Consider all aspects of the country's economy.

Third World countries are on the fringe of most world trade. With few manufacturing industries, they must depend on the export of their raw materials to earn money on world markets.

Figure 6.12 International Trade Can Work Against Third World Countries

25. (a) Examine Figure 6.12. What should the people in Ghana do to help solve this problem? Devise a ten-point plan of action.
    (b) What role might the First World have in helping to correct such problems?

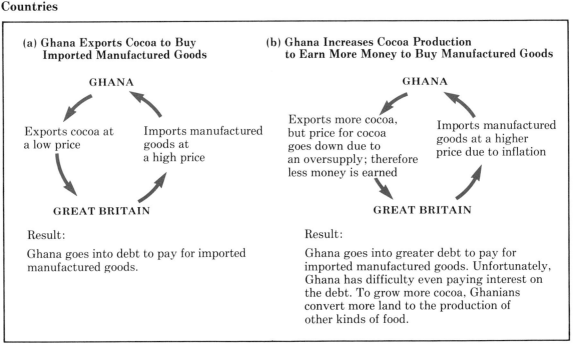

(a) Ghana Exports Cocoa to Buy Imported Manufactured Goods

GHANA

Exports cocoa at a low price

Imports manufactured goods at a high price

GREAT BRITAIN

Result:
Ghana goes into debt to pay for imported manufactured goods.

(b) Ghana Increases Cocoa Production to Earn More Money to Buy Manufactured Goods

GHANA

Exports more cocoa, but price for cocoa goes down due to an oversupply; therefore less money is earned

Imports manufactured goods at a higher price due to inflation

GREAT BRITAIN

Result:
Ghana goes into greater debt to pay for imported manufactured goods. Unfortunately, Ghana has difficulty even paying interest on the debt. To grow more cocoa, Ghanians convert more land to the production of other kinds of food.

Passenger Transportation

Automobile Transportation

Since the introduction of low-cost, mass-produced cars, the automobile has greatly changed the geography of the world. In North America especially, many cities have been built to accommodate cars (Figure 6.13).

During World War I and in the 1920s, most of our cities were still designed for people who walked or who rode in horse-drawn

Figure 6.13 Accommodating the Automobile in Urban Design. Our cities contain many expressways that use up valuable land.

carriages. Generally, the roads were poorly maintained and were too narrow for automobile traffic. After a heavy snowfall, it might take days before the roads were usable again. In the countryside, roads were often deeply rutted with little gravel to cover the surface.

With the increasing popularity of cars after World War II, city planners began to take the car into serious consideration in their planning. They made streets wider, introduced garages for many homes, and began creating large parking lots. By the 1950s, accommodating the car had become one of the most important factors in the design of cities.

26. From your own experience as well as from what you have seen near your home and school, write about 200 words to describe how the car has affected the Canadian landscape.

27. Some critics of the car have suggested that too much land has been wasted to accommodate it. Agree or disagree with this point of view, giving reasons for your answer. How and why might attitudes vary from one country to another?

How Cars Have Changed

Figure 6.14 An Early Steam-powered Automobile

During the late 1800s, a number of inventors in North America and Europe developed automobiles. These automobiles were different from other methods of transportation because they were self-propelling. In addition, the automobile was able to travel on any firm flat surface, rather than on steel rails. Some of the early cars were very unusual. A number ran on steam power (Figure 6.14); others used gasoline.

In 1913, Henry Ford produced the first Model T Ford on an assembly line. His factory was in Highland Park, Michigan, a city within Detroit. It was also in Highland Park that the first modern expressway was built to help test the Model Ts. From his assembly line, Henry Ford eventually produced a car that the average American could afford. By 1918, a car cost about $400.

28. Why do you think gasoline-powered cars became so widely used, whereas steam-powered cars almost disappeared?

29. Henry Ford has been described as the man who changed the face of North America with the assembly line. Explain how this statement is true.

Today, automobiles are no longer simply a means of transportation. Due to the widespread use of cars and their great impact on our society, many groups have pressured for changes to automobile design. Since 1979, a number of dramatic changes have been introduced to improve safety, mileage, and performance.

These changes include

- aerodynamic design
- lighter weight
- sturdier construction
- impact-absorbing bumpers
- pollution-control devices
- safer windshields
- more efficient transmissions
- some use of computers to control operations of car engines
- less noise
- improved trim and fit of doors and windows
- reinforced side doors
- rust-proofing

30. (a) **Consider the qualities that each of the following groups might like to see in cars:**
- **insurance companies**
- **car owners**
- **environmentalists**
- **automobile manufacturers**

(b) **What other interest groups would be concerned about car design? Explain what their interests might be.**

Highways

The multilane highways that have been built in Canada and the United States have led to great economic development. Most major highways in North America are four-lane **limited-access highways**. With this type of highway, cars or other vehicles can enter only at certain points (interchanges).

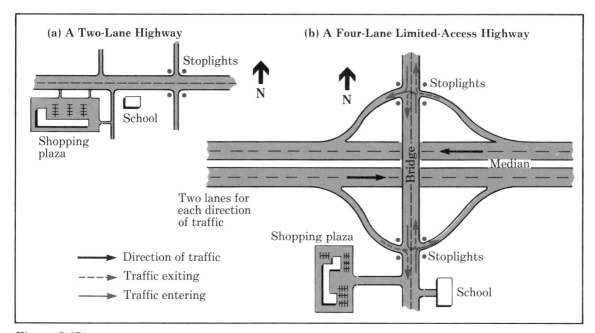

(a) A Two-Lane Highway

Stoplights

N

School

Shopping
plaza

Two lanes for
each direction
of traffic

→ Direction of traffic

--→ Traffic exiting

→ Traffic entering

(b) A Four-Lane Limited-Access Highway

N

Stoplights

Bridge

Median

Shopping plaza

Stoplights

School

**Figure 6.15
Two Types of
Highways**

31. Compare the two-lane highway and the four-lane limited-access
highway.

(a) Construct a table in your notes similar to the following one.
Fill in the answers from Figure 6.15.

FEATURES	TWO-LANE HIGHWAY	FOUR-LANE LIMITED ACCESS HIGHWAY
Safety		
Speed of traffic		
Cost of construction		
Suitability for long-distance travel		
Suitability for short trips		
Volume of traffic per hour		
Amount of land used		

SAMPLE ONLY

(b) Write one-quarter of a page to outline when a four-lane
limited-access highway is most suitable.

32. The map below shows a new interchange that will be built for a four-lane limited-access highway. After this interchange has been built, a number of different land uses will be developed along Highway 74 to serve those who exit.

(a) In your notebook, sketch an interchange similar to the one below.

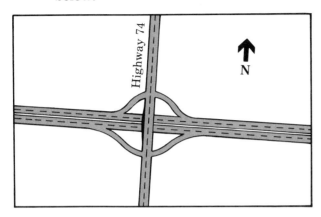

(b) Along Highway 74, mark on and label 15 land uses that would be developed to serve
- truck drivers and their trucks
- overnight travellers
- vacationing families with small children
- bus tours stopping for lunch

After highways are completed, they require a great deal of maintenance work. Repairing small problems as they develop is known as **preventive maintenance**. This means that maintenance of highways now will prevent major problems in the future.

Our Dependence on Cars

The car is very important to Canadians for travel within a city or a suburb, as is shown in Figure 6.16. North Americans use their cars more than any other form of transportation in spite of the fact that cars are expensive to drive (see Figure 6.17).

METHOD OF TRAVEL	% OF ALL TRIPS TAKEN
Car	74.2
Walking, bicycle, or motorcycle	12.0
Bus	9.1
Commuter train (to downtown)	1.6
Other	3.1

Figure 6.16
Method of Travel within a Typical Canadian Suburb

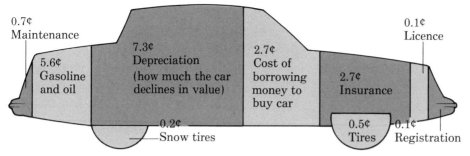

0.7¢
Maintenance

5.6¢
Gasoline
and oil

7.3¢
Depreciation
(how much the car
declines in value)

2.7¢
Cost of
borrowing
money to
buy car

2.7¢
Insurance

0.1¢
Licence

0.2¢
Snow tires

0.5¢
Tires

0.1¢
Registration

NOTE: It is assumed
that the car is driven
24 000 km per year.

The average cost of
driving a new,
medium-sized, six-
cylinder car is
19.9¢/km. The
various costs invol-
ved in driving a car
are shown here.

Figure 6.17
The Cost of
Driving a Car (Per
kilometre)

33. (a) In general, how does the popularity of the car compare with
that of other forms of transportation?
(b) What advantages would a car have over the following?
• a bus   • a bicycle   • a motorcycle   • walking
(c) For what type of trips would a bicycle be most suitable?
(d) Write a half-page essay discussing why Canadians prefer
their cars to other modes of transportation.

34. Many people think that the cost of running a car is mainly the
cost of gasoline.
(a) Is that statement true?
(b) Explain why many Canadians do not think of the other costs
of operating a car.

35. (a) Describe how the cost of operating an average car compares
with the costs of other types of transportation in your area,
such as
• bus   • taxi   • walking   • motorcycle
(b) Consider the cost of a 10-km trip along a main street in your
city or one near you. Rank the costs of the types of transportation listed in (a) from highest to lowest.

The extensive use of cars also involves other indirect costs, such
as highway construction. A large quantity of land in our cities has
been given over to roads. In Los Angeles, for example, one-third of
the land in the city has been used for highways or streets.

36. What other indirect costs are related to the use of cars, besides
road construction?

Public Transit
Public transit conserves more energy than cars, but it is very
expensive to operate. A single bus, for example, costs about
$130 000. The government usually pays almost 50% of the cost of

a

b

Figure 6.18
Various Forms of
Public Transit
(a) Monorail
(b) Bus
(c) Subway
(d) Streetcar
(e) Trolleybus

c

d

e

operating a public transit system. As a result, when you pay the fare on a bus, you are really paying only a small part of the real cost of operation.

37. (a) Which form of public transit in Figure 6.18 is most expensive to set up or build? Why do you think it is so expensive?
    (b) What advantages does it have?

Another reason that public transit systems are so expensive is that passengers do not travel in a steady stream throughout the day. Most passengers use public transit during **rush hours**, which are the hours in the morning and the late afternoon when people are going to and from work.

38. (a) Examine Figure 6.19. When are the rush hours for this intersection?
    (b) Why would these rush hours discourage some people from using public transit?
    (c) What could employers do to help change the patterns shown in Figure 6.19?

Figure 6.19 Number of Passengers Using Public Transit at a Typical Intersection

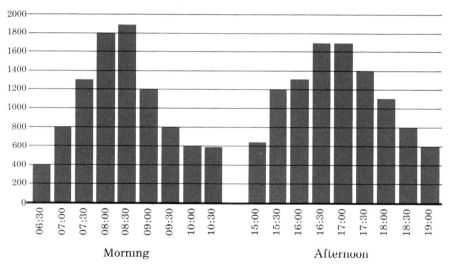

Number of passengers for each ½-hour period, commencing at time shown.

Who Should Pay for Public Transit?

There are usually two sources of income for transit systems in large cities—fares paid by passengers and money provided by government.

Assume that the transit system for the city of Winnipeg is under review and that four plans have been suggested to cover the costs of the system. These plans are:

1. The government pays 65% of the cost of the system and the users pay 35%.
2. The government pays 50% of the cost of the system and the users pay 50%.
3. The government pays 35% of the cost of the system and the users pay 65%.
4. The government pays 100% of the cost of the system and the users ride free.

Each of these plans has its drawbacks and advantages. For example, if the government pays for most of the cost of the transit system, the taxes for the public would increase, but the fares would be low. This would result in greater usage of public transit.

39. (a) **What would happen to taxes and the number of people using public transit in Winnipeg if the government paid only 35% of the transit system costs?**

   (b) **Which plan would each of the following groups support? In each case, give reasons for your answer.**
   - **downtown business owners**
   - **senior citizens living near the downtown area**
   - **city ratepayers (homeowners)**
   - **the owner of a Winnipeg factory that employs many unskilled workers**
   - **the owner of a downtown parking garage**

   (c) **Assume that you are one of the city politicians in Winnipeg. Which plan would you support? Give reasons for your answer.**

Intercity Travel

When people travel between cities in Canada, they most often use a car. Despite the cost, cars are very popular even for long-distance travel.

METHOD OF TRAVEL	% OF ALL TRIPS TAKEN
Car	81
Airplane	14
Bus	4
Train	1

**Figure 6.20
Method of Travel
from One City
to Another in
Canada**

40. (a) Using a graph, illustrate the information in Figure 6.20.
    (b) Convenience is often mentioned by people who drive
        cars from one city to another. Explain why cars are
        more convenient than
        • trains   • airplanes   • buses

Air Travel

Travelling by airplane is becoming more popular in spite of the high
price of tickets. Air travel is both fast and safe. For long distances,
such as across Canada, air travel is preferred by many. Business
travellers often choose air travel for its speed.

41. Use an atlas to answer this question.
    (a) Which region of Canada depends on airplanes for most of
        the year? Explain why other methods of transportation
        would not be suitable for this region.
    (b) Why would airplane travel be important for mineral explora-
        tion in northern British Columbia, northern Quebec, and
        northern Ontario?
    (c) What five other areas of the world would depend heavily on
        air travel? Suggest reasons for your selections.

42. Explain why airports are expensive to build and operate. Refer
    to Figure 6.21.

**Figure 6.21
The Many Services
Required in an
Airport**

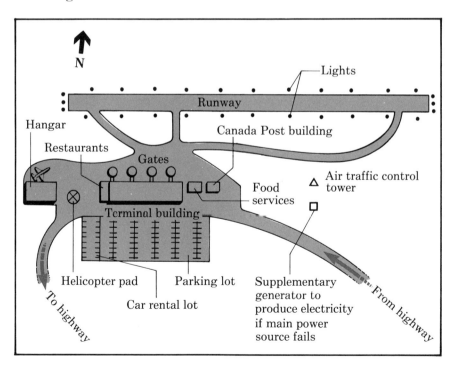

43. **Give three reasons why air travel is more important within Canada than it is inside the Netherlands. (Use an atlas for help in answering this question.)**

Impact of an Airport

A new international airport has just been built to serve the city of Maloneville. Built near the intersection of highways 7 and 14, the airport will serve both passengers and freight.

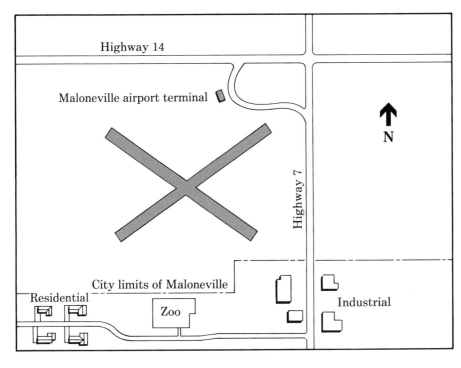

Figure 6.22 Maloneville International Airport

44. (a) Sketch the map in Figure 6.22 in your notebook.
    (b) Mark on and label 15 land uses, clearly related to the use of the airport, that would be developed nearby.
    (c) Add any roads that you feel are appropriate.
    (d) How do these land uses compare with those that you developed around a highway intersection earlier in this chapter? Explain the differences you observe.

45. Who would object to the construction of the airport? Explain your answer.

Passenger Trains

Train travel is not popular with most Canadians. The government-owned passenger rail company, VIA Rail, loses millions of dollars every year. In fact, almost all passenger-train systems in the world lose money.

But there are still a few train routes in Canada that are heavily travelled. Several **commuter trains** in Canada take people to and from work. And many of the trains linking the largest cities in the country remain popular. No train in Canada, however, can yet match the service of the TGV in France, one of the newest passenger trains in the world (Figure 6.23).

Figure 6.23 The TGV Train in France

The TGV

The TGV runs from downtown Paris to downtown Lyon, reaching speeds of up to 260 km/h. Passengers are unaware of the high speed and experience a smooth ride. The TGV allows a passenger to travel faster than by airplane, if the time for travelling to and from airports is considered.

The TGV is an electric train, and was very expensive to develop. A new track, designed with gentle curves and a smooth track bed, was laid through the countryside specifically for the TGV. The French government paid for most of the research for this train.

46. (a) Have you ever travelled by train?
    (b) If so, where did you travel? Would you travel by train again? Explain your answer.
    (c) What is your general impression of train travel?
    (d) What has kept you from using the train more often?

47. In which areas of Canada could passenger trains be most profitable? Explain your answer.

48. **What effects would high-speed intercity trains have on the airlines that provide services between these cities? Give reasons for your answer.**

VOCABULARY

break-of-bulk point	industrial linkage	protectionism
co-generation	limited-access highway	rush hours
commuter train	marshalling yard	tariff
free trade	piggyback	trade war
GATT	preventive maintenance	

RESEARCH QUESTIONS

To answer these questions, you will probably need to refer to library resources and other sources of information.

1. (a) Choose five families on whom to do a commuting survey. Use your own family and those of four other students, for example.
   (b) For each member of the family, find out his or her regular daily travelling habits (exclude those who do not commute). Fill in a table with the following headings:

Name	Approximate Age	Approximate Length of Journey (kilometres)	Between Which Places?	Mode of Travel
		SAMPLE ONLY		

   (c) Summarize your findings in a 200-word account. Draw conclusions where possible.

2. (a) Find out how much your local public transportation system (or that of a nearby city) is subsidized.
   (b) What would happen if this subsidy were removed?

3. Suggest improvements that could be made to your local public transportation system. Be specific about new routes (use a map), fare structures, timetabling, equipment, etc. Write up your proposals in a form suitable for presentation to the local authorities.

4. Design a wall chart that illustrates and briefly describes a futuristic transportation method.

SECTION III | **Cultural Geography**

The Spread of Culture, Ideas, Beliefs, and Races

Introduction

Look in, for a few moments, on the life of a typical Canadian teenager—Scott Newby. The following passage outlines Scott's activities from the moment he woke up one morning.

It was 07:30 on Thursday morning and the radio alarm jolted Scott out of a sound sleep. What a way to wake up! On came the radio with the news and weather, followed by rock music.

Barely awake, Scott struggled out of bed and stumbled to the bathroom. He turned on the water tap, splashed his face with water, and cleaned his teeth with an electric toothbrush. Scott caught sight of his reflection in the mirror but, feeling the way he did, he could hardly believe he was awake.

It seemed a struggle to get dressed that morning, but Scott managed it. "It's cold outside," he thought, as he slipped on his thick wool sweater and jeans. He stumbled down the stairs, still trying to open his bleary eyes.

At the breakfast table, Scott's dad was reading the morning newspaper and his mom was on the telephone talking to her secretary. They both would be leaving for work in a few minutes. Scott poured himself a bowl of sugar-coated cereal, covered it with milk, and gulped it down. He wanted to be at school early enough to see his girlfriend.

By 08:20 everyone had left the house. Scott's parents drove to work, and Scott and his brother went off to school.

Culture

Does the description of Scott Newby's morning sound familiar to you? Similar events probably occur in millions of North American households every working day. Scott's story reflects the North American **culture**. (In general terms, culture refers to the way of life of a group of people.) This early morning story shows some important aspects of North American culture:

- use of alarm clock radios, as well as of other electrical appliances
- popularity of rock music among teenagers
- warm clothes are worn for cool weather. Most people in the world live in tropical climates.
- diet that includes highly processed foods such as sugar-coated cereals
- dating. This practice is unknown to many people in the world. Many marriages in Asian countries such as India are still arranged by parents. In arranged marriages, the children are expected to marry the partner selected for them. Sometimes the marriage is arranged as soon as the children are born.

1. (a) **Reread the story of Scott Newby. Find and list in your notes four other aspects of his life which show that he lives in North America, rather than in another area of the world.**
   (b) **What five aspects of culture can you think of that people in poorer areas of the world would probably not have?**

Culture Realms

Canadians often assume that other people have a life similar to theirs, and that they think the way that Canadians do. They do not. In fact, North American culture affects only about 5% of the world's people. The map in Figure 7.1 shows 11 different **culture realms** around the world. A culture realm is a large area throughout which the way of life is much the same.

2. (a) **Which two culture realms are most similar to that of North America? Explain the similarities.**
   (b) **Name two cultures that are very different from North America's. Describe the differences.**

3. (a) **Which culture realm has the widest variety of culture within it? Explain your answer.**
   (b) **Which culture realm appears to have the least variety within it? Explain.**

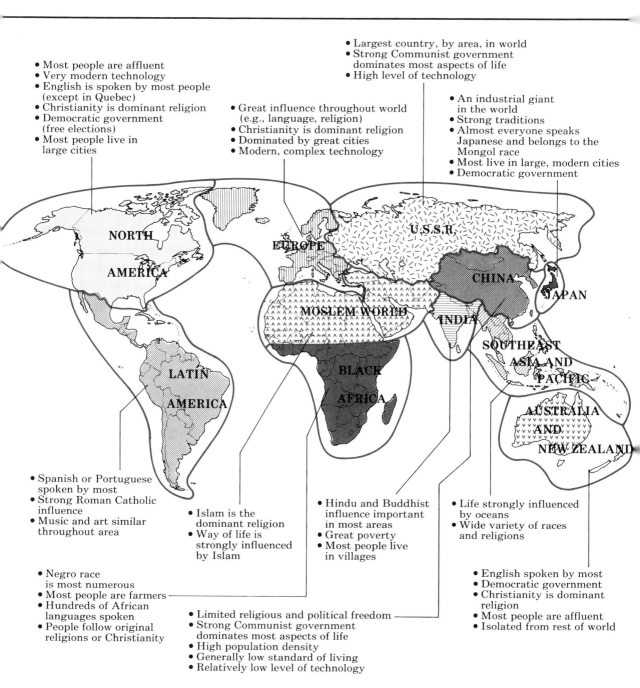

- Most people are affluent
- Very modern technology
- English is spoken by most people (except in Quebec)
- Christianity is dominant religion
- Democratic government (free elections)
- Most people live in large cities

- Great influence throughout world (e.g., language, religion)
- Christianity is dominant religion
- Dominated by great cities
- Modern, complex technology

- Largest country, by area, in world
- Strong Communist government dominates most aspects of life
- High level of technology

- An industrial giant in the world
- Strong traditions
- Almost everyone speaks Japanese and belongs to the Mongol race
- Most live in large, modern cities
- Democratic government

NORTH AMERICA

EUROPE

U.S.S.R.

CHINA

JAPAN

MOSLEM WORLD

INDIA

LATIN AMERICA

BLACK AFRICA

SOUTHEAST ASIA AND PACIFIC

AUSTRALIA AND NEW ZEALAND

- Spanish or Portuguese spoken by most
- Strong Roman Catholic influence
- Music and art similar throughout area

- Islam is the dominant religion
- Way of life is strongly influenced by Islam

- Hindu and Buddhist influence important in most areas
- Great poverty
- Most people live in villages

- Life strongly influenced by oceans
- Wide variety of races and religions

- Negro race is most numerous
- Most people are farmers
- Hundreds of African languages spoken
- People follow original religions or Christianity

- Limited religious and political freedom
- Strong Communist government dominates most aspects of life
- High population density
- Generally low standard of living
- Relatively low level of technology

- English spoken by most
- Democratic government
- Christianity is dominant religion
- Most people are affluent
- Isolated from rest of world

NOTE: There may be many differences between regions within a culture realm.

Figure 7.1 Culture Realms of the World

4. **What appear to be some of the key aspects of culture as shown in Figure 7.1? Name three.**

Culture Hearths

Each of the cultures around the world has roots in one or more **culture hearths**, centres where important aspects of culture were first developed. The first cities, for example, arose in culture hearths, as did the earliest forms of writing. Culture hearths were also early centres of religion, new technology, and trading. From these centres, new ideas and culture spread out to other areas of the world. To understand more fully what a culture hearth is, examine Figure 7.2.

**Figure 7.2
A Hearth and a
Culture Hearth**

(a) A Hearth

A *hearth* refers to the centre of a fireplace where conditions are most suitable for a fire to be started.

When the need arises, a spark is used to start a fire.

Wood (fuel) is supplied from outside to burn and provide heat.

Smoke rises up the chimney as new air is drawn from in front of the fireplace.

Hearth

The hearth is dry and protected from the weather, and thus suitable for starting a fire.

(b) A Culture Hearth

A *culture hearth* refers to an area of the world where conditions are most suitable for a new cultural idea to be started.

Culture spreads out from the hearth to areas around it.

New ideas come from outside world along trade routes.

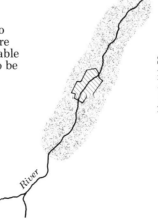

River

Trading centre, with more wealth than farming areas.

Suitable conditions here for developing new ideas. People are protected from the need to work every day for food.

Surplus food produced by surrounding farms is shipped to the city. This allows people to develop a culture with writing, religion, art, etc.
Culture hearth

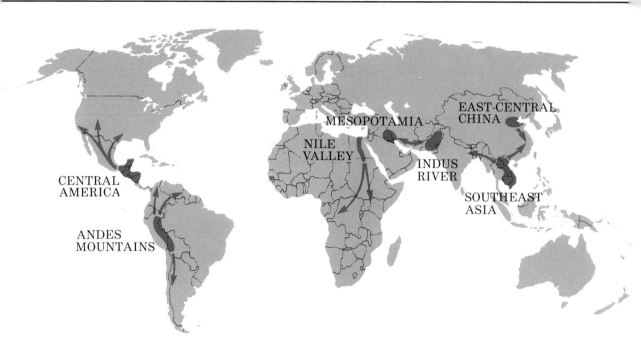

CENTRAL
AMERICA

ANDES
MOUNTAINS

NILE
VALLEY

MESOPOTAMIA

INDUS
RIVER

EAST-CENTRAL
CHINA

SOUTHEAST
ASIA

**Figure 7.3 Major
Culture Hearths
of the World**

5. Examine Figure 7.3, which shows the culture hearths of the
   world.
   (a) Which culture hearths appear to have influenced Europe
       most directly?
   (b) Which two culture hearths seem to have had little contact
       with each other or with other hearths?
   (c) Consider your answer to (b). What might be the result of the
       isolation of these two culture hearths on the development of
       their culture? Explain your answer.

   Culture has spread out from each of the culture hearths shown
in Figure 7.3. In fact, there has been some exchange of culture
between different hearths. But how does culture actually spread?
This next example will help to explain.

   Imagine that you are in a group of 1000 students standing
in your school gymnasium. Everyone is talking to his or her
friends so that there is a great deal of noise. There is no micro-
phone or public address system.

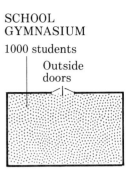

SCHOOL
GYMNASIUM

1000 students

Outside
doors

> At some point a man begins to hand out $10 bills at the outside doors of the gym. He does not move from his position at the doors. The first people who receive the $10 bills are those next to the doors. As the man hands out more money, the excitement builds. Everyone is eager to let others know what is happening. News about the give-away spreads quickly.

6. (a) In your notes, trace the outline of the gymnasium as in the illustration. Draw arrows to indicate how *news* about the $10 give-away would spread through the gym.
   (b) Describe, in your own words, how the news would travel in the gym.

The Spread of Culture

The process by which news travelled through the gym is referred to as diffusion. **Cultural diffusion** refers to the spreading of culture or ideas from person to person. On a world scale, of course, diffusion of culture would not take place as quickly as it did in the example of the gym. The process of diffusion in the gym, however, is similar to that which occurs in the world.

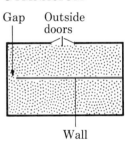

SCHOOL
GYMNASIUM

Gap   Outside
doors

Wall

7. (a) Draw the outline of the gymnasium again. In this illustration, draw a wall halfway down the gym with only one gap between the two halves of the gym. See the illustration to the right. This wall represents a geographic barrier such as a range of mountains. The gap in the wall could be compared to a pass (valley) through the mountains.
   (b) Assume that the same man began handing out $10 bills at the gym doors. Draw arrows on your illustration to show how news would spread.
   (c) What three other geographic barriers could be represented by the wall in the gymnasium? Explain how they would affect diffusion of ideas or culture.

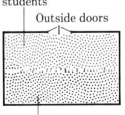

SCHOOL
GYMNASIUM

English-speaking students

Outside doors

Russian-speaking students

So far you have looked at the simple diffusion of ideas, as in question 6. In question 7, you looked at how barriers of geography can affect the simple diffusion of ideas. Now, see how factors such as language can also affect the spreading of culture.

8. (a) Draw the gymnasium once more as illustrated to the right.
   (b) Assume that the same man began handing out money at the gym doors. What would affect the diffusion of news about that man? Explain your answer.

(c) What would the English-speaking students have to do to let the Russian-speaking students know the news?

9. What aspects of culture besides language would affect the diffusion of ideas? Explain.

Figure 7.4 The Spread of a New System of Numbers

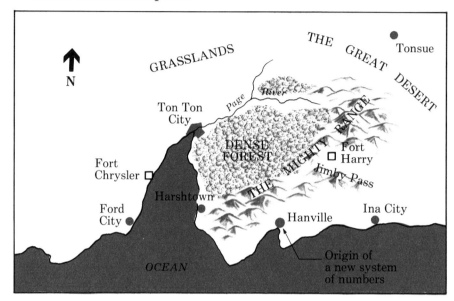

10. Figure 7.4 is a map of an imaginary region of the world. A new system of numbers has been developed at the city of Hanville. In which directions and by which routes do you think this counting system would spread? Explain. (Assume there is travel only on land by horse or by foot.)

Construct in your notes a table similar to the one below to help you to record your thoughts.

CITIES THAT RECEIVE THE NEW SYSTEM OF NUMBERS	NAME	ROUTE TAKEN TO REACH THAT CITY	WHY DID THE NEW SYSTEM SPREAD THIS WAY?
The first city is	_____		
The second city is	_____		
The third city is	_____	SAMPLE ONLY	
The fourth city is	_____		
The fifth city is	_____		

a   b

Culture is often spread along trade routes, as you have already discovered. Along these routes there are trading centres, each with its own markets. These markets are very important in the exchange of ideas and culture. Here, where new items from the out-side world are put up for sale, people meet, talk, and exchange ideas. As a result, markets throughout the world are centres of change.

One of the most famous of the early travellers was Marco Polo. In the 1200s, he left Italy and travelled to China along ancient trade routes. At markets along the way, he learned of new cultures and obtained items such as glass and paper, which he brought back to Europe.

In Canada, our shopping plazas have taken on a role similar to that of the markets in much of the Third World. Many Canadians spend a great deal of time at these plazas, not just to buy goods but to meet friends and exchange ideas and information. (See Figure 7.5.)

Figure 7.5 The Spread of Culture and Ideas through Markets
(a) A Market in Peru
(b) Canadians Socializing in a Shopping Centre

Migration and the Spread of Culture

Since the beginning of human existence, people have moved from one area of the world to another to live. Some of these migrations, or large-scale human movements, have been **voluntary**. This means that the people involved moved because of a free decision they made. Other migrations, however, have been **forced**. In this case, the people were ordered to leave their country or were transported from their homeland.

Regardless of whether a migration is forced or voluntary, immigrants bring along their own culture. Religion, music, lan-guage, and food preferences are aspects of culture that people carry with them. These are referred to as **cultural baggage**. Canada is, for the most part, a product of the various immigrant groups and the cultural baggage that they brought with them.

11. (a) List as many ethnic groups who have settled in Canada as you can.
    (b) Describe some of the cultural baggage of each group.

12. (a) Which ethnic groups are you aware of in your local area?
    (b) What evidence reveals the presence of these ethnic groups?

One way of tracing the migration of different groups to a new land is through the place names they bring with them. Canada, for example, has many place names brought from other countries. The first explorers or settlers in an area usually name the features there or the settlements that are established. Lancaster, New Brunswick, for example, was named after the city of Lancaster, England.

13. (a) Using the index in an atlas, look up the following place names from Nova Scotia. List the country outside of Canada where each place name is found. The country in which they are found is probably the source of settlers for that part of Nova Scotia. (Note: The place names in other countries may be spelled slightly differently.)

Halifax	Kentville
Dartmouth	Oxford
Liverpool	Colchester
Little Dover	Clyde River
Yarmouth	New Waterford
Truro	Lunenburg

    (b) The following place names are found in Nova Scotia as well. The origin of all these names is one country—which one?

Judique	Cheticamp
Michaud Point	L'Ardoise

Forced Migration

Forced migration has changed the face of many countries of the world. Australia, for example, received some of its earliest European settlers from British jails. During a period of about 50 years, over 150 000 British convicts were sent to Australia as punishment. Another example of forced migration occurred before and during World War II. More than eight million Europeans mostly of German origin and living in Nazi-occupied areas, were forced by the Nazi regime to move to Nazi Germany to work in the factories there. The goal was to increase the output of goods to help the German war effort.

14. **What attitude should a person forced to migrate have to successfully adapt to his or her new life? Explain.**

Much of the forced migration in the world has been due to slavery. Throughout history, there have been many examples where one group of people has been enslaved by another group. A **slave** is a person who is the legal possession of someone else and must do what he or she is told to do.

Throughout history, slaves have done work for other people that these people could not or would not do themselves. In the Roman Empire, for example, slaves built most large public buildings. Many of the slaves of Rome were brought from far-away areas of the empire. Modern-day France, Germany, and Spain were among the sources of Roman slaves.

CASE STUDY

The African Slave Trade

In its history, Canada has had little to do with slaves. Some of our neighbours, however, have been greatly affected by slavery. Thousands of slaves were brought into the United States, for example. Figure 7.6 illustrates the country of origin of African slaves and their main destinations.

Slaves were brought from Africa for mainly economic reasons. They were used to provide labour for tobacco or cotton farming, mining, or even road building.

Most slaves were forced onto ships along the coast of West Africa. They were brought from the interior as well as from the coastal areas and then sold to **slavers**. Slavers bought slaves and then transported them in ships to other countries, where they sold them at a profit.

Three general groups of blacks were sent as slaves across the Atlantic Ocean:

- people who were already slaves in Africa, possibly prisoners of war
- free individuals caught by white slavers or black workers
- those who were sold by their own tribes as punishment

Figure 7.6 The Movement of Slaves in the African Slave Trade

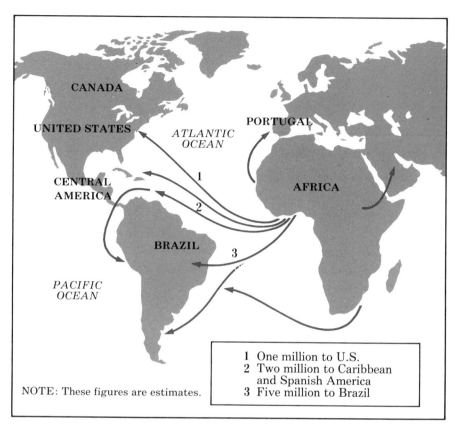

CANADA

UNITED STATES

PORTUGAL

ATLANTIC OCEAN

CENTRAL AMERICA

AFRICA

1

2

BRAZIL

3

PACIFIC OCEAN

NOTE: These figures are estimates.

1 One million to U.S.
2 Two million to Caribbean and Spanish America
3 Five million to Brazil

The trip across the ocean was among the most horrific experiences that a slave had to endure. Each slave was loaded onto a slave ship and branded with a hot iron. On board, each person had a space slightly smaller than a coffin (see Figure 7.7). The space given each male slave was approximately one-half metre high, one-half metre wide, and two metres long. Women and children received less room. As slaves lay on their backs in the ships, it was not unusual for them to feel rats running over their bodies. Many of the diseases that the slaves caught were carried by those rats.

Added to the crowded conditions were the stench of the air, the smothering heat, and the darkness of the lower decks. There were no showers or toilets. Every four or five days the slaves were allowed on deck for some fresh air. For the entire trip, they were chained to each other by shackles attached to their hands and feet. During the two-month voyage across the Atlantic, 25% to 50% of all the slaves died as a result of mistreatment or diseases such as measles, smallpox, or dysentery. Their bodies were simply thrown overboard, without ceremony.

Figure 7.7 Lower
Deck of a Slave
Ship

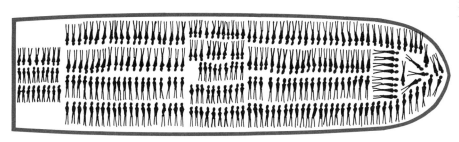

The arrangement of platforms
on which slaves had to lie

Once the slaves arrived in America, most were sold in auctions.
The slaves became the property of whoever bought them.

It is estimated that at least 15 million slaves made the voyage
to Europe and the Americas between 1451 and 1870. This number
is five times the population of Canada in 1870, or 13 times the
population of the city of Vancouver today.

15. Imagine that you were a black in Africa who was sold into
    slavery. Write 200 words to describe what you experienced
    after you boarded a slave ship. Be sure to include your feel-
    ings and emotions. Your story should end at a slave auction
    in America.

The slave trade had a great impact on Africa. Many tribes lost
their most able young people—hunters, farmers, and workers.
Numerous families were broken up.

On the other hand, the countries that received the slaves pro-
fited. The slaves provided cheap labour. Wherever the slaves landed,
they became involved in the life of that country. But they also
brought along their own music, language, and culture.

Voluntary Migration

Much of the large-scale movement of people on earth has been the
result of many individual decisions. Between 1820 and 1970, for
example, approximately 41 million people left Europe for North
America (Figure 7.8). Most came on a voluntary basis. Of that
number, 5 million came to Canada and 36 million to the United
States. During the same time period, almost 20 million European
immigrants arrived in South America. The total number of European
immigrants to the Americas is roughly the same as that of the
population of West Germany today.

Figure 7.8
Postwar European Immigrants Arriving in Canada

16. (a) What qualities would a person have who leaves home voluntarily to live in another country?
    (b) Why would the receiving country be eager to gain a person with the qualities outlined in (a)?

17. Compare the impact of a voluntary migration and a forced migration on the receiving country.

In recent years, there have arisen a number of obstacles that prevent the free movement of people in the world. One such obstacle has been the development of fixed boundaries of countries. As borders are more closely guarded, fewer people can enter new countries to live. National boundaries have become firmer, with less possibility of free crossing.

One of the obstacles that has prevented the movement of people from East Germany to West Germany is the Berlin Wall. Constructed in 1961, the Berlin Wall separates East Berlin and West Berlin. The wall was constructed by the East German government to prevent people escaping to freedom in the West.

Between 1945 and 1961, almost three million refugees flocked to West Berlin from East Germany. By June 1961, just before the wall was built, there were 1000 people per day crossing over to West Berlin. Since the completion of the wall, few have been able to escape to the West. Some people are still attempting to escape, however, using tunnels, ladders, racing cars, and even small aircraft.

There are other obstacles to migration besides boundaries. These include

- poor health
- lack of knowledge about where to migrate or how
- attachment to present home
- costs and risks of migration

18. **Select three of the obstacles listed above. Use these three factors to help you write a short letter to a friend. In this letter, explain why you will not move from where you live in Canada to the United States.**

Internal Migration in Canada

In addition to migration from one country to another, there is migration within a country. This is referred to as **internal migration**. Within large countries such as Canada or the United States, there is a great deal of room for such movement. On the average, Canadians move from one home to another every five years. Of course, some of these moves extend over only a short distance. There are, however, significant long-distance migrations, as Figure 7.9 shows.

Canadians today move from one region to another in Canada for many of the same reasons that immigrants move between countries: they move to obtain a job, higher pay, or a different lifestyle. Moving from one province to another, however, is much easier than moving from one country to another, because there are no government limitations on these moves.

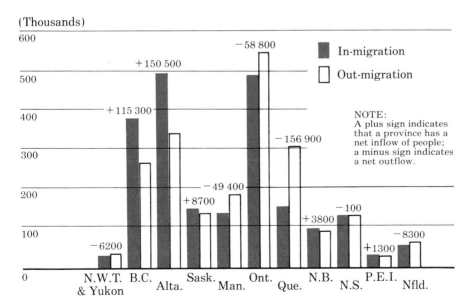

(Thousands)

In-migration
Out-migration

NOTE:
A plus sign indicates that a province has a net inflow of people; a minus sign indicates a net outflow.

+150 500
+115 300
−58 800
−156 900
+8700
−49 400
−100
+3800
−8300
−6200
+1300

N.W.T. & Yukon   B.C.   Alta.   Sask.   Man.   Ont.   Que.   N.B.   N.S.   P.E.I.   Nfld.

**Figure 7.9
Interprovincial Migration, 1976–81**

19. Examine Figure 7.9.
    (a) List the provinces that had a net inflow of people between 1976 and 1981.
    (b) List the provinces that had a net outflow of people between 1976 and 1981.
    (c) What conclusion can you draw from (b) about the economic health of the various provinces of Canada? Be specific about each province or group of provinces.

Population Shifts in the United States

After World War II, with many former soldiers returning to the United States looking for work, millions of Americans began to move to the northern states. The large industrial cities of the north, such as New York, Boston, and Chicago, grew quickly with the new arrivals. As the steel, auto, and oil-refining industries in these nor-

Figure 7.10 Percentage Increase in U.S. Population by State, 1970-80

State	%	State	%
Alabama	12.9	Montana	13.3
Alaska	32.4	Nebraska	5.7
Arizona	53.1	Nevada	63.5
Arkansas	18.8	New Hampshire	24.8
California	18.5	New Jersey	2.7
Colorado	30.7	New Mexico	27.8
Connecticut	2.5	New York	- 3.8
Delaware	8.6	North Carolina	15.5
Florida	43.4	North Dakota	5.6
Georgia	19.1	Ohio	1.3
Hawaii	25.3	Oklahoma	18.2
Idaho	32.4	Oregon	25.9
Illinois	2.8	Pennsylvania	0.6
Indiana	5.7	Rhode Island	- 0.3
Iowa	3.1	South Carolina	20.4
Kansas	5.1	South Dakota	3.6
Kentucky	13.7	Tennessee	16.9
Louisiana	15.3	Texas	27.1
Maine	13.2	Utah	37.9
Maryland	7.5	Vermont	15.0
Massachusetts	0.8	Virginia	14.9
Michigan	4.0	Washington	21.0
Minnesota	7.1	West Virginia	11.8
Mississippi	13.7	Wisconsin	6.5
Missouri	5.1	Wyoming	41.6
		U.S. Average	11.4%

thern cities grew, they gave employment to the new arrivals. Since 1970, however, conditions have changed and Americans have begun to move once more.

20. (a) From Figure 7.10, select and list the ten states that have grown most quickly.
    (b) List the ten states that have grown least quickly.
    (c) On a base map of the United States, using a red pencil, shade in the ten states that have grown most in population. Use a yellow pencil to shade in the states that have grown least.
    (d) On your map, draw several arrows from the slowest-growing states to the ones growing most quickly. These arrows suggest the probable movement of people. Label the arrows to indicate this.
    (e) Give the map a suitable title.
    (f) What two conclusions can you draw about the shift in population in the United States?

Other Modern Migrations

With any movement of these people there are push and pull factors. **Push factors** are those that encourage or force people to leave their homes. Included here are factors such as war, disease, starvation, or unemployment. **Pull factors**, in contrast, are those that attract people to a specific area or country. Friends, family, freedom, or a job all work to pull someone to a certain country.

In the case of slaves, force accounts for both the push and pull of their migration. **Refugees**, however, are faced with very strong push factors that force them from their homes. A refugee is a person who has been forced to leave his or her home, often with nowhere to go. The pull factors for a refugee could be relatively minor. Most migration to North America, however, involved people who had to weigh both push and pull factors in deciding to move.

The Canadian government has allowed many refugees to enter our country in recent years. Yet, only a very small number of all the refugees in the world are able to come to Canada. Many refugees leave their homes and end up living in camps in very poor conditions. Once a refugee has left his or her country, that refugee becomes an **exile** as far as the country of origin is concerned. Figure 7.11 shows the major concentrations of refugees and exiles around the world. The large numbers indicate the great amount of conflict that is taking place in the modern world.

1 FRANCE
132 000 refugees live here

2 WEST GERMANY
Since 1945, 14 500 000 have moved from East Germany to escape Communist rule

3 LEBANON
300 000 refugees live here; almost 500 000 exiles abroad

4 ISRAEL
85 000 refugees live here

5 PAKISTAN
300 000 refugees live here, all from Afghanistan

6 CHINA
230 000 refugees from Vietnam; 280 000 exiles abroad

7 CANADA
16 000 refugees arrived in 1982

9 UNITED KINGDOM
15 000 refugees from Vietnam

11 SAUDI ARABIA
200 000 refugees live here

8 UNITED STATES
Almost 900 000 refugees arrived in 1977 alone

10 PORTUGAL
750 000 refugees live here

12 JORDAN
650 000 refugees live here

13 VIETNAM
Hundreds of thousands of exiles abroad

15 CUBA
670 000 exiles abroad

14 INDIA
18 000 000 refugees from Pakistan in 1947; 9 000 000 refugees from Bangladesh in 1971; 100 000 refugees recently

16 EL SALVADOR
250 000 internal refugees

17 DOMINICAN REPUBLIC
300 000 refugees from Haiti

18 BRAZIL
200 000 refugees from Angola and Portugal

19 KENYA
110 000 refugees live here, mainly from Uganda

20 AUSTRALIA
62 000 refugees live here

21 URUGUAY
Nearly 800 000 exiles abroad

22 ZAIRE
Nearly 1 000 000 refugees live here

23 SUDAN
2 000 000 refugees live here

24 GHANA
1 000 000 refugees from Nigeria in 1983

25 SENEGAL
82 000 refugees live here

26 ZAMBIA
60 000 refugees live here

27 ETHIOPIA
500 000 refugees live here; 95 000 exiles abroad

28 BANGLADESH
10 000 000 refugees fled in 1971–72

29 TAIWAN
1 800 000 refugees from China

30 GABON
60 000 refugees from Equatorial Guinea

31 MOZAMBIQUE
70 000 refugees live here; 150 000 exiles in Portugal

32 THAILAND
Over 100 000 refugees live here

33 KAMPUCHEA (formerly Cambodia)
Millions forced out to farms from cities; tens of thousands of exiles

34 ANGOLA
250 000 refugees from Namibia and Zaire in 1977. Almost 700 000 refugees have left Angola; 350 000 refugees are still in country

35 SWAZILAND
Nearly 200 000 refugees, mostly from South Africa

36 SOMALIA
Almost 2 000 000 refugees live here

37 TANZANIA
150 000 refugees live here

38 INDONESIA
140 000 refugees from Portuguese Timor

39 HONG KONG
Nearly 2 000 000 refugees have arrived since 1974

NOTE: These figures are based on estimates made in 1984.

Figure 7.11 Refugees and Exiles around the World

21. (a) Which region of the world appears to have the greatest number of refugees today?
    (b) What does this indicate about that region?
    (c) What problems can that region expect in the future?
22. (a) Name the two countries that have received the greatest number of refugees since World War II.
    (b) What three problems would these countries have in dealing with the large number of refugees? Explain.
23. (a) Add together the number of refugees around the world to obtain an approximate total.
    (b) How does this compare with Canada's population of 25 million in 1985?

CASE STUDY

The Tran Family

Saigon, Vietnam, was home for Tan and his wife, Hoa. Although they were not rich, they owned their own home. Tan's father was an administrator in one of the provinces and was well respected in the Saigon area. In 1968, Tan joined the Marine Police, also working as a technician. Hoa had a responsible position with a local industry.

Then, the war in Vietnam spread right to the edge of Saigon. Each day brought more horror—bombings, killings, and mutilations—and great fear for the future. When would it all end? Finally, in 1975, the war did end. By that time, the Trans had two young children—a welcome addition to their life, but another reason for concern about the future.

No sooner did the war end than Tan was arrested and forced into a "re-education" camp. This camp turned out to be a concentration camp with hard labour, little food, and hours of lectures on Communism. Every six months, Tan was allowed to see his wife and family for half an hour. After three years, Tan was finally released from the camp, but then he couldn't find a job. The police kept track of him week by week.

By early 1980, Tan and Hoa had had to sell their home and furniture to have enough money to buy food. The future looked very bleak. There would be no freedom for them in Vietnam. Their children had no future either. Finally, Tan and Hoa made a difficult decision. They would leave their relatives, friends, and country, and take a boat toward freedom. The chances of surviving the trip were poor, but they took the risk.

In the summer of 1980, the Tran family and 51 others set out on the South China Sea in a 12-m motor boat with no food and little water. After five days and nights, they landed at an American oil rig. From there, they were sent to a tiny island with 11 000 other refugees. They applied to come to Canada, where they had relatives, and were finally accepted.

They now live in Canada where life is completely different. At first, the Trans had problems learning English and finding jobs. However, both Tan and Hoa have jobs now, and have bought a car. Most important, they live in freedom, away from the horrors of war and the restrictions of Communism. The Tran family is only one of millions of refugee families around the world.

24. (a) **Describe four push factors that led the Tran family to leave Vietnam.**
    (b) **What pull factors brought them to Canada?**

25. **In your opinion, which part of the Tran family's life was most difficult? Explain.**

26. (a) **In what four ways has your life been different from that of the Tran family?**
    (b) **What factors account for those differences?**
    (c) **What reasons might force you to leave Canada?**

Other Long-Term Migrations

There have also been major migrations on other continents. In

**Figure 7.12
Movement of
Bantu Tribes**

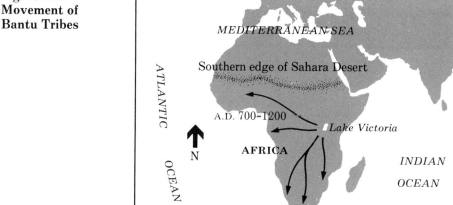

Africa, for example, Bantu tribes have been involved in slow but long-distance movements, as shown in Figure 7.12.

Between 1880 and 1914, nearly five million Russians moved out of European Russia into Siberia. Another example of mass migration is that of the Chinese into Southeast Asia. Today, there are about 12 million people of Chinese origin living in that area as a result of long-term migration.

Short-Term Migrations

It should be noted that not all migrations involve setting up a new and permanent home in a different location. Some migrations last for only a short term. In Western Europe, for example, millions of so-called "guest" workers from southern areas (North Africa, Turkey, and Greece) move north to work for a short period of time. Many of these workers do not bring their families, but return from time to time to visit them.

In Western Europe, there are also bands of gypsies constantly on the move. Living in trailers and tents, gypsies may stay in one location for only a few days or weeks before moving on.

The Lapplanders of northern Sweden are similar to many other nomad groups of the world. They move frequently with their reindeer in search of fresh pastures. As modern technology begins to affect these groups more and more, they often settle down to live in one place.

27. **What factors might account for the Lapplanders giving up their nomadic life to settle in one place?**

Mass Media and the Spread of Culture

The various means that are used to transmit information to a large number of people are called the **mass media**.

It has often been noted that we live in an electronic age. One of the features of this age is the rapid transmittal of information from one area of the world to another. Most of the people in the world are not far from a television or radio, which bring news from a great distance. The technology of radio and television is constantly improving, and as this happens, the number of people who can hear about events elsewhere in the world increases.

By the 1970s, for example, television programs could be beamed around the world through the use of satellites. The three examples in the following chart show how large worldwide audiences have grown.

EVENT AND LOCATION	DATE	ESTIMATED SIZE OF T.V. AUDIENCE
21st Olympic Games, Montreal, Canada	Summer, 1976	1 000 000 000
Pope's visit to Ireland	September, 1979	1 000 000 000
23rd Olympic Games, Los Angeles, U.S.	Summer, 1984	1 750 000 000

Other mass media, such as newspapers and magazines, also help to transmit information. Regardless of the form, mass media spread culture, moral values, and news, and speed up the rate at which culture changes and new ideas are exchanged.

It should be noted, however, that many people in the world do not have free access to the mass media. In Communist countries such as the U.S.S.R., Poland, and Czechoslovakia, the government **censors** the media. This means that only information with which the government agrees is released in the country. Some radio stations based outside these countries do manage to beam in information of which the government does not approve.

28. **Under what conditions do you think a government should be allowed to censor the mass media? Explain.**

29. **What impact would government censorship have on the people of a country?**

Religions of the World

As you have already discovered, there are many cultures around the world. One important aspect of culture is **religion**. Religion is very difficult to define because there are so many. In general, a religion involves these items:

- *A set of beliefs*: Whoever follows a religion will have some beliefs in common with others who also follow that religion.
- *Rituals*: are activities that people carry out to show what they believe.
- *Literature and organization*: In order to record beliefs and rituals, some organization and/or literature is usually necessary.

Figure 7.13 Hindu
Ritual: Bathing in
the Ganges River,
India

In some societies, religion and culture are almost the same.
In certain areas of East Africa, for example, eating, washing,
hunting, and even sleeping involve some form of ritual. In the
western world, however, daily religious ritual is less obvious. In
Denmark, for example, less than 2% of the population regularly
attend church.

Religion can strongly influence people's **moral values**. (Moral
values are the attitudes that people have about what is right and
wrong.) Stealing, for example, is considered to be wrong in Canada.

This attitude is rooted in Judæo-Christian moral values, and is reflected in our law.

30. **Make a list of ten moral values that you have (i.e., a list of ten human activities that you consider to be right or wrong).**

Moral values may vary from one religion to another. Different religions specify foods that should not be eaten by their followers. In the following chart, five major world religions are compared with reference to some of their food restrictions.

RELIGION	FOOD RESTRICTIONS
Judaism	No pork or pork products
Christianity	Generally, no restrictions
Hinduism	Great variations. Many Hindus do not eat beef; strict Hindus do not eat any meat.
Islam	Some variations. Generally, Moslems do not eat pork.
Buddhism	Great variations. Strict Buddhists do not eat meat.

31. **What impact would the various religious attitudes toward food have on farming in the countries where those religions are followed?**

Most of the major religions of the world are located in specific regions. Hinduism, for example, is largely concentrated in India. Japan and China contain most of the **adherents** to (followers of) Buddhism. Figure 7.14 shows the distribution of major religions in the world.

32. (a) **Which religion covers the greatest area?**
    (b) **Which religion covers the smallest area?**

33. **Compare figures 7.1 and 7.14.**
    (a) **Which two religions cover areas that are also culture realms? Briefly explain the significance of this overlap.**
    (b) **Which religion can be found in the greatest number of culture realms?**
    (c) **Briefly describe three different culture realms that follow the religion identified in (b). How do these culture realms differ from one another?**

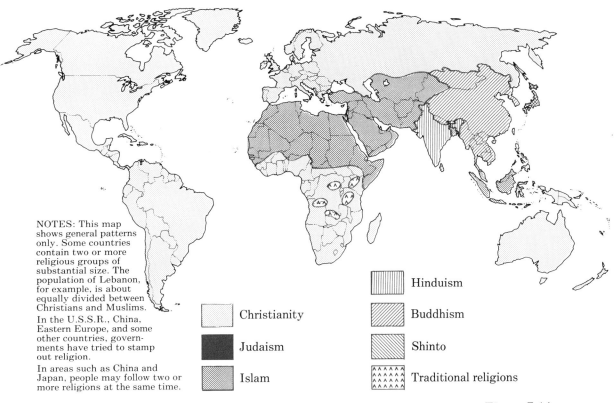

NOTES: This map shows general patterns only. Some countries contain two or more religious groups of substantial size. The population of Lebanon, for example, is about equally divided between Christians and Muslims.

In the U.S.S.R., China, Eastern Europe, and some other countries, governments have tried to stamp out religion.

In areas such as China and Japan, people may follow two or more religions at the same time.

Christianity

Judaism

Islam

Hinduism

Buddhism

Shinto

Traditional religions

**Figure 7.14
Distribution of
Major Religions
in the World**

The world contains a wide variety of religious groups. Most, however, fall into the broad categories that are shown below.

RELIGION	NUMBER OF ADHERENTS	PERCENTAGE OF WORLD'S POPULATION
Christianity	1 430 000 000	32.8
Islam	722 950 000	16.5
Hinduism	583 000 000	13.3
Buddhism	274 000 000	6.3
Judaism	17 000 000	0.4
Non-religions	716 000 000	16.4
Smaller religions	625 000 000	14.3

Hinduism

Hinduism is one of the oldest major religions in the world. One of its central beliefs is that all animals and humans have souls. They are all located on the "ladder" of life. If an individual is faithful to

Hindu beliefs and performs good deeds, that person will be born higher up the ladder in the next life. Otherwise, he or she will be reborn lower on the ladder. This belief is referred to as **reincarnation**.

There are great variations of belief within Hinduism. Some Hindus, for example, tend toward belief in one god. Others believe in many gods, including gods of trees and other natural objects.

The **caste system** of India is strongly tied to Hinduism. The castes are classes to which people and their descendents belong with little or no chance of ever changing their caste. There are seven major castes in India, with the Brahmin caste being the highest and most exclusive. There are also over ten million **untouchables**, who are people kept outside the caste system. Even today these untouchables have the most undesirable jobs in India, such as collecting and drying cow manure. They are not supposed to mix with most other Indians. Although it is now illegal to discriminate against the untouchables, problems still exist.

The landscape of India is marked by many colourful Hindu shrines and temples. Hindus consider some animals, such as the cow, holy, and these animals are seen everywhere. It is estimated that 200 million holy animals wander the streets of India. The Ganges River is also considered sacred, and bathing in the Ganges is an important part of Hindu ritual.

34. **Explain briefly the relationship between Hinduism and the culture of many people in India.**

Buddhism

Buddhism emerged in India as a reaction to Hinduism. After the death of Buddha in 489 B.C., Buddhism grew slowly at first, but by 200 B.C. was spreading quickly. Since that time, it has gradually moved into China and Japan. As it moved, Buddhism changed and evolved. It influenced other religions and also absorbed new ideas. In the areas where it is found today, people may follow Buddhism as well as one or more other religions.

A key belief of Buddhism is that a person can become enlightened by pursuing three things: knowledge of oneself, meditation, and pure thoughts. There is a strong emphasis on meditation and turning one's thoughts inward to discover oneself.

35. **Using an atlas, suggest routes that may have been followed by Buddhism from India to China and then Japan. Give reasons for your answers.**

Islam

Islam is the most recently developed of the world's major religions. Its focus is on the worship of Allah, the one god of the universe. The Islamic understanding of Allah is based on the teachings of the prophet Mohammed (A.D. 571 to A.D. 632), who is said to have received the truth directly from Allah. What Mohammed received from Allah was then written in the Koran, the Islamic holy book.

The Koran states that only Allah is holy and pure. He sees everything and knows everything and will judge every person at a final judgement, according to Islamic law. Central to the Islamic faith are the "five pillars" of Islam—five principles to be followed by faithful Moslems. These are

- frequent prayer to Allah
- observance of the festival of Ramadan, one month of daytime fasting (no eating or drinking) every year
- almsgiving (giving money to the poor)
- at least one pilgrimage (journey) to Mecca, the holy city of Islam, for each believer
- repetition of the basic beliefs of Islam

Moslems meet in mosques for Friday prayer as well as for social gatherings. Mosques are a notable feature of the landscape of Moslem lands (Figure 7.15). From its origin in a region that now forms part of Saudi Arabia, Islam has spread to cover an area larger than that of any other religion except Christianity.

36. (a) **What major differences exist between Islam and Hinduism?**
    (b) **Which of these differences might help explain the greater spread of Islam?**

Figure 7.15 The Dome of the Rock, Jerusalem. This mosque is considered one of the most beautiful buildings in the world.

Judaism

Judaism developed in a small area in the Middle East, probably in present-day Iraq, several thousand years ago. The Jews, one of a number of wandering tribes of that region, came to believe in one God. The Jews believed that they were chosen — God gave His law to all people, but that the Jews were the only ones to accept it.

Judaism first emerged as a religion before 2000 B.C. Since that time, the Jews have been faced with many problems. The world has never been a safe place for them, even today. Over the centuries, the Jews have been discriminated against, persecuted, and killed.

Central to their beliefs is a loving God who nevertheless disciplines them when they go wrong. The Jews continue to look forward to a Messiah who will save the world. The Jewish beliefs were set down in the Torah, or the five books of Moses, and in other writings, which also appear in the Old Testament of the Christian Bible.

Palestine (present-day Israel) was the homeland of the Jews for several thousand years. Its capital city was Jerusalem. According to the Torah, God gave Palestine to the Jews as their "Promised Land". In A.D. 70, however, the Romans destroyed Jerusalem, and the Jewish nation was dispersed throughout the world.

Over the next 19 centuries, however, the Jews always remembered Palestine as the land promised to them. By the second decade of the twentieth century, the Palestine population was mostly Arab, although the area was under British rule. The Balfour Declaration of 1916 opened the door for Jews to resettle. In 1948, after considerable conflict, the modern state of Israel was founded.

Once Israel was re-established as the Jewish homeland, thousands of Jews from all over the world settled there. To unite the Jews in Israel, the ancient language of Hebrew was modernized and declared the national language of Israel.

Today there are close to 3 400 000 Jews in Israel. There are also thousands of Jews living around the world, especially in the United States where there are approximately 7 260 000.

There has been much conflict in the Middle East since Israel was formed in 1948. The Palestinians Arabs who have lost their land want to reclaim it, and are supported by most of the Moslem countries that surround Israel. The support of the United States has been one factor that has prevented Israel from being destroyed.

The re-establishment of Israel is a major example of how religious belief can affect and unite a group of people who share the same religion but are often very different in terms of country of origin, culture, and lifestyle. The Jews' strong belief that Israel was their God-given land led eventually to the founding of that modern state.

Figure 7.16
(a) Jerusalem
   Today
(b) Parliament
   Buildings in
   Jerusalem

a

b

37. (a) Contrast Judaism and Islam.
    (b) Which characteristics of Judaism have allowed the Jews to
        survive, despite much opposition?

38. (a) What is the relationship between the beliefs of Judaism and
        and the existence of the modern state of Israel?
    (b) What conclusions can you draw about the impact of
        religious beliefs on a group of people?

Christianity

Christianity has a larger number of adherents than has any other major world religion. Over one thousand million people adhere, more or less, to the tenets of this religion.

Almost 2000 years ago, Christianity evolved out of Judaism, in and near the city of Jerusalem. It was founded on the teachings of Jesus, who was himself a Jew. According to tradition, Jesus lived on earth for only 33 years, had no formal education, never wrote a book, and never travelled more than 150 km from Jerusalem during his adult life. He lived in a relatively remote corner of the Roman Empire, in what is now the country of Israel, yet he had a great impact on the world.

Like Jews, Christians believe in one God. Jesus is believed by Christians to be the Messiah expected by the Jews. Unique among leaders of major religions, Jesus claimed he was the Son of God. Christians believe that "God so loved the world that he gave his only son so that whosoever believes in him should not die but have everlasting life." Christians believe that they are personally sinful, that Jesus died to save them from their own sin, that He rose again, thus conquering death, and that all who acknowledge their sins and believe in Jesus as their personal saviour, will have eternal life. The Christian way of life is based on this belief.

The Spread of Christianity

Today, there are Christians living in every country and territory of the world. The Christian Church has had three main periods of growth:

1. From the death of Jesus in about A.D. 30, to A.D. 500
2. From A.D. 900 to A.D. 1100
3. From A.D. 1500 to the present day

(Note: In North America and much of the world, the years are counted from the time Jesus was believed to have been born. For example, the year 1960 is about 1960 years after his birth. Recent research, however, indicates, that Jesus was probably born in the year now known as 4 B.C.)

39. Examine the world map in Figure 7.17. Also turn to a world map in an atlas. Make three lists, one for each of the periods of expansion of Christianity. Include countries, regions, or continents reached by Christianity.

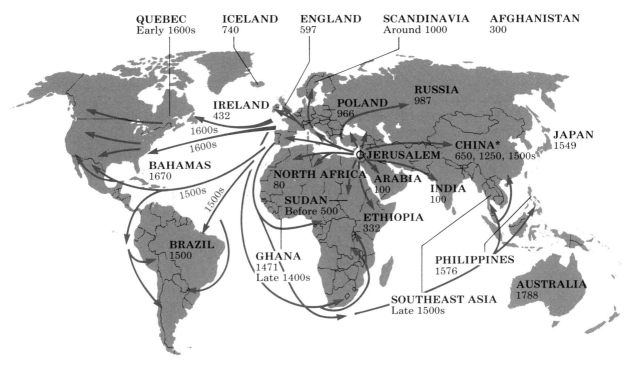

QUEBEC
Early 1600s

ICELAND
740

ENGLAND
597

SCANDINAVIA
Around 1000

AFGHANISTAN
300

IRELAND
432

POLAND
966

RUSSIA
987

JAPAN
1549

1600s

1600s

CHINA*
650, 1250, 1500s

BAHAMAS
1670

NORTH AFRICA
80

ARABIA
100

INDIA
100

1500s

1500s

JERUSALEM

SUDAN
Before 500

BRAZIL
1500

ETHIOPIA
332

GHANA
1471
Late 1400s

PHILIPPINES
1576

AUSTRALIA
1788

SOUTHEAST ASIA
Late 1500s

*Christianity reached China three times. The first two times the
churches were wiped out within a few hundred years.

NOTE: These dates are approximate. They represent the probable
date of the first arrival of Christianity.

**Figure 7.17 The
Worldwide Spread
of Christianity**

Several factors account for the spread of Christianity around
the world. One factor is the strong missionary efforts of many
Christian churches.

Paul, an early Christian apostle, travelled widely in the eastern
Mediterranean area. He preached, and set up many churches in
what is now Greece, Turkey and Lebanon. His example has had an
important influence on missionary work over the centuries.

Christianity had a strong appeal because it was not limited
to any one society. Anyone could believe in Jesus; people of all
countries of the world could relate to his teachings.

a

b

c

Figure 7.18 Christian Churches in Various Regions of the World
(a) Russian Orthodox Church in Sitka, Alaska
(b) Roman Catholic Church in Pisaq, Peru
(c) Anglican Church in England

Through the centuries, the Christian faith spread along trade routes. It was carried to the Americas, Africa, and Asia by Europeans as they established their empires. Christians spread the culture of Judæo-Christian society.

40. (a) Which major religion is tied most closely to a specific culture in its area of origin?
    (b) Consider your answer to (a). Explain how this factor might affect the spread of that religion.

41. (a) What similarities are there between Judaism and Christianity?
    (b) What importance do those similarities have today?

42. In your notebook, construct a table similar to Figure 7.19.
Complete the table.

	HINDUISM	BUDDHISM	ISLAM	JUDAISM	CHRISTIANITY
Countries or continents where it is located					
When it began					
Where it began					
Basic beliefs					
Similarities to other religions					
How it affects the landscape					

SAMPLE ONLY

**Figure 7.19
Comparison of the
Major Religions of
the World**

Languages of the World

An important aspect of culture is **language**. It is through language
that people can communicate with each other. They can also share
their way of life with others and learn from them. In addition,
culture is passed from parent to child through the use of language.
No culture can exist without a language of some type. In a **literate**
society, the importance of language is strengthened because it exists
in written form. Ideas and beliefs can be recorded and kept for
future generations.

There are approximately 3000 languages in the world. Some
of these are very similar to others and form a **language family**.
French, Spanish, Portuguese, and Italian are part of the Romance
language family, which owe their development to Latin, the
language spoken by the Romans. The chart on the following page
gives three examples of words that originally came from Latin that
now appear in the Romance language family.

	ROMANCE LANGUAGES			
LATIN	FRENCH	SPANISH	ITALIAN	ENGLISH
pater intelligens visitare	père intelligent visiter	padre inteligente visitar	padre intelligente visitare	father intelligent to visit

NOTE: English is a Germanic language, although some of its words have a Latin root.

The variety of languages in the world is astonishing. For example, nearly to 1000 languages are spoken in Africa alone. However, only a few languages are spoken by large numbers of people. The six most widely used languages are spoken by over 40% of the world's population (Figure 7.20). Figure 7.21 shows the distribution of major languages and language families in the world.

Figure 7.20 The Six Most Widely Spoken Languages in the World

LANGUAGE	APPROXIMATE NUMBER OF PEOPLE WHO SPEAK IT	A MAJOR LANGUAGE OF	WORDS IN ENGLISH FROM THAT LANGUAGE
Mandarin Chinese	675 000 000	People's Republic of China, and other countries	tea, typhoon, chow, ping pong
English	365 000 000	Britain, U.S., Canada, S. Africa, Australia, New Zealand, and many other countries	
Russian	240 000 000	U.S.S.R.	vodka, czar, steppe, ruble, sputnik
Spanish	225 000 000	Latin America, Spain, the Philippines	guitar, parade, barbecue, vanilla, banana, cannibal, cigarette
Hindi	220 000 000	India	shampoo, pajamas, jungle, loot, thug
Arabic	135 000 000	The Middle East	cotton, coffee, zero, mattress, giraffe, assassin

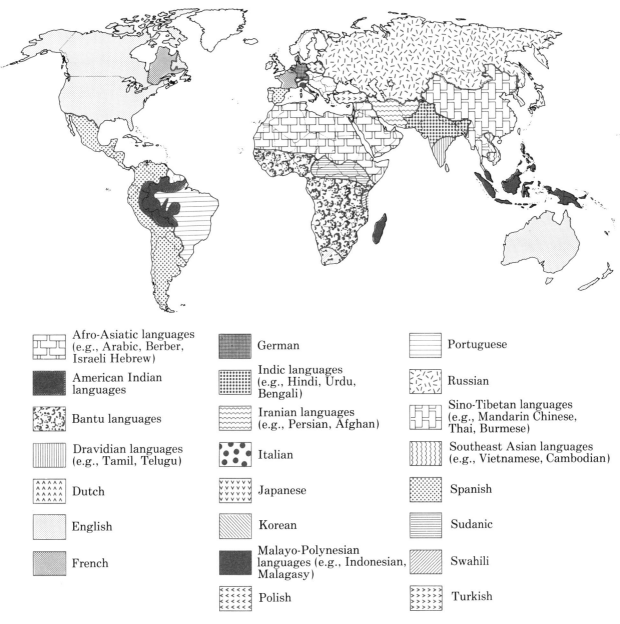

	Afro-Asiatic languages (e.g., Arabic, Berber, Israeli Hebrew)		German		Portuguese
	American Indian languages		Indic languages (e.g., Hindi, Urdu, Bengali)		Russian
	Bantu languages		Iranian languages (e.g., Persian, Afghan)		Sino-Tibetan languages (e.g., Mandarin Chinese, Thai, Burmese)
	Dravidian languages (e.g., Tamil, Telugu)		Italian		Southeast Asian languages (e.g., Vietnamese, Cambodian)
	Dutch		Japanese		Spanish
	English		Korean		Sudanic
	French		Malayo-Polynesian languages (e.g., Indonesian, Malagasy)		Swahili
			Polish		Turkish

NOTES: Areas with small populations, minor languages, or diverse languages have been left blank. Languages in Scandinavia include Danish, Norwegian, Swedish, and Finnish. Languages in Eastern Europe include Czech, Hungarian, and Greek.

This map shows only the predominant language or language family in a country or region. Many other languages may be spoken within an area. For instance, American Indian languages (e.g., Inuits, Algonquin) are spoken in parts of North America.

The official language of a country may or may not reflect what is widely spoken in that country. For example, the official language of Mozambique is Portuguese, but 95% of the population are Bantu-speaking.

Figure 7.21 Major Languages and Language Families of the World

43. (a) Examine Figure 7.21. Do the languages spoken in various countries influence how much Canada trades with them? Explain your answer.
    (b) Assume that a Canadian company wanted to sell goods to another country with a different language. Suggest three things that the company should do in this situation.
    (c) How might schools promote international trade?

44. What facilities are needed at the United Nations to deal with its members from countries around the world?

45. (a) Choose at random 25 words from an English dictionary, and list them, including their languages of origin.
    (b) What does your list show about the nature of the English language?
    (c) What might your answer to (a) show about the survival and development of English?

Monolingual Countries

A **monolingual** country is one in which only one language is spoken. Although few countries are truly monolingual, Poland, Japan, Uruguay, and Kuwait are all examples of countries that are nearly monolingual. Within each of these countries there are very few people who speak a language other than the national one.

A country might remain monolingual for a number of reasons, including geographic isolation or a government that resists contact with the rest of the world. (Both of these factors have led to a monolingual Japan.) New languages will only rarely be accepted by countries in which society has been slow to change from a rural to an urban way of life, for instance. This has been the case in Poland. The strength of Polish nationalism is reflected in the defence and development of the Polish language.

Multilingual Countries

In contrast to monolingual countries, those that are **multilingual** contain groups that speak different languages. Canada is officially bilingual, as it has two official languages: French and English. It is also a multilingual country, as numerous other languages are spoken in Canada. North American Indian languages such as Haida, Mohawk, and Ojibway are spoken by some Native Canadians. Other Canadians speak languages such as Italian, German, Ukrainian, Japanese, and Hindi. Because of the important relationship between culture and language, many of these groups try to maintain their language.

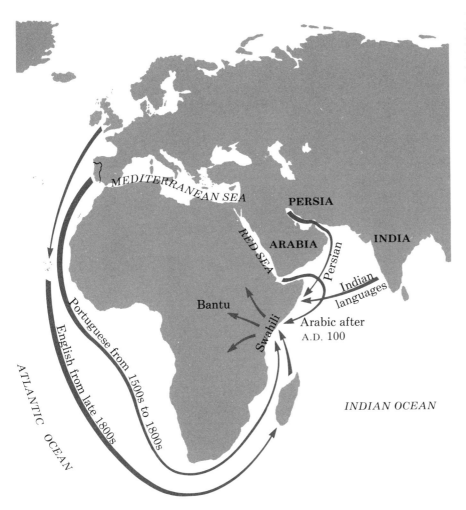

Figure 7.22
Languages That
Influenced the
Development of
Swahili

CASE STUDY

The Development of Swahili

Swahili is a language spoken by several million people in East
Africa. There are approximately 15 Swahili **dialects**, each one a
slightly different form of the language. A dialect usually corres-
ponds to a specific area of a country, where people speak with their
own particular accent and words.

    The structure of Swahili shows that it is in the Bantu langu-
age family, but a number of languages have influenced Swahili
over the last 1900 years (Figure 7.22). The first of these languages

was Arabic. From as early as A.D. 100, traders from southern Arabia brought goods as well as their language to the coast of East Africa. In fact, the word *Swahili* comes from the Arabic word *sawahili*, which means "coastal".

Traders from Persia (present-day Iran) and India also sailed to this area, bringing goods to trade—along with their language. Swahili has borrowed words from the languages of both of these countries.

In the early 1500s, the Portuguese also began to colonize East Africa, and established forts to protect their trading routes. Thus, Portuguese was introduced to the coastal peoples.

In the 1800s, as Arab trade continued, Swahili was taken inland along trading routes. Slaves and ivory from elephant tusks were brought out to the coast from the interior. The people who lived near the trading routes learned Swahili in order to trade with the Arabs.

By the time the British began to establish colonies in East Africa, Swahili was widely spoken. Since that time English has strongly influenced Swahili. The Roman alphabet, used in English, was introduced to Swahili, for example. Many words were also transferred from English to Swahili with little change, as shown below.

English	*Swahili*
July	Julai
shirt	shati
motor car	motoka
radio	radio
camera	kamera
O.K.	O.K.
tire	tire
picture	pitcha
cent	senti

As you can see from this short list, English provided words for Swahili to describe new technology as it arrived in East Africa. Before the arrival of English, Swahili had words to describe items and events common to its home, but not items such as radios and cameras, which were products of the English-speaking world.

46. The influence of English on Swahili occurred at the same time as other changes in the culture of East Africa. What were some of these?

The Origin and Spread of the English Language

Approximately 5000 years ago, a number of small groups of nomads roamed the plains of the Ukraine and southern Russia. They spoke a somewhat primitive language that is known as Proto-Indo-European. This language formed the basis of most languages of Europe, as well as those of Iran, Afghanistan, Pakistan, India, and Iraq. From that centre in the Ukraine, the language and its variations spread out, as is shown in Figure 7.23. Certain words in English are very similar to the corresponding words in a number of European and Indian languages.

Figure 7.23 The Origin and Spread of the English Language

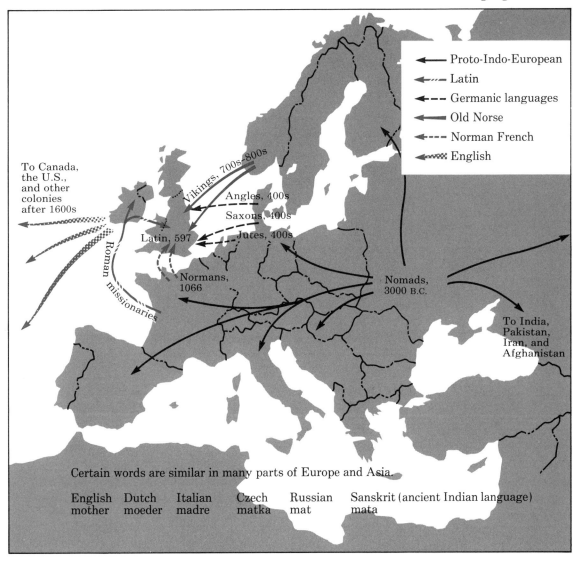

Certain words are similar in many parts of Europe and Asia.

English	Dutch	Italian	Czech	Russian	Sanskrit (ancient Indian language)
mother	moeder	madre	matka	mat	mata

47. **For many years after they arose, the languages of Europe were not written down, only spoken. Why is it logical that spoken languages would change so much?**

The English language has close to a million words, considerably more than most other languages. One reason for this enormous vocabulary is the large number of other languages that have influenced it (e.g., Latin, French, Saxon).

48. **Examine Figure 7.23. List the different languages that influenced English, with the approximate dates of their appearance in England.**

By the 1300s, the English language began to emerge as a distinct language. The English that was spoken and written at that time, however, was very different from that used today.

49. **(a) Read the following lines, which were written in the late 1300s. Translate them into modern English. (For the correct translation, see the end of this chapter.)**
    WHAN THAT APRILLE WITH HIS SHOURES SOOTE
    THE DROGHTE OF MARCH HATH PERCED TO THE ROOTE
   (b) Select five words from the above two lines. How have these words changed since the late 1300s?

In 1611, the King James Bible was published. It had been translated under the patronage of King James I of England. This bible is still in use today, and the language used in its original edition is considered to be the basis of modern English. The use of the printing press allowed thousands of copies of the Bible to be printed; the result was the widespread use of this form of modern English.

At the time of publication of the King James Bible, the United Kingdom began to establish colonies in Canada and the United States. As British settlers moved across the oceans to live in their colonies, they brought the English language with them. In its new environments, the English language developed new words and pronounciations.

North American English

Canadians have been involved in developing the English that is spoken on this continent. Following are examples of words that were introduced to English in North America. Words 1 to 9 originated in Canada.

1. prairie
2. toboggan
3. lacrosse
4. tamarack
5. dayliner
6. voyageur
7. gopher
8. portage
9. kayak
10. hamburger
11. mukluk
12. thruway
13. turnpike
14. moose
15. mosquito

50. (a) **Which of the above words do you recognize?**
    (b) **Explain the meaning of each word you know.**
    (c) **Find the meanings and origins of the words that you do not recognize. (Use a dictionary for reference.)**

The Origins of Canadian English

After the American Revolution in 1776, large numbers of settlers moved north from the United States into central Canada and the Atlantic provinces. These settlers were called **United Empire Loyalists** as they had remained loyal to a united British Empire and had opposed the American Revolution. As a result, they moved to Canada so that they could remain in the British Empire. The English language that they brought with them became the basis for modern Canadian English.

The United Empire Loyalists arrived by the thousands. They set up schools, farms, and churches and became involved in the government of Canada. By the time English, Irish, and Scottish immigrants came to Canada in the early 1800s, the English of the Loyalists was well established. It continued to dominate.

In the late 1800s, almost 100 years after the Loyalists settled in Ontario and the Atlantic provinces, the Canadian West was opened up. Many of the earliest settlers who moved across the Prairies were from Ontario. With them they brought Central Canadian English. For this reason, the English spoken from Ontario west to the Pacific Ocean has a similar accent and vocabulary.

Newfoundland's English developed in a somewhat different way. The language arrived from various sources, as shown in Figure 7.24. Once in Newfoundland, however, the language developed in unique ways. Along the coast of that province were many isolated fishing villages, each with its own small cove. There was little contact among the small groups of villages. As a result, each cluster

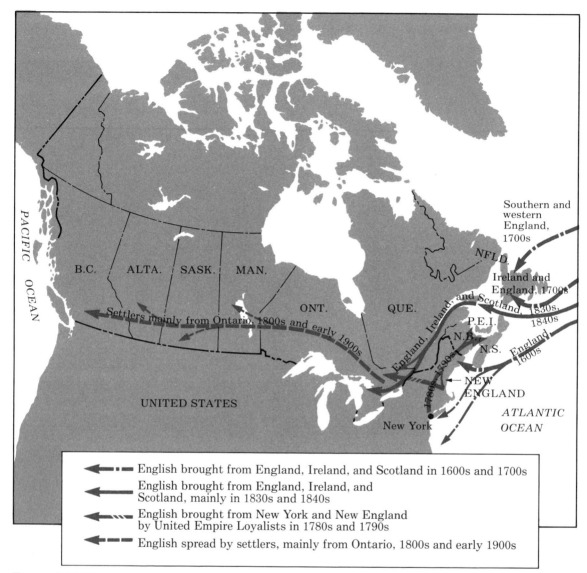

Southern and
western
England,
1700s

NFLD.

Ireland and
England, 1700s

and Scotland, 1830s,
1840s

P.E.I.

N.B.

N.S.

England
1600s

England, Ireland,

1700s 1790s

NEW
ENGLAND

ATLANTIC
OCEAN

New York

B.C.   ALTA.   SASK.   MAN.

ONT.   QUE.

Settlers mainly from Ontario, 1800s and early 1900s

UNITED STATES

PACIFIC

OCEAN

◄─·─·─ English brought from England, Ireland, and Scotland in 1600s and 1700s

◄───── English brought from England, Ireland, and
        Scotland, mainly in 1830s and 1840s

◄─▨▨▨─ English brought from New York and New England
        by United Empire Loyalists in 1780s and 1790s

◄─ ─ ─ English spread by settlers, mainly from Ontario, 1800s and early 1900s

**Figure 7.24 The
Origins of
Canadian English**   of villages developed its own accents and usage. With the influence
of television and radio, however, many of the unique characteristics
of accents in Newfoundland are being lost.

English: An International Language

English has become the international language of business and poli-
tics. The leaders of most countries of the world speak English, and
most international conferences use it. Almost 700 million people can
speak it, although only half that number speak it in their daily life.

The following are examples of how important English is around the world:

- Japanese business people in Kuwait speak in English.
- In September 1982, 11 of the top 20 record albums in Japan had English titles.
- Over 80% of all scientific research papers in the world are published first in English.
- In China, English is taught on television (one program is called "Yingying Learns English").

The great popularity of English may change the language in the future. Because English is spoken in so many countries with so many accents, it may break up into smaller languages, just as Latin once broke up into the Romance languages. Some people, however, believe that with modern communications, English will continue to expand its influence as a single language.

Races of the World

The population of the world consists of different groups called races, each of which has distinctive physical characteristics, such as skin colour (Figure 7.25), type of hair, and shape of eyes, nose, lips, or jaw.

Figure 7.25 How Melanin and Carotene Affect Skin Colour

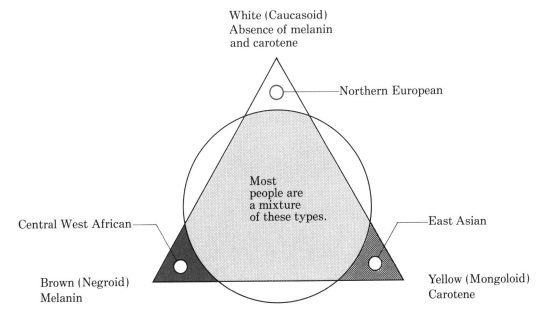

White (Caucasoid)
Absence of melanin and carotene

Northern European

Most people are a mixture of these types.

Central West African

East Asian

Brown (Negroid)
Melanin

Yellow (Mongoloid)
Carotene

There has been much debate and little agreement about the origin of the various races found in the world. Thousands of years ago, people lived in isolated groups and developed their own racial characteristics. It is likely that all racial groups had a common origin, probably in Asia (Figure 7.26).

The following are common theories proposed to explain the development of the various human races. All are based on the idea that people's physical characteristics have changed over the centuries to adapt to their environments.

- Dark-skinned people survive better in areas where the sun is strong, because melanin (see Figure 7.25) protects them from skin damage.
- Light-skinned people thrive in areas where the sun's rays are weak. Their skin is better able to absorb these rays. As a result, more vitamins are released to the body.
- Short, stocky people are better able to retain body heat and are more likely to survive in cold climates.

**Figure 7.26
Racial Groups
Likely Had a
Common Origin**

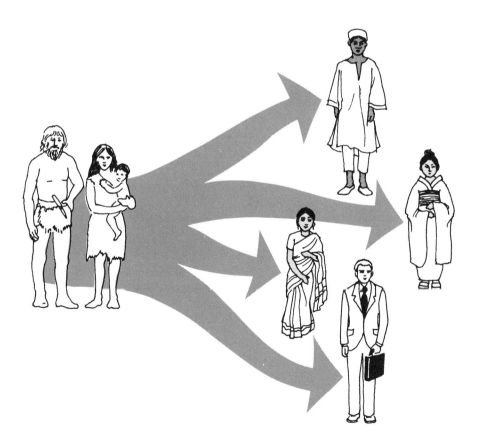

- Leaner people can keep cool more easily and so are able to survive better in a warm climate.

It is thought that, from a common origin, people moved around the world and encountered different environments. Evolutionists believe that those with bodies more suited to their new environment survived and produced children with the same characteristics. This process is called **natural selection**.

Conquest and trading have also led to the geographic spread of races beyond their regions of origin. In some cases, powerful groups have destroyed the environment upon which less powerful groups depended. Few of the Pygmies or Bushmen of Africa, for example, still survive. Their hunting grounds have been taken over by outside groups.

51. **How would racial characteristics affect the movement of people from one area to another?**

Sometimes, members of two different races intermarry and have children; this is referred to as **interbreeding**. The children of interbreeding have some characteristics of each race. In Polynesia and Brazil, there has been much interbreeding, to the point where the races have blended to a great extent.

52. **Why do you think some people would encourage interbreeding, as in Polynesia?**

Racism

Some racial groups in the world are subjected to prejudice or persecution. This is called **racism**.

South Africa is one country that has been cited for its racism. The whites in South Africa believe strongly in keeping the various races separate from one another. The government has specified which areas each racial group may live in, and intermarriage is illegal. The policy of racial separation in South Africa is referred to as **apartheid**.

Racism often stems from the false assumption that one race is superior to another. There is no scientific evidence to indicate that the races differ in intelligence or natural abilities. The differences that exist between various racial groups stem from cultural background, not racial characteristics.

Amerasians in Thailand

Sante Sarasadbancha is a 14-year-old Amerasian living in Bangkok. Apart from his Thai school uniform and the Buddha amulet that hangs from a chain around his neck, Sante looks like a young American.

Sante would like to be a lawyer, but does not have much of a chance. His fellow students taunt him because he looks different. He is hurt by the teasing and feels like staying away from school because of it. It is estimated that there are 20 000 Amerasians in the Far East. Their fathers were the white and black American soldiers who fought in the Korean and Vietnam wars. Their mothers were residents of the particular Asian country where the soldiers were stationed. Many of the Amerasians, however, are rejected by their mothers and discriminated against by government agencies. It is even more difficult for these young people in the rural areas, and they may end up with poorly paid jobs because of prejudice against them.

53. (a) **What examples of racism have you read about, seen on television, or experienced?**
    (b) **What reasons can you suggest for racism developing?**
    (c) **What would be three long-term effects of racism?**

54. **Suggest four ways in which racism could be fought in a country such as Canada or the United States.**

This is the correct translation of the lines that appear in question 49:

When April with his sweet showers
Has pierced the drought of March to the root

From Geoffrey Chaucer, *The Canterbury Tales*

adherent	Hinduism	push factor
apartheid	interbreeding	race
Buddhism	internal migration	racism
censor	Islam	refugee
caste system	Judaism	reincarnation
Christianity	language	religion
cultural baggage	language family	rituals
cultural diffusion	literate	slave
culture	mass media	slaver
culture hearth	monolingual	United Empire
culture realm	moral values	Loyalists
dialect	multilingual	untouchable
exile	natural selection	voluntary migration
forced migration	pull factor	

RESEARCH QUESTIONS

To answer these questions, you will probably need to refer to library resources and other sources of information.

1. Locate several books on the African slave trade.
   (a) Make notes on the following topics:
   - specific areas of origin of slaves
   - methods of slave capture
   - the trip across the Atlantic Ocean
   - life in the United States as a slave
   (b) Write a 300- to 500-word essay based on your research.

2. Conduct a survey in your class to discover the extent of the migration of your classmates' families within Canada. You will need a base map of Canada.
   (a) On your base map, mark and label the major cities of Canada. Use an atlas for help.
   (b) Talk to every member of your class and have each one put a red star on the map to represent any place else in Canada he or she has lived. Include any place where a classmate has lived even for a short period.
   (c) Draw straight red lines from each star to your present home area.
   (d) Write a half-page essay to describe your results. Include areas of Canada in which many of your classmates have lived, and those areas where no one in your class has ever lived.

3. Conduct a survey in your class to determine the areas of the world from which your fellow students' families originally came.
   (a) Obtain a base map for countries of the world.
   (b) Ask each student to identify the city or country outside Canada where his or her family or relatives originally came from. List these places, including a short description of each area of origin.
   (c) Mark on your map each city or country.
   (d) What cultural baggage has been brought to Canada by the families of students in your class? Be specific.
   (e) To what extent have students in your class been "Canadianized" (i.e., adopted Canadian values and culture)?

4. Locate a set of encyclopedias in your school library. Your area of research is the major denominations within the Christian Church.
   (a) Within Christianity, there are three major divisions: Roman Catholicism, Protestantism, and Orthodox Christianity. List the subdivisions of each of these categories.
   (b) On a world map, mark the areas in which each of these three major divisions dominates.
   (c) Contrast the major beliefs of each of these three divisions.

5. Your area of research is Islam. Using your library resources, investigate the following topics:
   (a) the characteristics of the Sunni and Shia branches of the religion
   (b) the expansion of Islamic influence in Africa
   (c) the impact of the resurgence of Islam in Iran and Saudi Arabia
   (d) the importance of oil to the political power of Moslem countries

6. Investigate the apartheid policy of South Africa under these headings:
   (a) the details of the policy, including its enforcement
   (b) the black African homelands program
   (c) the white versus the black way of life
   (d) attitudes of First World countries to South Africa
   (e) future problems and prospects for South Africa
   (f) black opposition to apartheid

Lifestyle, Leisure, and Mass Media

Lifestyles

A World View

A person's **lifestyle** grows out of the culture in which he or she lives. The work, recreation, and various activities that fill a person's time determine his or her lifestyle. Around the world, there is a multitude of lifestyles. In fact, each person has a lifestyle that is slightly different from everyone else's. Only the significant differences in lifestyle concern us here. Figure 8.1 illustrates some examples of various lifestyles around the world.

1. Select two people described in Figure 8.1 who have very different lifestyles. Write about 75 words to describe the differences. Use an atlas for help in answering the question.

2. Imagine that you decide to write a letter in English to Maria in Brazil. Explain to Maria how your lifestyle differs from hers. Suggest four places near your home that she might like to see that would show her your lifestyle. Describe each place briefly. Your letter should be about a page long.

3. (a) If you could trade lifestyles with anyone in Figure 8.1, who would it be? Explain.
   (b) Whose lifestyle in Figure 8.1 would you least want to have? Explain.

Imagine that the world population was represented by 100 people. That group of 100 people would represent, in actual proportion the populations of continents and countries around the world.

1 **Maria**, 14, lives on a farm in northern Brazil. She is one of nine children and has had two years of formal education. Each day, she eats one meal and works 12–14 h. She is very poor.

2 **Mohammed**, 31, has 12 years' education. He is a technician, earning $10,000 a year. He is in good health and has an excellent diet. He has travelled in the Middle East. He is a strict Moslem.

3 **Jacqueline**, 51, belongs to the French Socialist party. She works in a Paris bookstore, eats three meals each day, owns a car, T.V., and radio. She is divorced. She has travelled to Moscow and many European countries.

4 **Gabi**, 26, is married with one child (the official maximum in China). She works on a very poor farming commune. She eats mainly rice. Once a month she has meat. She has never seen a T.V.

FRANCE 3

MEXICO 5

KUWAIT 2

CHINA 4

7

NIGERIA 6

INDIA

10 THAILAND

BRAZIL 1

COMORO ISLANDS 9

8 ARGENTINA

5 **Juan**, 17, lives in a small village, 100 km from Mexico City. His father is dead and he helps his mother on the farm. His diet consists mainly of bananas and corn. He had eight years of education at a school run by U.S. nuns. He hopes to get a job as a factory worker in Mexico City.

6 **Emmanuel** is an oil worker in Lagos. He earns $900 a year and owns a T.V. and radio. He has two meals each day. He has a wife and four children. He speaks Yoruba and can read and write.

7 **Sidar**, 22, is a very poor woman in New Delhi. She works 12 h a day sewing blankets. She also cooks for her family. Her family earns $300 a year.

NOTE: These descriptions are composites.

8 **David**, 35, lives in Buenos Aires with his wife and two children. He owns a four-bedroom house and runs his own company. He has an English background and his children go to an English private school. His diet and health are excellent.

9 **Ahmed**, 21, lives on the Comoro Islands. Over one-half of the population is younger than Ahmed. He has never been to school and he fishes for a living. He has never seen a T.V. nor been treated by a dentist or a doctor.

10 **Sarak**, 8, works 13 hours each day in a clothing factory. He earns 75¢ a day. He has no formal education and has never left Bangkok. He is one of a family of ten children. His main diet is rice, with chicken as a rare treat. He has never been treated by a doctor.

Figure 8.1 Examples of Lifestyles around the World

The ages of the people in the group would also reflect the ages of people in the world. Figure 8.2 illustrates this representative group.

Figure 8.2 One Hundred Representative World Citizens

CONTINENT OR COUNTRY	NUMBER	DESCRIPTION
Europe	11	• 36 people are under 15;
U.S.S.R.	6	6 are over 65
North America	6	• radios are owned by 20
China	22	• 5 people have a car
India	16	• 7 people have a T.V.
Asia (excluding India,		• in the next year, there
China, U.S.S.R.)	16	will be 1 death, 3 births,
Middle East	4	and 1 marriage
Latin America	8	
Africa	10	
Australia, New Zealand, Pacific	1	

4. (a) **Examine Figure 8.2. How much of the description applies to you? What does it show you about your lifestyle?**
   (b) **Which three continents or countries, when added together, have over 50% of the world's population? How would that fact probably affect their lifestyles?**

5. **Imagine for a moment that the 100 people in Figure 8.2 could be brought together to live in one village. Imagine also that you were one of the North Americans in the group.**
   (a) **How would births, deaths, and marriages affect you?**
   (b) **How would this reaction compare with your current reactions to events affecting people around the world?**

Lifestyles in Canada and the United States

Even within Canada and the United States there is a great variety of lifestyles. Since our countries are wealthier than most in the world, some people can choose their own lifestyle. Other people, however, have had their lifestyles forced on them by certain conditions. Figure 8.3 gives examples of the variety of lifestyles in Canada and the United States.

1 **Daryn**, 23, and **Elizabeth**, 22, live with their two small children in a town house in a suburb of Winnipeg. They both work. He is a machinist, and she manages a small office. They do not go out much and have not travelled far. Their vacations are spent camping in Manitoba.

2 **Brian**, 18, lives in a ghetto. He is unemployed. At 16, he dropped out of Grade 10. Brian lives at home with his mother and five of his seven sisters. He is black. He has never left Detroit.

3 **Ann**, 31, and **Tom**, 30, live in a log cabin in the mountain wilderness of B.C. Tom hunts for food, traps animals for fur, and fishes. Ann looks after their four children. They have a small garden and live "off the land". They love living in the wild and seldom leave home.

4 **Harman**, 60, and **Gretchen**, 55, run a dairy farm near Peterborough. They work long hours. Gretchen is receiving treatment for cancer. Their children have grown up and live near Toronto. Harman and Gretchen have little free time but a fairly high income.

5 **Otto**, 55, is a diplomat based in Washington. He has travelled widely, speaks seven languages, and has a Ph.D. As part of his job, Otto attends parties and other functions almost every night. He is married with no children.

6 **John**, 30, lives in San Diego, where it never snows and where there is a warm climate year-round. He owns his own house with a swimming pool and has another home in the mountains. He is single and works for a computer company. He is very well paid. He has travelled around the world. John loves warm-weather sports.

7 **Ellen**, 32, is a single parent. She is divorced and has two children. She works full time to support her family. She does not travel much. She lives in a small apartment in Calgary.

8 **Alice**, 95, lives in a nursing home in Halifax. Though her mind is bright, she is seriously crippled. Confined to a wheelchair, Alice watches a lot of television. She cannot even write now. She leaves the home only at Christmas to visit her children. She has 26 great-grandchildren.

9 **Francine**, 43, lives in a high-rise apartment in Manhattan. She shares the large apartment with two other women. She is a secretary and loves New York and its theatres, concerts, and shopping. She always carries a revolver in her purse for safety. She loves to travel.

NOTE: These descriptions are composites.

Figure 8.3 Examples of Lifestyles in Canada and the United States

6. (a) Examine Figure 8.3. Which of the people described have the greatest freedom to choose the lifestyle they want? Explain why they have this freedom.
   (b) Which people have little freedom to choose a lifestyle? Explain the factors that have limited their freedom.

7. (a) In your notes, construct a table similar to Figure 8.4.

Figure 8.4 Factors Affecting Lifestyle

NAME	LOCATION OF HOME	CLIMATE	NUMBER OF CHILDREN (IF ANY)	AMOUNT OF TRAVELLING	OTHER FACTORS THAT AFFECT LIFESTYLE
1.					
2.					
3.					
etc.					

SAMPLE ONLY

   (b) Fill in the table you have constructed for the nine individuals or couples in Figure 8.3.
   (c) Select four individuals or couples from Figure 8.3. In what way does the location of their home and the type of home affect their lifestyle?

8. (a) Describe your own lifestyle in about 100 words. Refer to your age, home, interests, hobbies, travel, and family.
   (b) What factors affect or limit your lifestyle?

Using statistics, a fictitious average Canadian can be created. (See Figure 8.5.) No one, of course, fits this description exactly because it deals with averages. It can, however, be useful in helping to understand Canadian life.

Figure 8.5 An Average Canadian

- drinks 5.46 cups of coffee per day
- borrows 4 books from a public library per year
- works 30 h per week
- visits a museum 2-6 times per year
- at home there are 0.6 people per room
- is married
- family size is 3.5 people
- does not have a dishwasher
- has at least some high-school education
- spends over $44 per year on potato chips
- lives in a city
- eats 515 potatoes per year
- travelled on a Canadian airline once this year
- goes to 4.3 movies per year
- man will live to 69 years of age
- woman will live to 76 years of age
- home has T.V., radio, refrigerator, record player
- does not have a vacation home, snowmobile or snowblower
- speaks English

9. (a) Which statistic in Figure 8.5 surprised you? Explain your answer.
   (b) List those statistics that describe you and your life.
   (c) Which statistics do not describe your life?

10. What is misleading about using statistics to determine what an average Canadian is like?

Leisure

Leisure forms an important part of the lives of most Canadians. Leisure time is time that is not committed to work or school.

Naturally it is important to eat and sleep during leisure time. As a result, not all leisure time is available for you to do whatever you want. Some people have almost no time in which they have the freedom to do whatever they want.

11. Rank these five people according to the amount of time in which they have complete freedom to do whatever they want. Place first the individual who has the greatest total amount of freedom in leisure per year. Give reasons for your answers.
    • minister, pastor, or priest
    • high-school student
    • mother of four young children who stays at home
    • baseball player
    • single office worker who works eight hours a day

Leisure in History

During most of human history, there has been little leisure time available for the average person. As we saw in Chapter 2, the average person spent most of his or her time working for basic survival. During the period of hunting and gathering, for example, people had to spend much time searching for food and had practically no time for leisure. As agriculture developed, more people could afford much more leisure time. The vast majority of the population, however, still had to work long hours to survive.

Conditions have changed greatly since then, and today most people in Canada have at least some leisure time. As would be expected, leisure time brings with it a number of benefits. But it also causes some problems.

Leisure in North American Society

The amount of leisure time has increased for the average North American, and a number of businesses have developed to provide leisure-time activities. The variety of leisure activities has also increased as the income of North Americans has grown.

12. (a) Examine the headings listed below. For each one list ten hobbies or leisure-time activities:
    • group entertainment activities
    • activities involving instruction
    • seasonal sports
    • individual activities or hobbies
    (b) Of those leisure activities listed in (a), select ten and describe the special sites or facilities necessary for each.
    (c) For each of the ten activities you selected in (b), describe the age group or type of individual who might be involved in it.

13. What negative aspects might there be to a rapid increase in leisure time in our society?

Theme Parks

In the First World, many kinds of centres have been created for leisure-time activities. **Theme parks** are among the most popular of these centres. A theme park is an entertainment complex with rides and activities developed around a theme, or central idea. There are several dozen theme parks across North America. Canada's largest theme park is Canada's Wonderland, which opened in 1981 just north of Toronto. The most famous theme park is Disney World.

CASE STUDY

Disney World

Just outside Orlando, Florida, is the tourist attraction that draws more visitors per year than any other single site in the Western world. With 14 million visitors a year, Disney World is an extraordinary leisure-time industry. At this rate, in just two years, Disney World attracts more tourists than there are people in Canada.

Disney World was first developed around cartoon and fairy tale characters such as Mickey Mouse and Cinderella. This theme park offers a world of fantasy in which a visitor can "leave" the real world for a few hours or a few days. Clean, well kept, and attractive, Disney World offers a wide range of entertainment. If you are interested in shopping, eating, golfing, watching a movie or a parade, or taking a ride on a train, boat or rollercoaster, Disney World might appeal to you.

14. Examine the map of Disney World in Figure 8.6.
    (a) Name the different areas within Disney World. Briefly describe the activities within each area.
    (b) Disney World is said to appeal to the whole family. Describe features of Disney World that would appeal to
        • children   • teenagers   • adults

15. Using an atlas, describe the year-round climate (high and low temperatures, etc.) of central Florida.

Figure 8.6 Disney World

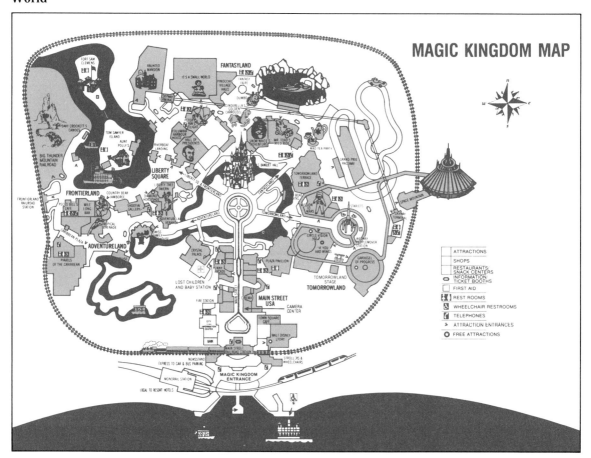

The focus at Disney World, as at other theme parks, is on making every tourist's visit as enjoyable as possible. At the same time, the owners of Disney World have the goal of making money; therefore they have created an environment that is so enjoyable that visitors will not mind spending money, as they will feel that they are receiving value from the money they spend. On average, one visitor spends $25 per day at Disney World.

The people who designed Disney World and those who now run it have paid great attention to the tiniest details of the park. This ensures that visitors experience total leisure. One such detail is garbage collection. There is almost no litter. Workers, in costume, quickly pick up all garbage and then deposit it in one of several centres (see Figure 8.7).

16. **What advantages would there be to having underground tunnels for**
    - **the people in costume?**
    - **the truck drivers?**

**Figure 8.7
Underground at
Disney World**

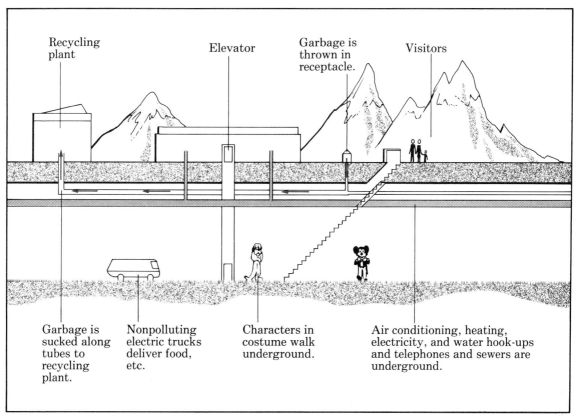

The planners of Disney World took great care to ensure that its construction would not damage the environment around it. The 110 km² of Disney World were originally swampland. Although some of the swamplands were drained, the original lakes, forests, and drainage patterns were preserved as much as possible. All of the garbage and sewage produced in Disney World is disposed of or purified on-site. For example, water hyacinth, a naturally occurring water weed, is used to purify sewage water. Disney World produces one-third of its own electricity and one-third of its own food. Part of this electricity is produced by solar cells.

17. **How has the development of Disney World been different from that of many cities? Explain.**

In October, 1982, EPCOT was opened next to the original Disney World. (EPCOT stands for Experimental Prototype Community of Tomorrow.) Included in EPCOT are centres representing many different countries such as Canada and Mexico. EPCOT also contains buildings that relate to new technology and science.

Next to Disney World are several resort hotels and campsites. These provide the accommodation necessary for tourists to spend a week or more in the area. With all of these facilities available, Disney World can be considered a single-destination resort. A family could come to Disney World and find plenty of activities for a stay of several days.

18. **In what way has Disney World brought together the interests of the owners and tourists?**

19. **Some people have expressed concern about the drainage of the swamps and forests to make way for Disney World. Imagine that you are one of the owners of Disney World. Write one half of a page to explain why you feel Disney World is worthwhile and presents little serious threat to the environment.**

20. **When Disney World opened in 1971, the government had provided few facilities to serve it. What do you think the government has provided to serve Disney World since 1971? (Hint: Most visitors arrive by car, but many come using other forms of transportation.)**

21. **Design your own theme park. To do so, follow these steps.**
    (a) Re-examine the map of Disney World in Figure 8.6.

(b) Decide on a main theme and a name. The theme should appeal to a wide number of people, including whole families. Some examples are World of Music, Countries of the World, Canada's History, and World of the Future.

(c) Once you have completed (b), decide on smaller theme areas within your park. For example, if your major theme was Countries of the World, your smaller theme areas might be Canada, the United States, Australia, China, and the Jungles of Uganda (Africa). You should have four or five smaller theme areas.

(d) Draw a rough map of your park. Allow for one main entrance.

(e) Within each theme area, create rides, stores, restaurants, parks, movies, etc. If one of your theme areas is the Jungle of Uganda, for example, you could have a jungle restaurant, a ride down a jungle river, and stores selling hot-weather clothing.

(f) Include walkways, etc., for tourists. They should provide easy access to each smaller theme area. Use sufficient trees and bushes to separate one area from another.

(g) When you have completed your rough map, put the final plan on a standard sheet of bristol board.

Other Tourist Centres in North America

Certain locations have become tourist centres because of their special features. St. Joseph's Oratory in Montreal, for example, is a major religious shrine for Roman Catholics. Tombstone, Arizona, has become well known because of its colourful "wild west" background. The gunfight at the O.K. Corral, for example, took place in Tombstone.

22. What three places near your home are tourist attractions? Briefly explain the reason for the importance of each one.

National Parks

The governments of Canada and the United States have developed a wide range of national parks across North America. The original goal for the establishment of these parks was the preservation of areas of extraordinary natural beauty or special interest. Yellowstone National Park in the United States is the location of remarkable hot-water geysers. Some of Canada's most spectacular mountain scenery can be seen in Banff National Park in Alberta.

a

b

Figure 8.8
National Parks
(a) Yellowstone
    National Park,
    Northwestern
    United States
(b) Nairobi National
    Park, Kenya

Many nations in the Third World have also developed national parks. Kenya, India, and Zimbabwe, for example, each have parks to preserve natural environments as well as to protect wildlife.

Since the establishment of the first national parks in North America, there has been increasing pressure for other land uses to be permitted within these parks. The controversy that has developed now involves many Canadian parks.

23. **Which of the following land uses should be allowed in national parks? Explain your answers fully. Outline conditions that might apply to allowing each land use in a park.**
   (a) **farming**
   (b) **airports**
   (c) **oil wells**
   (d) **mining**
   (e) **forestry**
   (f) **ski resorts**
   (g) **private cottages**
   (h) **golf courses**

Exotic Travel

People in First World nations often wish to travel outside their own country, and even outside the First World. Those fortunate enough to be able to afford it can explore exotic places located in remote areas of the world. The jungles of South America, for example, have great appeal for some travellers.

Machu Picchu

Set in the jungle-covered mountains of Peru, Machu Picchu is one of the most spectacular ruins in the world. Built by the Incas as a religious centre in the A.D. 800, Machu Picchu is perched on a mountain ledge 1000 m above the Urubamba River, a branch of the Amazon. It cannot be seen by people walking alongside the Urubamba River.

In the 1530s, the Spanish arrived in Peru and eventually destroyed the Inca Empire. Spanish troops marched along the Urubamba River, but did not notice that Machu Picchu was nearby. Separated from the rest of the Inca Empire, the inhabitants of Machu Picchu died off, and the jungle grew to cover the site for almost 400 years. In 1911, an American researcher called Hiram Bingham discovered this lost city by chance. A young boy apparently told Bingham of some unusual rocks at the top of a nearby ridge. This led to Bingham's discovery.

Today, tourists leave Cuzco to travel by train to this ancient site.

Figure 8.9 Machu Picchu, Peru

24. Describe the appeal that Machu Picchu has for a Canadian tourist.

25. If a tourist were to travel from your home area to Machu Picchu, what would be his or her
    • interests?   • probable level of income?
    Explain your answer briefly.

26. Besides being a tourist centre, what other value might Machu Picchu have for Peruvians? Explain your answer.

The Package Deal

Many tourists who like to travel prefer to avoid the small details of planning a trip. For these people, the **package deal** trip has been designed. With a package deal, almost all the major travel arrangements are made by a tour operator. Figure 8.10 outlines the details of two such trips. Package deals may cost less than a trip for which the traveller has made his or her own arrangements.

**Figure 8.10
Examples of
Package Deals**

27. **In your own words, describe the two package deals in Figure 8.10.**

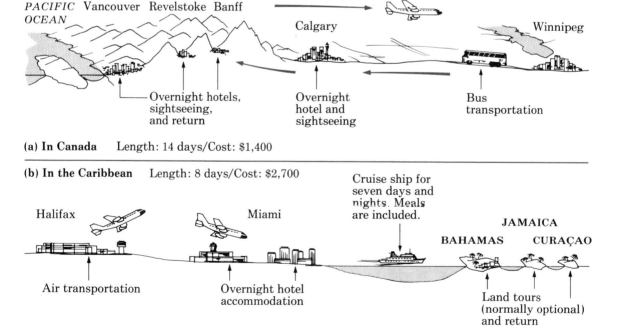

(a) **In Canada**   Length: 14 days/Cost: $1,400

(b) **In the Caribbean**   Length: 8 days/Cost: $2,700

28. Why might some people not enjoy a package deal trip?

29. Create a newspaper advertisement for each of the package deals in Figure 8.10. Be sure that the advertisement is attractive and full of information. Each advertisement should be 12 cm x 25 cm.

Package deals have meant, in some cases, that large numbers of North Americans and Europeans have flooded into poorer areas of the world. Most people view this tourist trade as positive because it brings a lot of money into these poor areas. Tourism is also looked upon favourably because it is considered a clean industry, generally adding little pollution to the environment. Catering for thousands of visitors in some Caribbean Islands, however, has resulted in untreated sewage from hotels polluting beaches and killing coral reefs.

30. (a) From the point of view of the tourist, what would be the benefits of an economical package deal to a Third World country?
    (b) What benefits would the tourist trade bring to the Third World country? Mention industries that would be helped, as well as other factors such as employment and taxes.

31. (a) Imagine that you are a poor resident of Acapulco, Mexico. The hot climate, sunshine, and beautiful beaches of Acapulco draw hundreds of thousands of Canadian and American tourists every year. Write a short description of your reactions to these "wealthy" tourists coming to your city.
    (b) If you were a Canadian tourist in Mexico, how would you feel about the poverty that you saw in Acapulco?

Figure 8.11 Low-Income Area in the Third World: Caracas, Venezuela

Mass Media

Modern technology has brought about enormous changes in the ways in which people communicate with one another.

**Figure 8.12
Different Methods
of Communication**

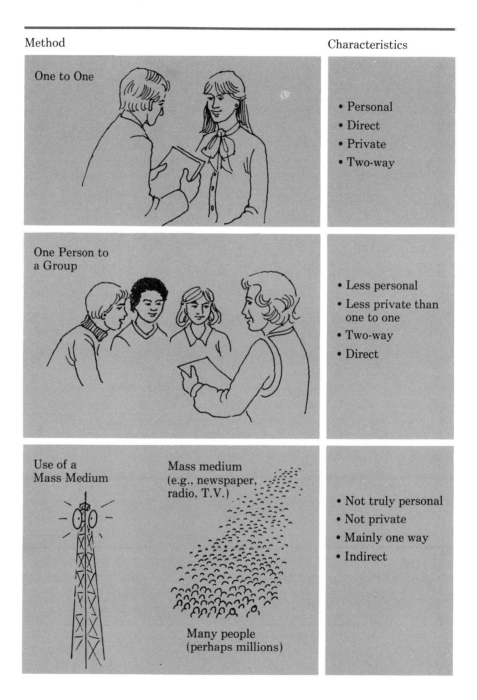

Method	Characteristics
One to One	• Personal • Direct • Private • Two-way
One Person to a Group	• Less personal • Less private than one to one • Two-way • Direct
Use of a Mass Medium — Mass medium (e.g., newspaper, radio, T.V.) — Many people (perhaps millions)	• Not truly personal • Not private • Mainly one way • Indirect

32. (a) Examine Figure 8.12. Describe the circumstances under which each method of communication is most effective.
   (b) Briefly describe when you last experienced each type of communication.

Mass media are the various means used to transmit information to a large group of people. Mass media are not used only for leisure-time activities. Business and government use mass media to relay a wide variety of information. So much information is now available in society that the situation has been described as **information explosion**. Yet, despite the rapid increase in knowledge and its communication, the average Canadian is often unaware of how to go about finding the information that he or she needs.

33. (a) What advantages do you have living in a world that has access to so many mass media and so much information?
   (b) In what ways do the mass media not actually benefit you?

Newspapers

Many people prefer newspapers to other sources of information because they can read an article over several times or even cut it out. In addition, newspapers often carry a wide variety of information. They are inexpensive to buy and are widely available.

34. There is a wide variety of newspapers available in Canada.
   (a) List five newspapers with which you are familiar. Describe the area or audience to which each appeals.
   (b) Outline eight different types of information that you could derive from a newspaper and the usefulness of each type.

35. (a) If newspapers were to disappear in Canada, what positive and negative effects might result?
   (b) What other media might emerge or expand in scope to replace newspapers?

36. In general, which generation reads newspapers more often—yours or that of your parents or guardians? Explain.

37. (a) Obtain a copy of a newspaper published in a large centre near you. Read the advertisements in the newspaper, taking note of the cities or towns mentioned in the ads. For example, you could note the location of various stores advertised. List at least 30 urban centres.

(b) Obtain a map of your province or territory. Plot your list from (a) on the map.

(c) Shade in the area around the city in which the newspaper is located. Include in the shaded area the various centres marked on your map. The map will now give you some indication of the area of influence of the newspaper and of the city in which it is located. Give your map a suitable title.

(d) In what ways might the map of the area of influence of your newspaper be inaccurate? Give reasons for your answer.

CASE STUDY

The Globe and Mail

The Globe and Mail, a daily newspaper based in Toronto, Ontario, serves not only the Toronto area but also a number of cities across Canada (Figure 8.13).

38. (a) Before the use of laser beams and satellites, how do you think that *The Globe and Mail* was moved across the country?

Figure 8.13 How *The Globe and Mail* Prints Its National Edition

The Globe and Mail prints editions in four Canadian cities as well as in Toronto.

Laser beams carry information at the speed of light. One page is sent each minute.

Anik satellite stays in orbit over the equator.

Vancouver Calgary Moncton Ottawa Toronto

(b) Since the satellite/laser system came into use, what advantages might there have been for
- a reader in Vancouver?
- companies that want to advertise in the newspaper?
- the owners of *The Globe and Mail*, who are concerned about selling more newspapers?

(c) Who might be opposed to this expansion by *The Globe and Mail*?

(d) What are the harmful effects that could result from the national distribution of newspapers?

Radio

Both AM and FM radio stations are widespread in Canada. AM stations can generally send their messages further, but the AM sound is less "clear". (This is because it is more subject to atmospheric interference.) In recent years, FM radio stations have been gaining listeners at the expense of AM stations.

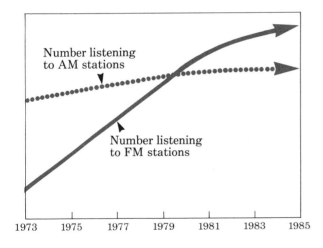

Number listening to AM stations

Number listening to FM stations

1973 1975 1977 1979 1981 1983 1985

**Figure 8.14
Changing Radio Listening Patterns in Canada**

39. Examine Figure 8.14. Suggest reasons for the changes in radio listening patterns. Your own listening habits may help you to answer this question.

Almost 99% of Canadian households have AM radios, while 86% also have FM radios. Most cars and trucks contain radios.

Along with the growth in the number of radios in the last 50 years, there has been an increase in the number of radio stations.

The first **commercial radio station** in Canada that still operates is CFCF, Montreal. (A commercial radio station is one that is operated to make money.) The second is CKOC in Hamilton, Ontario. When it started in 1922, CKOC broadcast for 20 min each day and its 20-W transmitter reached only the local community.

40. (a) Tastes in radio listening change as people grow older. Describe the type of music and programs that would appeal to people of the following ages:
    • 16
    • 30
    • 65

41. The largest portion of Canada's population was born during the baby boom—from 1946 to 1961.
    (a) What ages would these people be today?
    (b) Consider your answer to question (a). In what significant family-related activities would these people be involved?
    (c) What products would advertisers want to advertise on radio to appeal to the baby-boom age group? List at least 25 items.

42. What advantage does radio have over newspapers for reporting news items? Explain.

43. In your atlas turn to a map showing population distribution.
    (a) Where would you expect most radio stations to be located in Canada? Explain.
    (b) Since FM radio signals travel only about 50 km, where would most FM radio stations be located? Explain.

CASE STUDY

CJOB, Winnipeg, Manitoba

When CJOB was established in March 1946, it became the third privately owned radio station in Winnipeg. The call letters CJOB stand for "Canada" and "John Oliver Blick", the station's original owner. Originally, the station was staffed by veterans of World War II. Then, as now, CJOB broadcasted news, information, and music to its Winnipeg area audience.

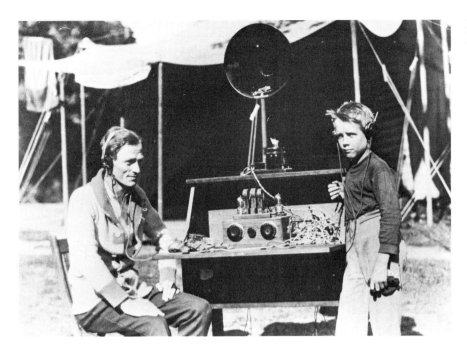

Figure 8.15 An
Early Radio

CJOB has broadcast non-stop since 1946, and even operated
during the spring of 1950 when the Red and Assiniboine rivers
flooded Winnipeg. Although the radio station building was flooded
by about a metre of water, a transmitter was set up on top of the
building and the station continued broadcasting when no other
Winnipeg stations could.

When CJOB began broadcasting, its signal sent out a power
of 500 W and the station operated 24 h a day. (Some earlier radio
stations broadcast programs only a few hours a day.) Today,
CJOB's signal has a power of 50 000 W. This power is needed not
just to travel the distance to an audience but also to overcome
interference from sources such as trucks, machinery, and airplanes.

When the radio signal is sent out from the transmitter of any
radio station, it follows a certain pattern. Figure 8.16 illustrates
this pattern.

Some radio signals travel upward to the atmosphere and are
reflected back to earth by the ionosphere (one of the upper layers
of the earth's atmosphere). These radio signals are reflected back
to earth from over 3000 km away (Figure 8.17).

During the day, the signals reflected by the ionosphere are
quite weak. After sunset, however, the reflected signals are usually

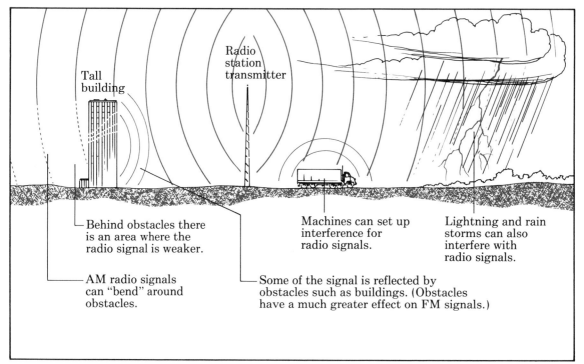

**Figure 8.16
Transmission of
AM Radio Signals
through the Air
at Low Levels**

Tall
building

Radio
station
transmitter

Behind obstacles there
is an area where the
radio signal is weaker.

AM radio signals
can "bend" around
obstacles.

Machines can set up
interference for
radio signals.

Some of the signal is reflected by
obstacles such as buildings. (Obstacles
have a much greater effect on FM signals.)

Lightning and rain
storms can also
interfere with
radio signals.

strong. As a result, at night CJOB cuts back its power, thereby
reducing the size of the area in which its signal is received. This
limits interference with other radio stations sharing the same
frequency. Other radio stations that share CJOB's frequency of

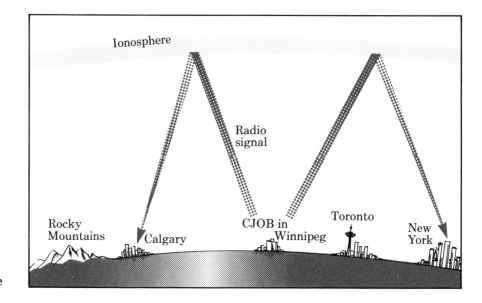

**Figure 8.17
Transmission of
Radio Signals by
Bouncing Them
off the Ionosphere**

Ionosphere

Radio
signal

Rocky
Mountains

Calgary

CJOB in
Winnipeg

Toronto

New
York

680 are located in Gravelburg, Saskatchewan; San Francisco, California; and the New England states.

44. (a) What other obstacles besides tall buildings reflect radio signals? Name five.
    (b) Think of the times you have listened to a car radio. When did you find the AM radio signal to be weak? Give two examples.

45. (a) Suggest three ways in which CJOB could discover the size of its listening area.
    (b) Which method would be the simplest? Explain.

46. If you were preparing a weather report for CJOB, what cities or towns would you mention? Explain.

Figure 8.18 The Main Listening Area for Radio Station CJOB, Winnipeg

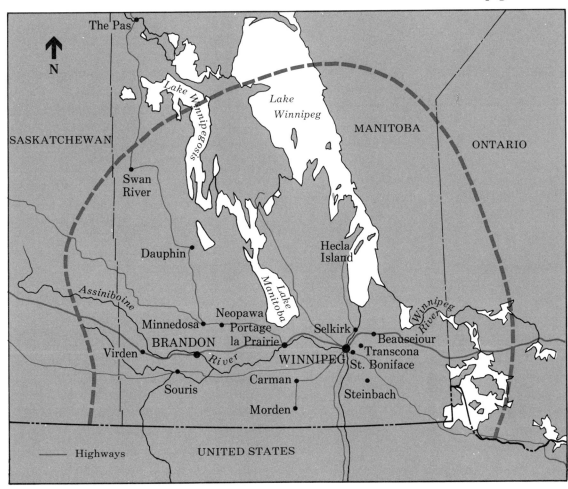

47. (a) Select a radio station you can listen to at home. What cities, towns, or regions are mentioned in its news, public affairs, and weather broadcasts?

(b) Obtain a map of your local area. On the map, mark the cities, towns, or regions from (a). Shade in the listening area that you have determined.

(c) What conclusions can you make about the area of influence of the centre from which that radio station broadcasts?

(d) Compare the map you have constructed in (b) with the one from question 37. Explain.

Television

Television is the most important of the various mass media in Canada, and it is extremely versatile, as shown in Figure 8.19.

48. Which of the functions listed in Figure 8.19 have you used or are you familiar with? Explain how they are used.

There are approximately 850 television stations in Canada, many of which belong to **networks**. The two major Canadian networks are CBC (Canadian Broadcasting Corporation) and CTV (Canadian Television Network). CBC is owned by the federal

Figure 8.19 The Many Uses of Television

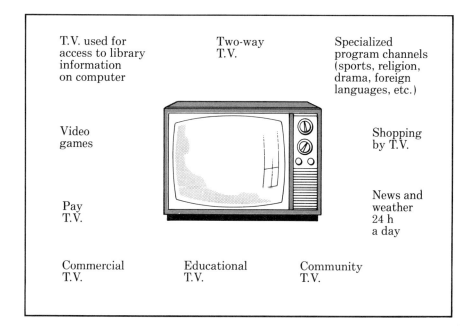

T.V. used for access to library information on computer

Two-way T.V.

Specialized program channels (sports, religion, drama, foreign languages, etc.)

Video games

Shopping by T.V.

Pay T.V.

News and weather 24 h a day

Commercial T.V.

Educational T.V.

Community T.V.

government and CTV is privately owned. Most Canadians can receive programs from both networks. In addition, there are other independently owned stations and a few publicly funded television systems (such as TVOntario, which broadcasts programs without commercials). Pay T.V., so-called because viewers pay local cable stations an additional fee to receive special channels, was introduced in Canada in early 1983.

**Figure 8.20
Television Coverage in Canada**

CBC and Affiliated Stations

English

French

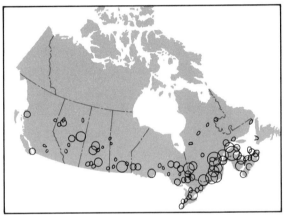

The CBC has many repeater stations and Anik satellite rebroadcasters to service remote areas of Canada, especially the North.

CTV Affiliated Stations, English

Global, TVO Networks

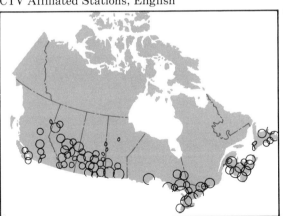
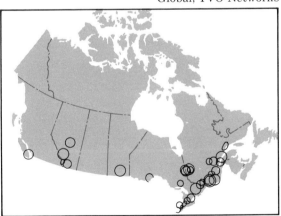

These stations also have repeater stations, mainly in the south.

49. It has been said that television demands more of the viewer than radio does of the listener. Do you agree with this statement? Explain.

50. (a) How many hours of television do you watch per week? Calculate your average television viewing hours per day, then determine your weekly total.
   (b) There are 168 h in a week. Of that time, on average you would sleep 56 h. How many hours per week do you spend at school or working? Subtract the total of sleep, work, and school hours from 168. That number represents the total number of leisure hours you have per week. What percentage of your leisure time do you spend watching television?

$$
\begin{array}{rr}
\text{Example: Total hours per week} & 168 \\
\text{sleep} & -56 \\
\hline
 & 112 \\
\text{school and work} & -48 \\
\hline
\text{Total leisure} & 64 \\
\end{array}
$$

Total watching T.V.   24

Percentage of leisure
spent watching T.V. $\dfrac{24}{64} \times 100 = 37.5\%$

   (c) Imagine that all television suddenly disappeared. How would you spend the time that you had once spent watching television?

51. Television, in itself, is neither good nor bad. It is the way in which television is used that determines whether it has a good or bad effect. Although millions of Canadians spend many hours watching television, many critics believe that T.V. programs are largely negative in their impact. Write a 300- to 400-word essay to discuss
   (a) the positive and negative aspects of television
   (b) your conclusion about television's overall impact on Canadians
   Consider all aspects of television programming, as well as the lifestyles shown and the values portrayed in the shows.

Television's New Uses

The inventor of television, John Logie Baird from Helensburgh, Scotland, and those who refined his invention had little idea of the many uses that would be developed for this medium. Recent developments involving television include two-way television, access to library information on computer, fibre optics systems, and satellites.

Two-Way Television

Two-way television is a system that connects a television studio by cable to a large number of homes with television sets. People in each home can send a message to the studio along the cable (Figure 8.21).

Figure 8.21 Two-Way Television

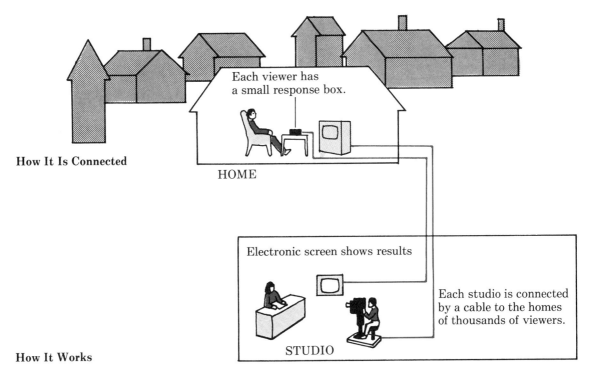

How It Is Connected

Each viewer has a small response box.

HOME

How It Works

Electronic screen shows results

Each studio is connected by a cable to the homes of thousands of viewers.

STUDIO

1. The person on T.V. asks "Do you think the mayor of our city is doing a good job?"

The home viewers push either the "yes" or "no" button.

The results of the voting are recorded on the electronic screen in the television studio.

2. The viewers are asked at the end of a T.V. show to rank the quality of that show. The number 1 represents "very poor" and 10 represents "very good".

The viewers at home push numbered buttons to indicate their rating of the show.

The show is rated by its viewers in less than a minute.

52. In what specific ways is two-way television different from the type of television with which you are familiar?

53. (a) Suggest four ways in which two-way television could be used, other than the ways described in this text.
    (b) To what groups would two-way television appeal?
    (c) How might two-way television be paid for?
        Explain your answers.

54. (a) In what ways is two-way television similar to a meeting of people in a town hall?
    (b) What happens to people's concern about distance when they use two-way television?

55. (a) How might two-way television be used to invade your privacy and possibly to exert control over you?
    (b) What should be done to try to limit the use of two-way television to protect your privacy?

Access Through Television to Library Information on Computer

It is 20:00 on a Monday. Vimla Gupta, a high-school student, has decided to do some research for a geography essay. She turns on the television and flicks a switch to connect to the computer at her local library. On the television screen appear a number of general topics, each with numbers beside it. Vimla pushes the number for the topic she wants on the small control she has. After a few more choices, the information that she wants on the Rocky Mountains appears on the television screen.

---

56. What three advantages does this use of television have over other methods of research?

Fibre Optics Systems

In general, television signals travel less than 100 km from their transmitter. As a result, cable television has been introduced to much of Canada. Nearly 60% of Canadian homes had cable television in 1983. Cable television brings a wide variety of programs from stations that are distant from your home. In Saskatchewan, some cable television is carried on a **fibre optics** system. Such a system involves the use of tiny strands of glass that carry laser light beams (see Figure 8.22).

This system can also carry telephone and data messages along the same cable. The two copper wires connected to most Canadian telephones are able to carry only one conversation at a time.

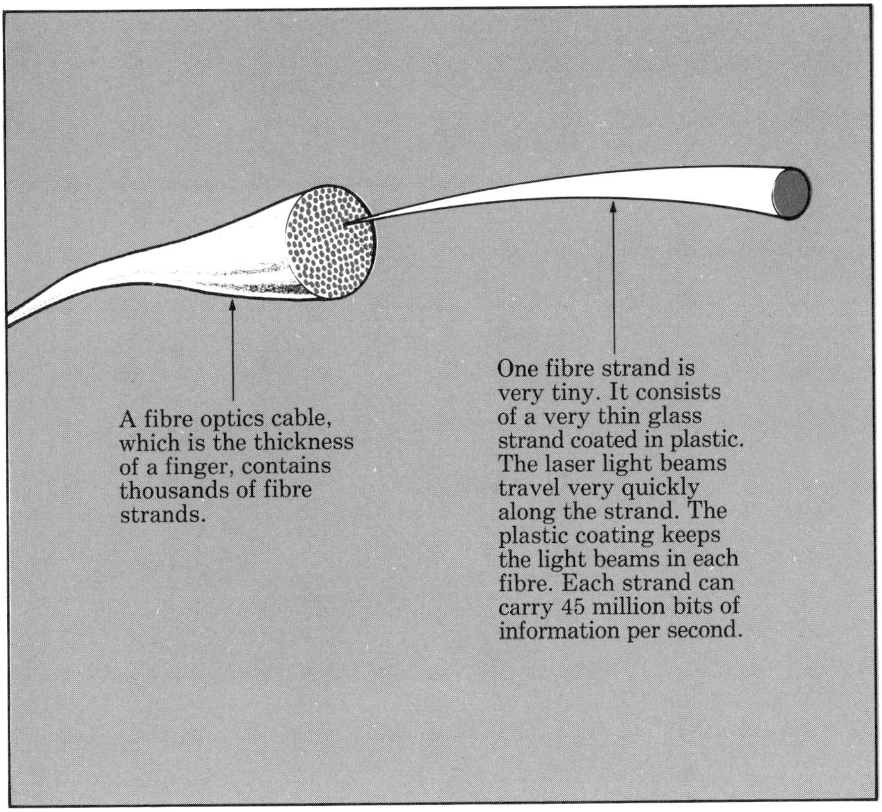

Figure 8.22
A Fibre Optics
System

A fibre optics cable, which is the thickness of a finger, contains thousands of fibre strands.

One fibre strand is very tiny. It consists of a very thin glass strand coated in plastic. The laser light beams travel very quickly along the strand. The plastic coating keeps the light beams in each fibre. Each strand can carry 45 million bits of information per second.

Once the fibre optics cable system is connected to more homes, those who live in smaller towns will be able to have as much variety on television as people who live in cities. The cable system will also allow people to enjoy new uses of television, such as shopping, two-way television, and access to library information on a computer.

57. Using an atlas, examine a map of your province. Which areas of your province would benefit most from the introduction of cable television?

58. As the fibre optics system expands in Saskatchewan, in what ways can the people in small centres develop lifestyles similar to those of people in large cities?

Satellites

Another type of technology affecting television in North America is the satellite. Television stations can use satellites to send their signal across the continent (see Figure 8.23).

Figure 8.23
The Use of
Satellites in
Television
Transmission

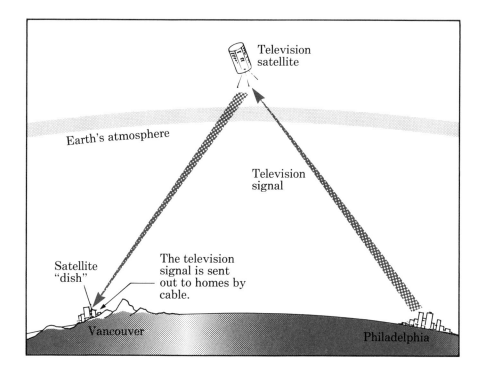

COMSAT is the American corporation that operates television satellites. One major Canadian group of satellites is called Anik. *Anik C3* is a powerful communication satellite that was launched in November 1982 from the U.S. space shuttle *Columbia*. It carries educational programs to communities in northern B.C. and northern Canada.

Figure 8.24
A Satellite Dish

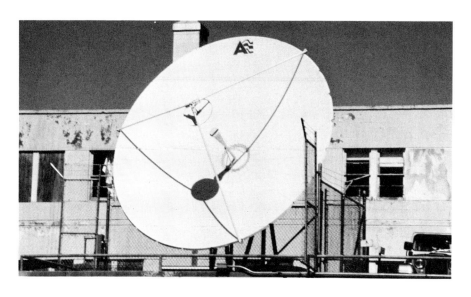

59. Consider your favourite television shows. Many of these, especially those produced in the United States, are shown on television in the Third World.
   (a) What impression would someone in Quito, Ecuador, have of North American life, based solely on those television programs?
   (b) What attitudes might people in Ecuador develop about their own lifestyle, based on their reaction to American-made programs?
   (c) Suggest ways in which television might be used in a positive way in a country such as Ecuador.

60. (a) What relationship is there between the size of a city and its influence through mass media, such as television?
   (b) Select four cities that you think have a significant influence, through mass media, on people who do not live in them. Give the reasons for your choice.

Cellular Radio

Only a small number of Canadians have telephones in their cars. Plans are being developed, however, to allow the average Canadian

**Figure 8.25
A Typical
Cellular
Radio System**

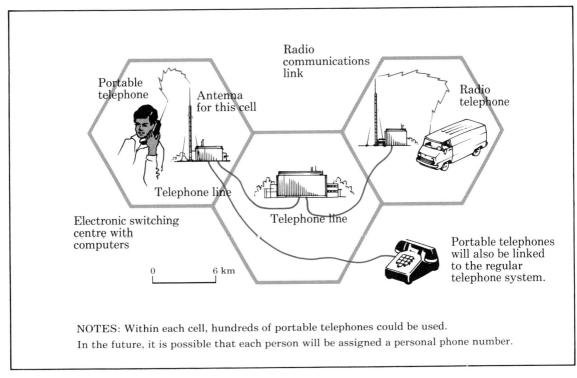

NOTES: Within each cell, hundreds of portable telephones could be used.
In the future, it is possible that each person will be assigned a personal phone number.

to buy and use a portable telephone. A system that allows people to use a portable telephone in or out of a car is called **cellular radio** (Figure 8.25). Due to the great expense of setting up these systems, only Canada's largest cities will receive cellular radio at first.

Although cellular radio is not a mass medium, it is a form of communication that will become increasingly important.

61. (a) **In your own words, explain how the cellular radio system operates.**
    (b) **What three advantages does this system have over radio systems in use today?**
    (c) **How will cellular radio change the way in which people think of time, distance, and their city?**

VOCABULARY

baby boom	information explosion	package deal
cellular radio	leisure	theme park
commercial	lifestyle	two-way television
radio station	mass media	
fibre optics	networks	

RESEARCH QUESTIONS

To answer these questions, you will probably need to refer to library resources and other sources of information.

1. Use books and encyclopedias in your library to research this question. Your answer should be between 300 and 400 words in length.
   (a) Briefly describe the way of life of people in these civilizations or societies:
   - ancient Rome
   - ancient Egypt
   - Canada from 1750–1810
   (b) How much leisure did the average person have in these civilizations or societies? What forms did it take?
   (c) Compare these examples with the situation in Canada today.

2. Using the following guidelines, research the topic of *hobbies* in Canada.
   (a) List 15 popular Canadian hobbies.
   (b) Give a brief description of each.
   (c) To which key group, if any, does each hobby appeal?
   (d) What expenses are involved in this hobby?

3. Select three national parks in North America or elsewhere that have not been discussed in this book. For each park,
   (a) describe the location
   (b) outline the specific features (e.g., specific types of animals, landforms, etc.)
   (c) give a brief history
   (d) outline the type of person who probably would be interested in visiting that park

4. Obtain a copy of a major daily newspaper, preferably one that is printed near your home. A weekend edition would be most suitable.
   (a) Select ten package deals from the travel section.
   (b) For each one, record the destination, cost, length, and special features.
   (c) Assuming that you had the money, which one would you choose? Give reasons for your selection.

SECTION IV

The Impact of Economic and Cultural Geography on the Environment

9 | Environmental Concerns

Introduction

The quality of your environment has an enormous influence on your health and happiness. In the relatively short time that people have existed on earth, there have been great changes in the environment. Increasing developments in technology have raised the living standards of people in industrial nations. However, a price has been paid for this comfort. The quality of the environment has declined (Figure 9.1).

Figure 9.1
Problems Resulting from a High Standard of Living
(a) Air pollution
(b) Garbage
(c) Heavy traffic
(d) Loud noise

a

b

c

d

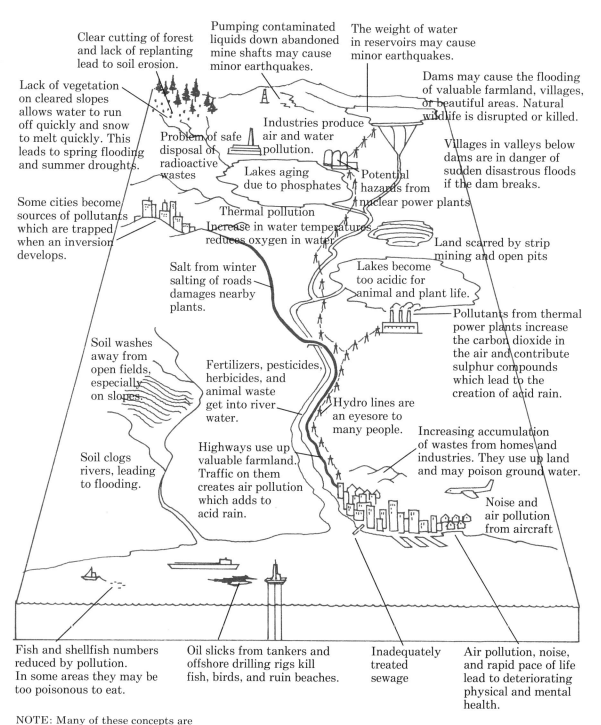

Clear cutting of forest and lack of replanting lead to soil erosion.

Pumping contaminated liquids down abandoned mine shafts may cause minor earthquakes.

The weight of water in reservoirs may cause minor earthquakes.

Dams may cause the flooding of valuable farmland, villages, or beautiful areas. Natural wildlife is disrupted or killed.

Lack of vegetation on cleared slopes allows water to run off quickly and snow to melt quickly. This leads to spring flooding and summer droughts.

Problem of safe disposal of radioactive wastes

Industries produce air and water pollution.

Lakes aging due to phosphates

Potential hazards from nuclear power plants

Villages in valleys below dams are in danger of sudden disastrous floods if the dam breaks.

Some cities become sources of pollutants which are trapped when an inversion develops.

Thermal pollution Increase in water temperatures reduces oxygen in water

Land scarred by strip mining and open pits

Salt from winter salting of roads damages nearby plants.

Lakes become too acidic for animal and plant life.

Pollutants from thermal power plants increase the carbon dioxide in the air and contribute sulphur compounds which lead to the creation of acid rain.

Soil washes away from open fields, especially on slopes.

Fertilizers, pesticides, herbicides, and animal waste get into river water.

Hydro lines are an eyesore to many people.

Increasing accumulation of wastes from homes and industries. They use up land and may poison ground water.

Soil clogs rivers, leading to flooding.

Highways use up valuable farmland. Traffic on them creates air pollution which adds to acid rain.

Noise and air pollution from aircraft

Fish and shellfish numbers reduced by pollution. In some areas they may be too poisonous to eat.

Oil slicks from tankers and offshore drilling rigs kill fish, birds, and ruin beaches.

Inadequately treated sewage

Air pollution, noise, and rapid pace of life lead to deteriorating physical and mental health.

NOTE: Many of these concepts are further explained later in this chapter.

Figure 9.2 How Technology Contributes to Pollution

Environmental problems are not restricted to First World nations. The proper management of resources is also of vital concern in many poorer nations. However, environmental problems affected the wealthier nations first, as they were the first to industrialize.

Figure 9.2 illustrates how complex environmental problems are in an industrial nation such as Canada. Most of them result from a very high standard of living. To produce increasing quantities of consumer goods, more and more resources are needed. The removal of these resources often damages the land. Transporting and manufacturing these resources creates wastes, some of which are extremely dangerous. In homes, solid and liquid materials are discarded, as are human wastes. All of these wastes can pollute the air and water on which everyone depends for life.

1. (a) **List ten items that are commonly discarded in your household.**
   (b) **Are any of these potentially dangerous? Which ones?**
   (c) **What can be done to reduce the danger of the items listed in (b)?**
   (d) **Is it possible to recycle any of the ten items? Explain how.**

Almost every human activity affects the environment. Figure 9.3 shows the impact of the production of paper on the environment.

Figure 9.3 How Paper Production Affects the Environment

Air pollution

Pulp and paper mill

Air pollution

Water pollution

River

Erosion along logging roads

Soil erosion

Logging causes damage to new trees, bushes, grass, which are food for deer, moose, etc.

Air pollution

Noise pollution

Air pollution

Slope of land may need to be changed to build railway tracks

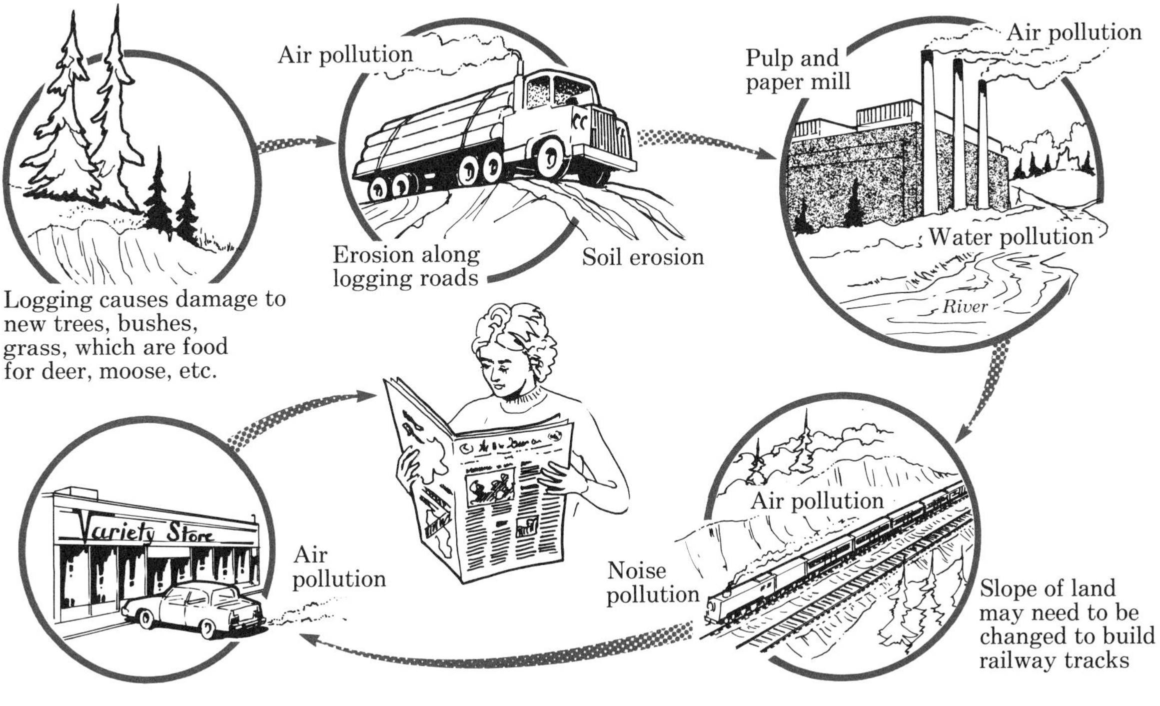

2. Suggest and describe fully four ways in which the environmental damage shown in Figure 9.3 could be reduced.

3. Select another industry and list the changes in the environment as a result of that industry. Note that some of the changes in the environment are not harmful.

Environmental Concerns in Everyday Life

Hazards in the Home

Most people are well aware of the many hazards that threaten the environment. Newspapers, magazines, and news programs inform their audiences of air and water pollution, of garbage problems in our cities, and of the dumping of dangerous industrial chemicals

Figure 9.4 Causes and Effects of Air Pollution in a Typical Canadian Home

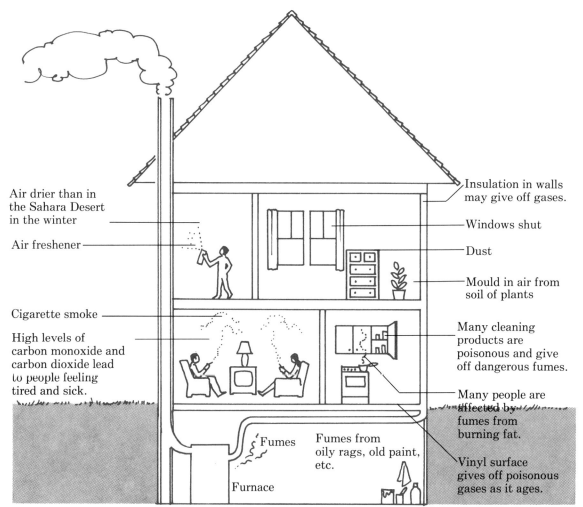

Air drier than in the Sahara Desert in the winter

Air freshener

Cigarette smoke

High levels of carbon monoxide and carbon dioxide lead to people feeling tired and sick.

Insulation in walls may give off gases.

Windows shut

Dust

Mould in air from soil of plants

Many cleaning products are poisonous and give off dangerous fumes.

Many people are affected by fumes from burning fat.

Vinyl surface gives off poisonous gases as it ages.

Fumes

Fumes from oily rags, old paint, etc.

Furnace

on land and in water. Your home may seem to be a refuge from such problems. Yet, even within the home there are many hazards (see Figure 9.4).

4. **Examine Figure 9.4. Suggest three ways in which the quality of air in this Canadian home could be improved. Be specific.**

Recently, it has been discovered that common tap water could possibly be hazardous. People in Canada obtain their water from wells, from unpolluted lakes or rivers, or from main supplies that have been treated with chlorine.

Chlorine is used to kill bacteria, which might spread diseases such as typhoid, dysentery, or diphtheria. It does not, however, remove the dangerous chemicals that result from dumping by industrial plants. Tap water originating from the Great Lakes, for example, that has passed through normal chlorination, may still contain small, but measurable quantities of many chemicals (see Figure 9.5).

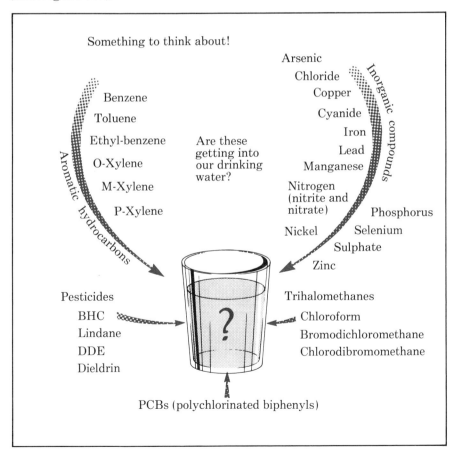

Figure 9.5 Chemicals in Water Taken from the Lower Great Lakes

Figure 9.6 How Well Water Is Contaminated

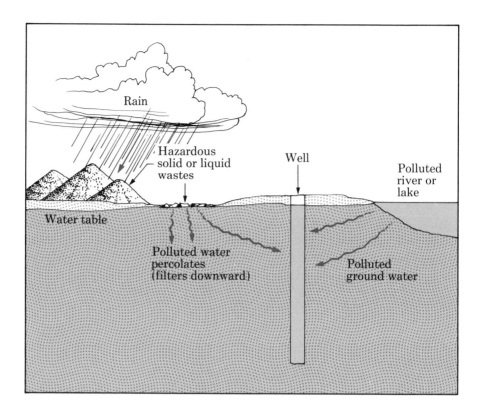

People who use their water from wells are also in some danger. Ground water, which flows into wells that are drilled, may be contaminated by solid and liquid wastes deposited on the surface (see Figure 9.6). For example, concern has been expressed about the seepage of polluted water from mining sites in British Columbia. (Mine tailings may contain toxic chemicals, which enter the local ground water through the action of rain.) Other mining operations have also contributed to the pollution of ground water. In late February 1982, waste water containing oil and grease spilled into the Athabasca River near Fort McMurray. The result was extensive pollution of the river and contamination of fish.

The salt, used to melt ice on many highways in winter (Figure 9.7), is also filtering into our water supplies. Although high levels of salt in drinking water certainly do not present the same kind of hazard as chemical contamination, such levels can be dangerous for people with a history of high blood pressure or heart disease. In water from wells close to highways, salt concentrations have been found to be nearly eight times as high as is recommended for those on controlled-salt diets.

Figure 9.7
Salt spreading equipment, dwarfed by a mountain of road salt.

Unsafe substances can also be hidden in many of the foods commonly consumed. Although strict laws keep these hazards to a minimum, you should be aware of their presence. In order to prevent **botulism**, a deadly form of food poisoning, some cured meats such as bacon, hot dogs, and ham are preserved with nitrites. Nitrites, however, are suspected of being **carcinogens**, cancer-causing agents. Researchers have discovered, however, that Vitamin C stops the formation of dangerous compounds from nitrites.

In addition, many fish taken from Canadian lakes and rivers contain high quantities of mercury. When eaten in large enough quantities, mercury causes nerve and brain damage.

These are but a few of the hazards that are faced by people every day in their homes. There are many others. Later in this chapter, the sources of pollution will be examined in more detail.

5. (a) **Make a list of five hazardous substances in your home. You might want to begin by listing cleaning products. In your notebook, construct a table with the following headings and then complete the table.**

PRODUCT	DANGER	FIRST-AID TREATMENT
	SAMPLE ONLY	

(b) **What could be done to control the danger of having these substances in our homes?**

Stress

Stress affects people in all aspects of their lives—in homes, schools, places of work, recreation areas, and on trips. You will recognize many of the symptoms of stress outlined in Figure 9.8.

**Figure 9.8
Some of the
Symptoms of
Stress**

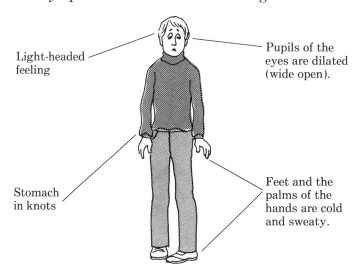

Light-headed feeling

Pupils of the eyes are dilated (wide open).

Stomach in knots

Feet and the palms of the hands are cold and sweaty.

This reaction to an uncomfortable situation is natural. It occurs when adrenalin is secreted into the blood. Adrenalin raises the blood pressure and readies the body for extra physical or mental effort. Occasional stress, according to medical experts, is tolerable and may even be helpful. When stress continues at high levels, however, it may have a negative effect on a person's mental or physical health.

Psychologists have attempted to put a stress value on different life events. The scale in Figure 9.9 was devised by Dr. Thomas Holmes. It is not foolproof, for stress affects different people in different ways. Many events not listed here may also cause stress.

6. **Examine Figure 9.9. Add up the total for all events that you experienced during the last year. A score of below 150 is average. You have a 30% chance of serious illness. A score of 150–300 increases your chance of illness to 50%. Over 300 means that you have an 80% to 90% chance of illness. (These events may be more or less stressful to you than this chart indicates.)**

7. **According to this list, which sources of stress are more common among older people (such as your parents) than among your peer group?**

8. **What factors would lead to stress for a young child? Name at least four.**

EVENT	POINTS	EVENT	POINTS
Death of spouse	100	Son or daughter leaving home	29
Divorce	73	Trouble with in-laws	29
Marital separation	65	Outstanding personal achievement	28
Jail term	63	Spouse begins or stops work	26
Death of close family member	63	Begin or end school	26
Personal injury or illness	53	Change in living conditions	25
Marriage	50	Revision of personal habits	24
Fired at work	47	Trouble with boss	23
Marital reconciliation	45	Change in work hours or conditions	20
Retirement	45	Change in residence	20
Change in health of family member	44	Change in schools	20
Pregnancy	40	Change in recreation	19
Sex difficulties	39	Change in church activities	19
Gain of a new family member	39	Change in social activities	18
Business readjustment	39	Small mortgage or loan for lesser	
Change in financial state	38	purchase (e.g., car, T.V.)	17
Death of a close friend	37	Change in sleeping habits	16
Change to different line of work	36	Change in number of family	
Change in number of arguments		get-togethers	15
with spouse	35	Change in eating habits	15
Large mortgage or loan for major		Vacation	13
purchase (e.g., house)	31	Christmas	12
Foreclosure of mortgage or loan	30	Minor violations of the law	11
Change in responsibilities at work	29		

Figure 9.9 Stress Values of Selected Life Experiences

9. (a) **Devise your own stress scale for students of your age group. Work in a small group to answer this question. Arrange your list from most stressful to least stressful event.**

   (b) **Choose one of the stresses that you listed in (a) that results from your school life. Suggest and carefully explain a practical way in which this stress could be reduced.**

Noise

The noise that people experience in their daily lives adds to stress, and it can make people short-tempered, sick, or even deaf. Simply living in a modern city affects people's hearing, and listening to very loud noises for even short periods of time may cause permanent damage. Sounds louder than 75 dB (decibels) increase the human pulse rate and cause a person to breathe more quickly and become more aggressive and irritable. Loud noises at night disturb sleep and may affect a person's mental state if the situation continues.

As you will observe from Figure 9.10, people are subjected to dangerous noise levels in almost every area of their lives. Protective hearing devices are compulsory for some workers.

**Figure 9.10
The Decibel Scale**

CAUSE OF NOISE	INTENSITY (dB)	OBSERVATION
Space rocket at 100 m	180	Noise causes pain and may damage unprotected ear.
	170	
	160	
	150	
Jet aircraft at 10 m	140	
	130	Prolonged exposure results in irritation, stress, and eventual damage to hearing.
Rock band at 10 m	120	
	110	
Power lawn mower at 1.5 m		
Snowmobile	100	
Heavy diesel truck at 6 m	90	
Vacuum cleaner at 1.5 m	80	
Dishwasher at 3 m	70	Acceptable noise level in industry
Busy traffic	60	
	50	Urban residential area
Inside average home	40	Quiet residential area
	30	
Soft whisper at 1 m	20	Noise level in rural area
	10	
Hearing threshold	0	

NOTE: The decibel scale is logarithmic. In this case, this means that each time the number on the scale doubles, the sound intensity increases ten times.

10. **List ten types of employment that you consider should have hearing protection.**

11. **(a) To what hazards is your hearing exposed?**
    (b) How could you reduce the risk of damage to your hearing?

Environmental Concerns in Industrialized Nations

Everything that people use or consume originated from resources in the natural environment. The more goods that are used, the greater are the demands placed on the environment. In industrialized nations, the processing, manufacturing, use, and disposal of goods produce wastes that pollute the air, land, and water. Current environmental problems have resulted from unwise practices in the past. It is important to deal with these problems now, before they become too serious or cause damage that cannot be reversed.

Air Pollution

In Rome, Italy, the ancient marble buildings in the Roman Forum are crumbling. Age is not the problem—they are being eaten away by air pollution. In Tokyo, Japan, police who direct traffic downtown during rush hours take an "oxygen break" every hour. They go inside a nearby building to breathe some oxygen to clear their lungs of polluted air.

Pollutants are found in the air of every region of the world today. Even the Arctic and Antarctic are beginning to be affected by significant air pollution. Major wind systems, which circle the globe, spread pollutants through the atmosphere. Most of the sources of air pollution are in the urban areas of the world. In general, air pollution results from the activities outlined in Figure 9.11.

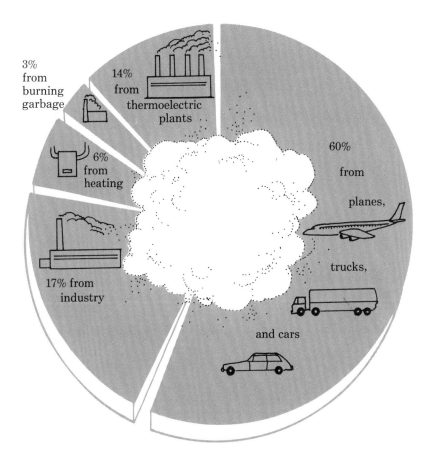

**Figure 9.11
Major Sources
of Air Pollution
in the World**

3% from burning garbage

14% from thermoelectric plants

6% from heating

17% from industry

60% from planes, trucks, and cars

Under certain weather conditions, pollutants become trapped in a city, sometimes building up to the point where they cause illness and death. The weather condition that traps pollution is referred to as an **inversion** (see Figure 9.12).

Cities located in valleys or beside lakes experience inversions from time to time. If a warm air mass moves over an area of cold air, the cold air becomes trapped below the warm air. Any pollutants remain confined within the cold air mass. The inversion may last for many days, with a continual build-up of pollutants. The problems disappear only when weather conditions change.

Figure 9.12 Two Causes of Inversion

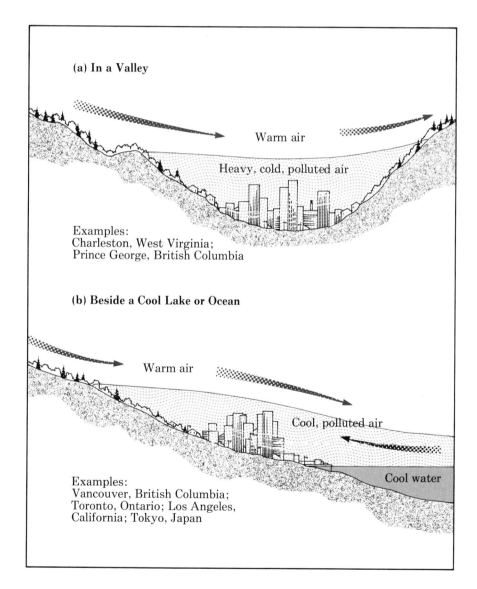

(a) In a Valley

Warm air

Heavy, cold, polluted air

Examples:
Charleston, West Virginia;
Prince George, British Columbia

(b) Beside a Cool Lake or Ocean

Warm air

Cool, polluted air

Cool water

Examples:
Vancouver, British Columbia;
Toronto, Ontario; Los Angeles,
California; Tokyo, Japan

The most serious instance of this occurred in 1952 in London, England. Here is a first-hand account.

> I remember feeling my way along the iron railings on my way home from school. This was the fourth day. The dank air smelled foul and was a thick pea-green colour. At home, the windows were shut tight, and a cheerful fire warmed the air. The smog lasted one more day. When it was over, 4000 people had died.
>
> C. Hannell

The air over London is much cleaner now as a result of the *Clean Air Act* of 1956, which outlawed the burning of coal to heat homes. This was perhaps the most significant source of air pollution in London. The *Clean Air Act* led to a switch from coal to other, cleaner sources of heat.

12. **Think of the worst air pollution that you have experienced.**
    (a) **Describe, as accurately as you can, when it occurred—the time of day, season, and year.**
    (b) **Explain what the pollution looked like and how it smelled.**
    (c) **Try to explain the probable cause(s) of this pollution.**

Air pollution presents a major concern in many cities around the world. Provincial laws have been successful in causing a reduction of pollutants in many Canadian cities. Many industries have installed pollution control equipment. As a result, the levels of some pollutants have been significantly reduced, as in the case of sulphur dioxide (see Figure 9.13). There are also stricter controls on automobile exhaust now than in the past.

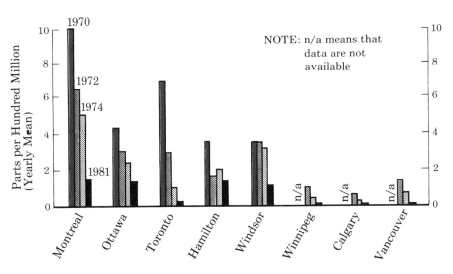

**Figure 9.13
The Reduction in Sulphur Dioxide Levels in Selected Canadian Cities**

Sour Gas Emissions in Alberta

"Sour gas" is a natural gas that contains impurities such as hydrogen sulphide. Most of Alberta's natural gas is "sweet", but enough sour gas is drilled in the province that there are nearly 50 processing plants, where sour gas impurities are removed. The purification process makes the gas suitable for sale, but it poses another problem. As the gas is processed, a number of air pollutants, including sulphur dioxide, are emitted. Sulphur dioxide has been linked with conditions such as asthma and rashes. It has also been cited as contributing to poor crops and local acid rain.

The petroleum industry has raised some doubts about the seriousness of air pollution coming from sour gas processing plants. Almost 98% of the sulphur dioxide is removed before plant emissions are released into the air.

Accidental release of toxic emissions from sour gas plants is of some concern to Alberta residents, however. In 1982, a sour gas plant blowout near Lodgepole resulted in sulphur dioxide drifting toward Edmonton (see Figure 9.14). Sixty-eight days went by before the escaping gases were brought under control.

Figure 9.14 The Area Affected by the Sour Gas Plant Blowout of 1982 near Lodgepole, Alberta

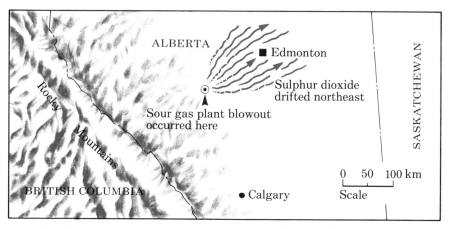

Particulate matter consists of tiny solid and liquid particles that stay suspended in the air. This matter comes from burning processes, such as those carried out by thermal power plants (Figure 9.15), and is clearly visible. The smallest particulates are especially dangerous because they carry poisonous substances. When a person breathes particulates, they can travel deep into the lungs. On a normal day in a city such as Montreal, a citizen could breath up to 500 g of dust particles! In heavy coal-burning areas of the world,

Figure 9.15
Pollution from a
Thermal Power
Plant

the concentration of particulate matter can be up to five times
that amount.

It has been estimated that it would take a train 600 cars in
length to haul away the coal soot given off each year in Peking,
China. Coal is widely used in Chinese homes for heating and
cooking, and is also used in many industries. As a result, many
people suffer from illnesses related to breathing problems. Blowing
your nose after a wintry walk through a Peking park will turn a
clean handkerchief black. Currently, however, the Chinese appear
to consider that industrial progress is more important than
environmental concern.

13. (a) In your own words, explain what is meant by the last
        sentence above.
    (b) Why would the Chinese have this attitude?

14. What developments do you think will have to occur in China
    before the government will take measures to decrease air pollu-
    tion levels?

The Arctic region of Canada is currently experiencing a great
increase in air pollution. Pollutants from industries in Siberia
(U.S.S.R.), Europe, and North America are responsible for a haze
that hangs in the air over northern Canada and Greenland every
winter. Airplane pilots have observed that on some occasions
visibility is reduced from 300 km to 30 km by these pollutants.

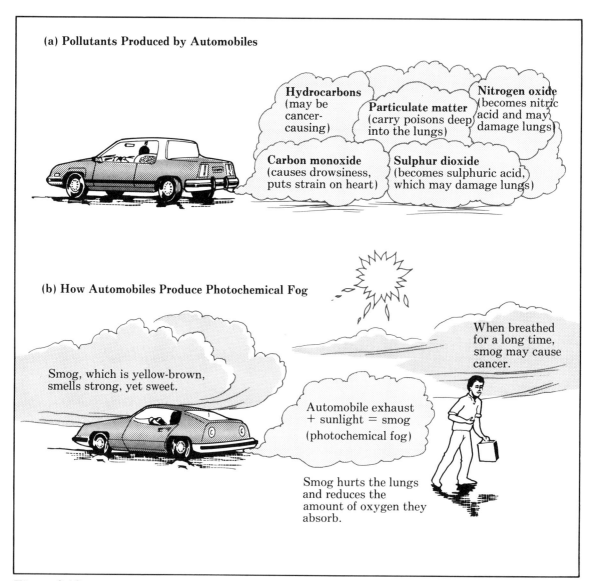

(a) Pollutants Produced by Automobiles

Hydrocarbons (may be cancer-causing)

Particulate matter (carry poisons deep into the lungs)

Nitrogen oxide (becomes nitric acid and may damage lungs)

Carbon monoxide (causes drowsiness, puts strain on heart)

Sulphur dioxide (becomes sulphuric acid, which may damage lungs)

(b) How Automobiles Produce Photochemical Fog

When breathed for a long time, smog may cause cancer.

Smog, which is yellow-brown, smells strong, yet sweet.

Automobile exhaust + sunlight = smog (photochemical fog)

Smog hurts the lungs and reduces the amount of oxygen they absorb.

Figure 9.16 Effects of Automobile Pollution

Figure 9.16 shows how automobiles pollute the major cities of the world and cause **photochemical fogs**.

Los Angeles has a geographic location similar to the one in Figure 9.12(b). Inversions are common in Los Angeles in the summer, when there is a great deal of intense sunshine. When the sunshine acts on the automobile exhaust in Los Angeles, photochemical fog results (Figure 9.17). Photochemical fog can also develop in cities such as Denver, Colorado; São Paulo, Brazil; Mexico City, Mexico; and Toronto, Ontario.

Figure 9.17
A Photochemical
Fog in
Los Angeles

15. Why are photochemical fogs rare in Canada?

16. What could and should be done to reduce the occurrence of photochemical fogs in cities like Los Angeles?

Carbon monoxide is a gas commonly inhaled by those who drive in heavy traffic. In small amounts, carbon monoxide can cause fatigue, headache, confusion, and dizziness. It also puts a strain on the heart and poses a danger to anyone with heart disease. In large concentrations, carbon monoxide is lethal.

Air Pollution in the Workplace

Employees in many factories and refineries suffer from the effects of air pollution. Miners in particular experience serious problems from air pollution while on the job. Miners who work in underground mines face a number of dangers in the air that they breathe. Heavy equipment used underground emits diesel fumes. The drilling and explosions that break down rocks also release dust and fibres into the air. Yet, in spite of daily contact with these pollutants, it often takes 20 to 30 years for serious diseases to appear in a worker after he or she has been exposed.

DISEASE	PROBABLE CAUSE
Asbestosis and mesothelioma	Breathing asbestos fibres
Black lung	Breathing coal dust
Silicosis	Breathing dust from hard-rock mining
Cancer	Exposure to a wide variety of pollutants

NOTE: Cancer rates among miners are higher than average.

Recently, laws have been passed in an attempt to reduce air pollution problems in mines. Measures include:

- increased ventilation (circulation of air to the outside)
- wearing of protective masks
- measuring and recording of dust levels

Cubatao, Brazil

**Figure 9.18
The Location
of Cubatao**

Countries in the Third World also experience serious air pollution problems in and around certain cities or industries. Cubatao is one such city. It has major steel and fertilizer plants, and is also one of the most important oil-refining centres in South America. In addition, it is one of the most polluted communities in the world.

Each day 1000 t of toxic (poisonous) gases are pumped into the air of the coastal area. A range of hills about 600 m high stops these fumes from being dispersed. One environmental group has labelled this area "the valley of death". In the Cubatao area, the rate of respiratory diseases, infant deaths, and **still births** is very high. (A still birth occurs when a baby is born dead.)

The World Health Organization (WHO) has carried out measurements of the air pollution there. WHO has concluded that the air is so seriously polluted that it is a threat to the health of everyone who lives there. But nothing has been done to decrease the pollution.

The state government has laws in place to fine polluters, but it has not enforced those laws. The government is concerned that if the laws were enforced, some companies might move out and jobs might be lost. Many workers are more concerned about earning money than about the long-term effects of pollution on their health. Some people doubt that the air pollution is that serious. Others may not think much about it at all. In Brazil, air pollution has been seen as a sign of progress.

Cubatao does have the highest income per person of any city in Brazil. This wealth, however, does not reach many of the city's inhabitants. One-third of the population live in **shanty towns**. Such shanty towns are areas of slum housing with many shacks and lean-tos. Little clean water is provided for them, and little or no sewage disposal or electricity.

17. What do the shanty towns show about Cubatao, Brazil? Mention two main ideas.

18. If Canada buys steel from Cubatao, Brazil, how is it encouraging air pollution there?

19. Imagine that you live in Cubatao, Brazil. Write a half-page letter to a friend in Canada to explain why the pollution laws are not enforced.

20. Why do you think serious pollution would more likely occur in the Third World than in a country such as Canada?

Visual Pollution

Visual pollution refers to the clutter and ugliness created by civilization as it develops industrially. Visual pollution may occur in cities or in the countryside, or wherever human activity has spread (Figure 9.19).

**Figure 9.19
Examples of
Visual Pollution
(a) Cluttered industrial area next to residential area
(b) Power lines
(c) Exposed garbage dump
(d) Excavated area**

a

b

c

d

21. (a) Write three lines to describe each scene shown in Figure 9.19. In each case, explain what has caused the visual pollution.
    (b) Explain what could be done to improve the attractiveness of each scene.
    (c) Examine the following scale.

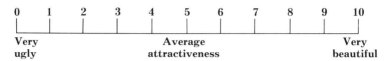

For each photo, assign a number on this scale to represent its general attractiveness.

22. (a) Select an area near your school or home that is visually polluted. Write four lines to describe what has caused the visual pollution.
    (b) Rank the area that you selected, using the scale in question 21(c).
    (c) What improvements could be introduced to increase the attractiveness of the area that you selected?
    (d) Why has this area not been improved visually before?

Figure 9.20
(a) Housing Area with Overhead Wires
(b) Housing Area with Buried Lines

As you examined the photos in Figure 9.19, you were thinking about the **aesthetic** value, or the beauty or general attractiveness, of each scene. Improving the aesthetic value of any landscape, however, usually involves a cost. For example, a residential area can be made more attractive by burying the power distribution lines rather than installing them overhead (Figure 9.20). Burying the

a

b

lines, however, is a more expensive method. In the case of high-voltage transmission lines, burying costs much more because it requires considerable technical skill, labour, and machinery (Figure 9.21).

TWO-CIRCUIT LINE	OVERHEAD	BURIED
230 kV	$186 000	$2 112 000–$4 000 000
500 kV	$373 000	$10 000 000

Figure 9.21
Costs of Installing
High-Voltage
Electric Lines
(per kilometre)

23. **List the advantages and disadvantages of overhead and buried electric lines during and after installation.**

The Use of Chemicals and Pesticides

There is growing concern in society about the long-term effects that chemicals, pesticides, and fertilizers may have on health. People absorb these substances through drinking water and through the food that they eat. Gradually these chemicals can build up in their bodies.

Some people have developed strong **allergies** to these chemicals. An allergy occurs when someone's body reacts negatively to a substance. Even with a strict diet, an allergic person may not be able to avoid all such chemicals.

There is a much more serious side to the issue of using chemicals and pesticides. Some chemicals are used before their long-range effects on humans can be known. The result can be catastrophic, as the case of agent orange shows.

CASE STUDY

Agent Orange

Agent orange, a mixture of 2,4,5-T and 2,4-D, is a chemical that contains deadly dioxin. It became the centre of controversy when it was sprayed in Vietnam from U.S. aircraft. The chemical was used to kill vegetation so that the Vietcong guerrillas could not hide in the forests. Unfortunately, many Vietnamese and Americans were also exposed to agent orange.

The same chemical has been used in Canada since the 1950s. For example, agent orange was used for 30 years to clear routes for hydro lines. To stop trees from growing back, the chemical was sprayed beneath the lines.

Wherever agent orange was used, few precautions were taken. Some workers describe how they used to douse each other with agent orange to keep cool! Now the people who worked with this chemical are showing the results of their exposure. Dave Taylor, for example, spent 14 years spraying agent orange. He has since had serious stomach problems, five heart attacks, open heart surgery, and his gall bladder removed. He suffers from pains in all of his joints and itching all over his face and neck and around his hairline.

Mr. Taylor is not alone. Such complaints are typical of workers who have been exposed to agent orange.

24. **List the advantages and disadvantages of using agent orange as a way of stopping plant growth.**

25. **Present arguments for and against the use of agent orange in warfare.**

26. **Assume that a definite link is established between a chemical such as agent orange and problems such as Dave Taylor's. What form of compensation should a court award to such an individual? Give reasons for your answers.**

Transporting Dangerous Chemicals

The transportation of hazardous materials is another environmental concern in our society. Many regulations govern the transportation of dangerous chemicals, but accidents still occur. A train derailment in Mississauga, Ontario, in 1979, involving the leakage of chlorine gas, forced the evacuation of 250 000 people. Improved laws will reduce incidents such as this, but probably will never eliminate them.

27. **Imagine that a spill of chlorine gas has occurred on a road 1 km from your school. All people within 5 km are to be evacuated. You are in charge of evacuation procedures.**
    (a) **Draw a rough map of your school area. On it mark where the spill has occurred and a circle with a radius of 5 km around that point.**
    (b) **Explain how you would communicate with people in the area. What would you tell them?**
    (c) **What arrangements would you make to move the people?**

(d) How would you care for those who had no friends or relatives to help them?

(e) Which groups or organizations would you call in to assist you? What responsibilities would you give to each?

(f) After the danger was over, how would you let people know they could go back?

Disposal Hazards

Disposing of Municipal Garbage

Once a week in most Canadian communities, you will see garbage put out at the roadsides for collection. Each Canadian on average produces 400 kg of waste per year, or 1.1 kg per day. Taxes pay for it to be collected, but where does it go?

One commonly used disposal method is called **sanitary landfill**. The municipality (local government) first buys land for the landfill site. Each working day, trucks bring in garbage, which is compacted (pressed together) by machines and covered with a 15-cm layer of soil. Landfill sites, however, use up land that is needed for building and agriculture. Many large cities face critical problems in trying to acquire landfill sites. Garbage may have to be trucked considerable distances. Many small communities near large cities refuse to have garbage dumped in their areas. One imaginative use of garbage has resulted in ski hills in otherwise flat areas, such as Blackstrap Mountain near Regina, Saskatchewan.

Figure 9.22 Ski Hill Made from Landfill

Landfill sites not only waste land, they also make it impossible to retrieve valuable resources for recycling. The sensible answer for the future is to reclaim and reuse as much garbage as possible.

SWARU, Hamilton, Ontario

In 1971, SWARU (Solid Waste Reduction Unit) was opened to serve the city of Hamilton, Ontario, and the surrounding area (Figures 9.23 and 9.24). Each day, 500 t of municipal waste passes through the unit. After shredding, the waste is moved through three main stages.

1. The magnetic stage separates out ferrous metal wastes, which make up 5% of the garbage.
2. In the semisuspension stage, much material is burnt at about 1200°C. This heat is used to create steam, which in turn is used to produce electricity. Air pollution is kept low through the use of **precipitators**. They remove many of the pollutants from the air before it is released to the outside.
3. Heavier glass and other metals drop down and are recovered.

Figure 9.23 Flow Chart Showing Garbage Disposal in SWARU

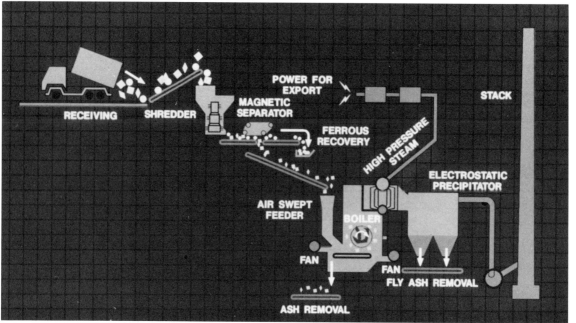

SWARU deals with 75% of the region's waste. The unit reduces the need for landfill sites, recovers valuable resources, and uses energy released in the burning process. The system has two major drawbacks, however.

1. It costs considerably more to dispose of garbage in SWARU than by conventional landfill methods. Costs were approximately $34/t in SWARU compared to $25/t in landfill sites in the 1979-83 period. When the costs for landfill sites are included, however, the difference is reduced to about $2/t. Also, when one landfill site is filled, it has to be monitored and a new dump site acquired.
2. Emissions of deadly dioxins and other air pollutants from the smokestack are both unpleasant and dangerous for nearby residents. New precipitators at a cost of $4 million could rectify this problem.

Figure 9.24
SWARU Process-ing Plant in Hamilton, Ontario

Possible future strategies for SWARU include:

1. Let SWARU continue to operate with no change.
2. Reduce the amount processed by SWARU to reduce the costs and pollution.
3. Close SWARU for a period so that new precipitators can be installed.
4. Close SWARU permanently and return to landfill disposal.
5. Close SWARU and build a more efficient system, at an estimated cost of $40 million to $50 million (the original plant cost $8.8 million in 1970 and 1971). This system could also be used for the disposal of garbage from other nearby communities.
6. Expand the present SWARU to process more garbage, including that from nearby communities.

28. **For this question, you are to imagine yourself a regional councillor. You are answerable to**
    - **residents affected by pollution and landfill sites**
    - **municipal taxpayers**
    - **environmentalists**

    (a) **Read over the list of six proposals for SWARU.**
    (b) **List the proposals in order of your preference.**
    (c) **Carefully explain why you ranked the proposals the way you did. Your answer should be about two pages in length.**

The Conserver Society and the Consumer Society

Among the various solutions to our energy problems, **conservation** is very attractive. In many instances, it costs little or nothing! Conservation refers to using fewer resources and less energy, through wise planning and use of what Canada has.

Another advantage of conservation is that it can be practised by everyone. If every Canadian uses less energy, then Canada as a whole will use less.

Canada is basically a **consumer society**, that is, a society in which the main goal is to increase industrial production and the standard of living. Canadians have benefited greatly from the consumer society in this country. There are, however, limits to the increase in use of resources. Energy and resources are often wasted in order to increase the standard of living.

In a **conserver society**, the goal is to do more with less—to increase the standard of living, but to do it using fewer resources (Figure 9.25). This is possible by designing technology and lifestyles to use resources more efficiently.

**Figure 9.25
The Conserver
Society**

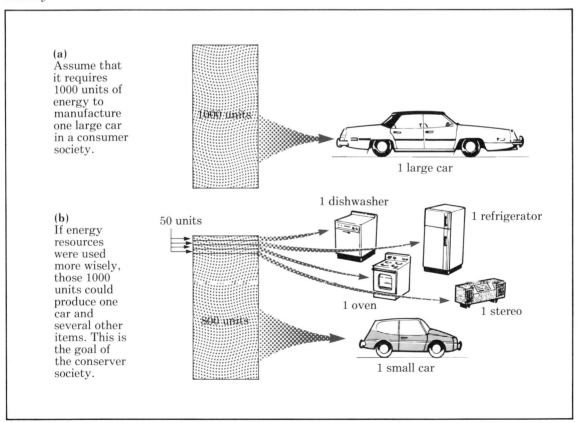

(a) Assume that it requires 1000 units of energy to manufacture one large car in a consumer society.

1000 units

1 large car

(b) If energy resources were used more wisely, those 1000 units could produce one car and several other items. This is the goal of the conserver society.

50 units

800 units

1 dishwasher

1 refrigerator

1 oven

1 stereo

1 small car

Recent increases in energy prices, especially the price of oil, have forced companies and individuals to use resources more wisely to save money.

29. **List 15 ways in which your family, or companies or stores near your home, could make changes to help move toward a conserver society.**

30. **Waste production has increased continuously over the past 20 years. Much of this waste occurs in the form of excessive packaging. Some packaging is vital to ensure cleanliness. List and briefly explain five examples of excessive packaging.**

31. **Think about each of the following items. Suggest improvements that would reduce the waste involved in their use and/or the disposal of the finished or used-up product.**

milk	car tires	disposable diapers
newspapers	furniture	paper towels

32. **(a) List five products used in your home that are packaged in plastic or glass. Suggest one or two uses for each package.**
   (b) What would happen if every Canadian reused packages in the way that you suggest?

Disposing of Hazardous Wastes

Hazardous wastes from industries, nuclear power production, and household sources are increasing in quantity and variety. They may be solid, powdered, or liquid. The disposal of hazardous wastes, which are dangerous to people, animals, and plants, is of growing concern. There are many ways of disposing of these wastes. They can be stored, buried, put into surface disposal sites, or allowed to flow directly into creeks, rivers, lakes, or oceans. What is ultimately at risk is the water supply. Health depends on that vital resource.

Until recent years, the disposal of these wastes by burying them or by putting them in special sites was thought to be safe. Now it is known that such methods only delay the pollution of the water supplies. In some cases these methods hide the water pollution, but the pollution still exists.

As rainwater moves down through the wastes, it carries chemicals with it into the ground water in the soil and rocks. The polluted water slowly moves downhill to form a polluted **plume** (point) of water. Wells downhill from the waste disposal area are usually the first to be affected. (See Figure 9.26.)

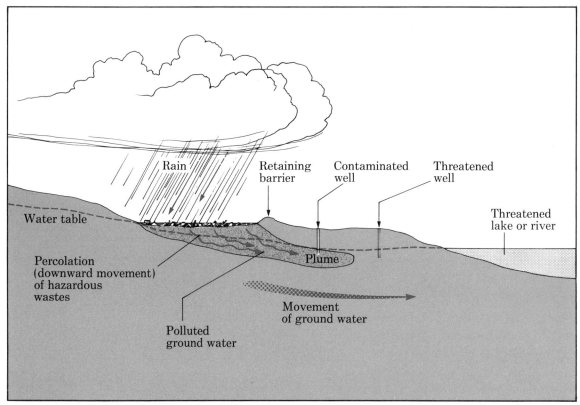

Figure 9.26
Ground Water
Pollution by
Hazardous
Wastes

In 1972, toxic chemical wastes were dumped in a 10-ha site, 10 km northwest of Atlantic City, New Jersey. By the time that the dump was closed 18 months later, more than 40 000 000 L of chemicals had been poured into the pit. The plume that formed is **contaminating** (poisoning) more and more of the wells that, at one time, supplied 90% of Atlantic City's water. Now only 50% of the water supply comes from wells because of the contamination. The rest of the water for the city is piped in from reservoirs.

The contaminated water in the wells of Atlantic City is foul smelling. It also blackens cooking pots, turns laundry yellow, and at times fizzes like soda pop. Residents are convinced that the contaminated water is responsible for the high rates of cancer, kidney disease, and epilepsy in the area. Tests have shown that the contaminated water contains benzine, arsenic, and other chemicals that are known to contribute to such disorders.

Ground water supplies one-half of the drinking water in the U.S., where chemical contamination has forced the closure of hundreds of private and community wells. Canadians are realizing that they face similar problems. It is estimated that Canadian

industry produces 10 000 000 t of waste each year, of which
1 000 000 t are hazardous. More than 50 000 chemicals are used by
Canadian industry, of which 35 000 are or could be hazardous.
These chemicals have been described as a "time bomb". Since 1930,
it has been known that such wastes are being dumped into landfill
sites. It was not until the 1960s that some concern was voiced.

Among the most hazardous liquid wastes in Canada are acids,
oils, dangerous chemicals such as PCBs (polychlorinated biphenyls),
and dioxin, the deadliest of all substances made by people. Ontario
has the greatest concentration of industry in Canada, and also
produces nearly one-half of the country's industrial waste. (Figure
9.27 shows how this waste was disposed of during one year.) Ontario
is not alone in encountering problems with hazardous waste disposal,
however. Liquid wastes from Winnipeg, for example, are shipped
to storage tanks and warehouses far out of the city. Waste containing PCBs is shipped to special storage facilities outside
Manitoba. PCBs can be disposed of through high-temperature
incineration, or using molten sodium or salt, which strips the
chlorine molecules from the PCBs. However, none of these methods
has been used extensively in Canada.

METHOD	%
Incinerated (burned) near Sarnia	27
Dumped in landfills	19
Recycled	12
Shipped to U.S., to disposal companies in Niagara Falls, N.Y.	8
Spread on farmland (as fertilizer) or roads	4
Treated in sewage plants	3
Unaccounted for	27

Figure 9.27 Disposal of Ontario's Industrial Liquid Wastes, 1980–81

NOTE: These data are for the period August 1, 1980 to July 31, 1981.

Across Canada, wastes are dumped illegally into sewers, waterways, or fields by people referred to as "midnight dumpers". The
effects on ground water, creeks, and lakes can be serious.

Landfill sites, however, are of greatest concern. Any hazardous
liquid wastes that they contain continue to leak after dumping.
Of the 2000 landfill sites in Ontario in 1971, 500 have been closed.
Even these closed sites continue to be a problem.

Outside Perkinsfield, near Midland, Ontario, 13 solvents were
dumped in the early 1980s. Some of these are cancer-causing and
have contaminated well water there. Residents of the area now bring
in drinking water from 17 km away, and their health has improved.

Love Canal

On August 2, 1978, 240 families were evacuated from their homes within two blocks of an abandoned canal, the Love Canal, in Niagara Falls, New York (Figure 9.28). Dangerous concentrations of poisonous and cancer-causing chemicals were oozing from the canal. Tests showed that the air, water, and soil were affected. The air in the basements of some houses was particularly dangerous.

The source of the dangerous chemicals was the Hooker Electro-chemical Corporation, now named the Occidental Chemical Corporation. Between 1947 and 1952, Hooker had dumped almost 20 000 000 kg of chemical wastes into the canal. Among these were

- 6 000 000 kg of lindane, a cancer-causing pesticide
- 2 000 000 kg of chlorobenzenes, which cause two serious diseases (aplastic anemia and leukemia)
- 40 000 000 kg of TCP (trichlorophenol), heavily contaminated with TCDD (tetrachlorodibenzo-para-dioxin). Less than 200 g of TCDD could kill the entire population of New York City!

The experiences related by local residents are like fictional horror stories—only they were true.

- The fumes took the bark off trees and turned white paint pink.
- Plants would not grow.
- Holes in the ground that had filled up with a brown-black liquid "smelled like Hooker Chemical."
- People had sludge in their swimming pools.
- Sump pumps corroded as they pumped foul water out of basements.
- The smell from the basements of the houses was so strong it made people's eyes water.

The results of the last 18 pregnancies in the area revealed serious problems: two produced normal children, nine produced children with birth defects, four ended in spontaneous abortions, and three ended in still births.

The Environmental Protection Agency of the U.S. government says that there are at least a thousand "Love Canals" in that country. In Ontario, there are probably 800 forgotten dumpsites, and perhaps twice that number across Canada.

33. **Discuss the cartoon in Figure 9.29. Write five lines outlining what the main point is.**

**Figure 9.28
Location of
the Love Canal**

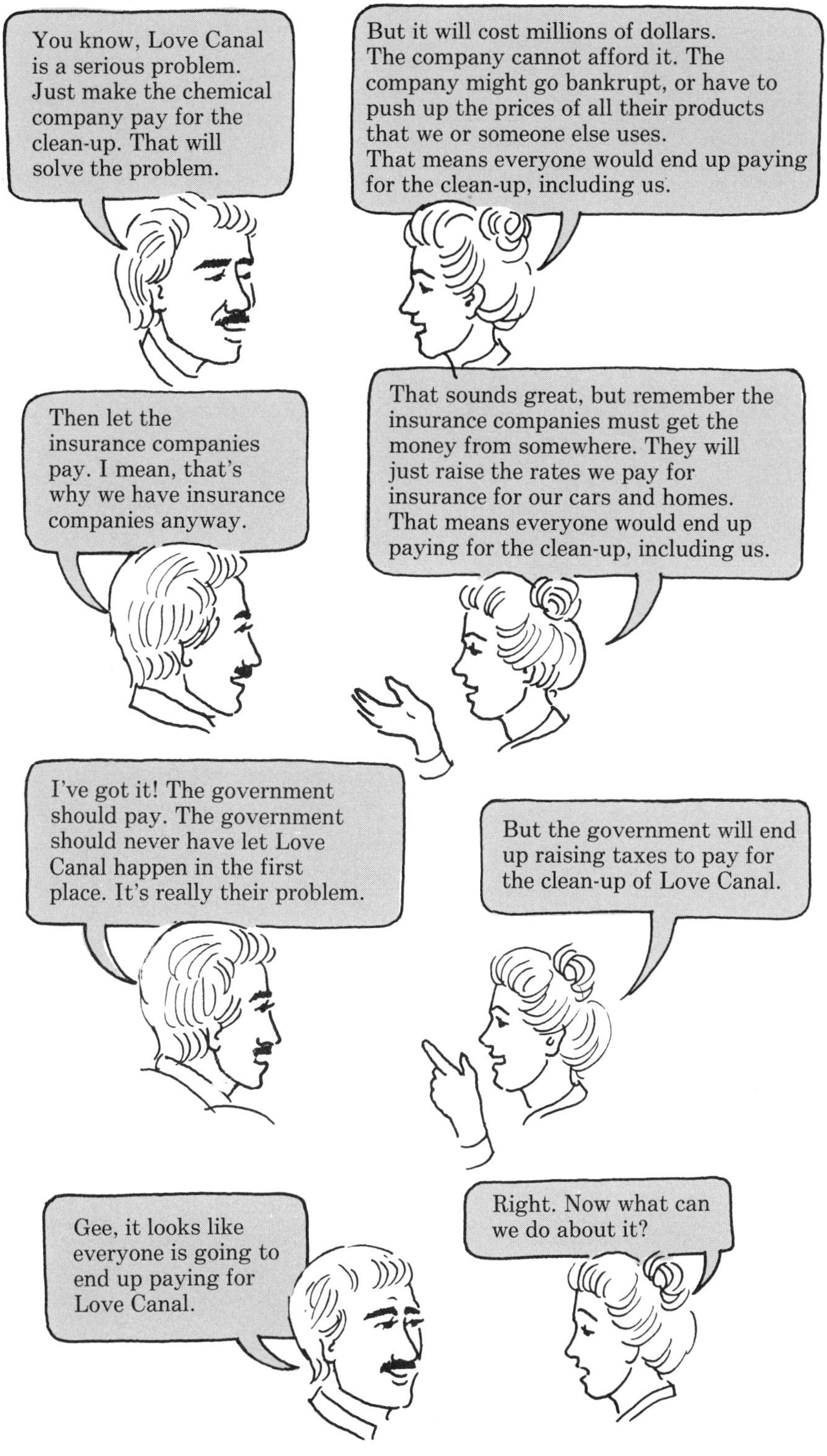

Figure 9.29 Who Pays for the Clean-up of Love Canal?

34. **What does this cartoon say about the clean-up of any pollution?**

Disposing of Radioactive Wastes

Disposing of radioactive wastes and partly used radioactive materials is of particular concern to many people. Radioactive wastes are produced during the processing of uranium at mines, and in nuclear reactions involving uranium in power plants. Exposure to radioactive materials leads to serious health problems. Cancer and genetic disorders are among the known effects of exposure to radioactive materials.

According to the Ontario Public Interest Research Group (OPIRG), "creeks, rivers, and entire watersheds have been contaminated by the 85 million tonnes of toxic uranium mine **tailings** [wastes produced in mining] that have been dumped near the community of Elliot Lake, Ontario. There are no fish living 90 km downstream in the Serpent River system." On the other hand, sworn testimony by mine representatives indicates that the water and fish of the Serpent River are no more polluted than those from other rivers of northern Ontario. The mining companies at Elliot Lake have begun to spend enormous amounts of money to contain and filter radioactive tailings (Figure 9.30).

Clearly, a solution must be found to the problem of disposal of radioactive wastes. For example, the nuclear power plants in Ontario produce 200 kg of used uranium every day. The accumulated waste has now reached about 3500 t. At the present time, there is no effective method of disposing of this waste. It is being contained in water-filled pools in the nuclear stations.

**Figure 9.30
New Tailings
Pond at Elliot
Lake, Ontario**

The same method of waste disposal is used at the Point Lepreau nuclear power station in southern New Brunswick. Scientists are investigating the possibility of burying radioactive wastes in special vaults, deep in the rock of the Canadian Shield. Many people are concerned that this waste could still escape to pollute nearby ground water.

During construction of the Point Lepreau power station, further safety concerns were raised when earthquakes shook parts of New Brunswick. Occasional "heavy water" leaks have also occurred at this station and at nuclear power stations in Ontario. Some power station officials do not consider these to have been a major hazard.

35. **Explain why the disposal of hazardous wastes is a recent problem.**

36. **Work in small groups to formulate five laws that you think should be enacted to control hazardous wastes.**

Our Endangered Rivers, Lakes and Oceans

All of the pollutants emitted into the air or dumped in or on the land end up in rivers, lakes, and oceans. Earlier in this chapter, it was explained how hazardous chemicals are contaminating ground water supplies. This ground water eventually seeps into marshes and creeks. Sooner or later it reaches rivers, lakes, and ultimately the oceans (Figure 9.31). In addition, some wastes go directly into these bodies of water.

Figure 9.31 The Final Destination of Most Pollutants Is the Ocean

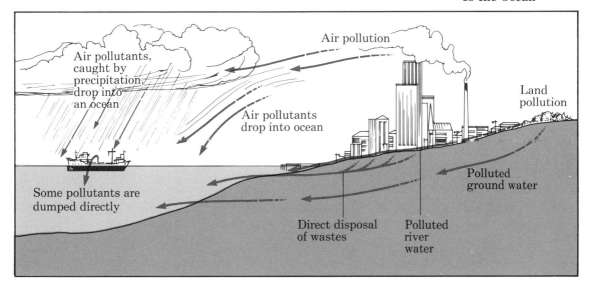

Air pollution

Air pollutants, caught by precipitation, drop into an ocean

Air pollutants drop into ocean

Land pollution

Some pollutants are dumped directly

Polluted ground water

Direct disposal of wastes

Polluted river water

Sewage Pollution

Sewage is a pollutant that flows directly into rivers, lakes, and oceans. A town with a population of 10 000 discharges about 100 kg of solids in its sewage each day. If permitted to build up in waterways, sewage causes great problems. In addition, several diseases are carried in untreated sewage water, including polio, infectious hepatitis, typhoid, gastroenteritis, and dysentery.

Figure 9.32 A Modern Sewage Disposal Plant. Envirex, a Rexnord Company, is located in Waukesha, Wisconsin.

Figure 9.33 Stages Involved in Sewage Treatment

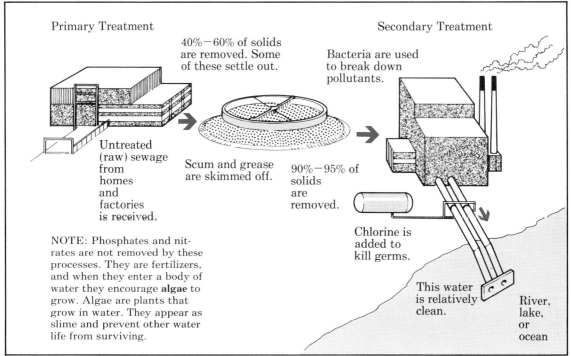

Primary Treatment

40%−60% of solids are removed. Some of these settle out.

Untreated (raw) sewage from homes and factories is received.

Scum and grease are skimmed off.

90%−95% of solids are removed.

NOTE: Phosphates and nitrates are not removed by these processes. They are fertilizers, and when they enter a body of water they encourage **algae** to grow. Algae are plants that grow in water. They appear as slime and prevent other water life from surviving.

Secondary Treatment

Bacteria are used to break down pollutants.

Chlorine is added to kill germs.

This water is relatively clean.

River, lake, or ocean

Our lakes and rivers are a major source of drinking water; therefore, any inadequate treatment leads to the spread of disease. In November 1953, for example, there was an outbreak of polio in Edmonton. The cause was traced to the general water supply. Polio had occurred in Devon, a town upstream from Edmonton, earlier in the year. Devon's sewage discharge had not been chlorinated sufficiently, and the virus had managed to survive water purification in Edmonton.

Although some North American cities do have modern sewage disposal plants (Figure 9.32 and 9.33), many Canadian cities do not adequately treat their sewage. Examine the following table.

QUALITY OF SEWAGE RELEASED TO NEARBY WATER BODY	CITIES
Untreated sewage	Halifax, St. John's, Hull, Quebec City
Some treatment	Dartmouth, Saint John, Montreal, Saskatoon, Victoria, Labrador City, Oromocto, Laval, Kamloops
Primary and secondary treatment	Toronto, Brandon, Edmonton, Calgary, Winnipeg

37. (a) **Why do you think that so many Canadian cities do not treat their sewage before allowing it to flow into nearby bodies of water?**
    (b) **What could you or your class do to encourage more sewage treatment in your city or one nearby? Explain.**
    (c) **Are you aware of water near your home that is noticeably polluted? Describe that water.**

Industrial Pollution

Many industrial processes require large quantities of fresh water. Manufacturers in these industries tend to locate beside rivers and lakes. To keep costs low and profits high, some manufacturers do not treat polluted water before it is returned to the river or lake. This leads to the accumulation of many chemicals in these bodies of water. In recent years, hundreds of chemicals have been identified in Canadian lakes and rivers. High levels of dioxins have been found in fish in some bodies of water. As a result, it has been recommended that adult males should eat lake trout only once a month. It is further recommended that children of less than 15 years and women between 15 and 45 should not eat lake trout at all.

Figure 9.34 shows some different types of water pollution concerns across Canada.

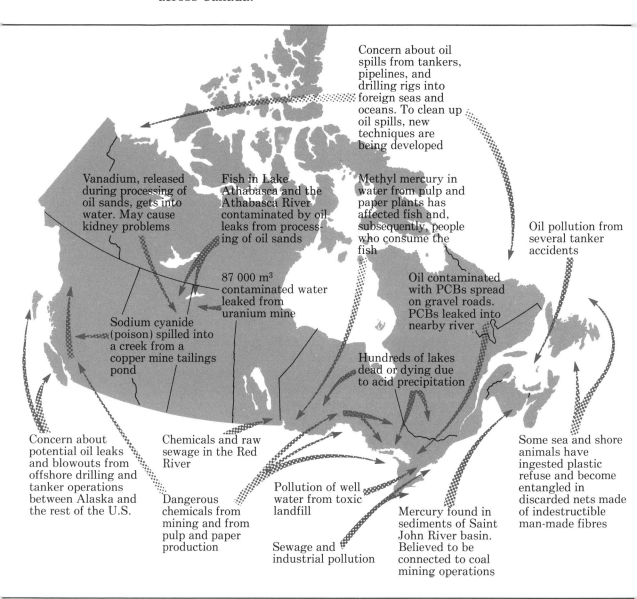

Concern about oil spills from tankers, pipelines, and drilling rigs into foreign seas and oceans. To clean up oil spills, new techniques are being developed

Vanadium, released during processing of oil sands, gets into water. May cause kidney problems

Fish in Lake Athabasca and the Athabasca River contaminated by oil leaks from processing of oil sands

Methyl mercury in water from pulp and paper plants has affected fish and, subsequently, people who consume the fish

Oil pollution from several tanker accidents

87 000 m³ contaminated water leaked from uranium mine

Oil contaminated with PCBs spread on gravel roads. PCBs leaked into nearby river

Sodium cyanide (poison) spilled into a creek from a copper mine tailings pond

Hundreds of lakes dead or dying due to acid precipitation

Concern about potential oil leaks and blowouts from offshore drilling and tanker operations between Alaska and the rest of the U.S.

Chemicals and raw sewage in the Red River

Dangerous chemicals from mining and from pulp and paper production

Pollution of well water from toxic landfill

Sewage and industrial pollution

Mercury found in sediments of Saint John River basin. Believed to be connected to coal mining operations

Some sea and shore animals have ingested plastic refuse and become entangled in discarded nets made of indestructible man-made fibres

**Figure 9.34
Types of Water Pollution Concerns and Incidents (1980-1985)**

The pulp and paper industry has been associated with many water pollution problems, as well. In British Columbia, for instance, each pulp mill uses about 190 million litres of water a day. The pulping and bleaching processes can pollute lakes and rivers with fibrous wastes and with chemical wastes such as chlorine compounds.

Such pollution poses a potential hazard to the salmon that spawn in affected B.C. rivers. In the past, mercury pollution has also resulted from the pulping and bleaching processes. Figure 9.35 shows the effect that this type of pollution had on people living in Grassy Narrows, northwest of Thunder Bay, Ontario. Some of the residents of Grassy Narrows contracted **Minamata disease** (methyl mercury poisoning) from eating fish contaminated with mercury.

Research is being carried out to reduce the pollutants originating from pulp and paper mills. The law now requires that new mills recycle wastes and water. In Thunder Bay, Ontario, for instance, a closed-cycle plant is currently in use. So far, however, very few pulp mill owners have committed themselves to making changes that will substantially decrease pollution.

Figure 9.35 Minamata Disease at Grassy Narrows, Ontario

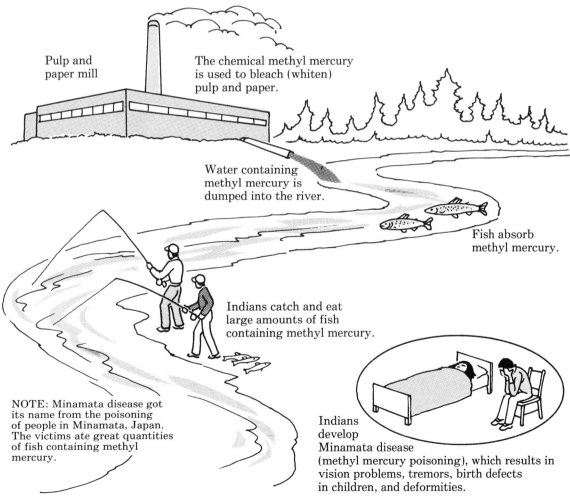

Pulp and paper mill

The chemical methyl mercury is used to bleach (whiten) pulp and paper.

Water containing methyl mercury is dumped into the river.

Fish absorb methyl mercury.

Indians catch and eat large amounts of fish containing methyl mercury.

NOTE: Minamata disease got its name from the poisoning of people in Minamata, Japan. The victims ate great quantities of fish containing methyl mercury.

Indians develop Minamata disease (methyl mercury poisoning), which results in vision problems, tremors, birth defects in children, and deformities.

38. Many of the pulp and paper mills in Canada are old. Why do you think that the owners hesitate to install extensive pollution-control devices?

39. (a) In half a page, explain how Minamata disease developed among Indians at Grassy Narrows.
    (b) What solutions can you propose for the Grassy Narrows problems? Explain each one.

40. What do you think should be done if a company continues to dump pollutants after it has been warned and/or fined? Explain.

Acid Rain

A topic of continuing concern in North America and many other parts of the industrial world is acid rain. Acidic lakes that result from acid rain were first noticed in Canada in the 1950s. The problem had been recognized in the Adirondack Mountains of New York State 20 years before that. The problem came to light in Sweden and Norway in the 1960s.

Rain is naturally acidic because it dissolves carbon dioxide. The amount of acid in solutions is measured by the **pH scale** (Figure 9.36). As you move down the scale, the degree of acidity increases greatly. For example, a solution with a pH of 3 is ten times more acidic than one with a pH of 4.

Figure 9.37 shows the characteristics of a typical acidic lake.

Figure 9.36
The pH Scale

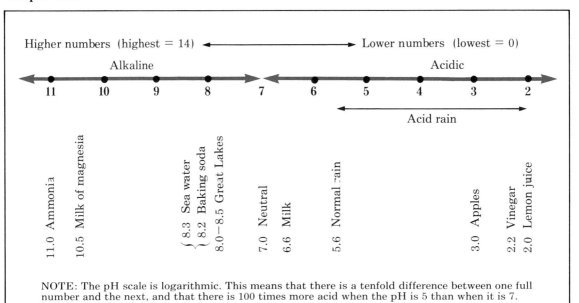

NOTE: The pH scale is logarithmic. This means that there is a tenfold difference between one full number and the next, and that there is 100 times more acid when the pH is 5 than when it is 7.

Some lakes are surrounded by limestone rocks, which are able to reduce the lakes' acidity or bring it close to neutral. Lakes located on granite are unable to do this (Figure 9.38).

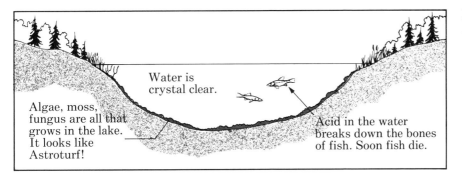

Figure 9.37 An Acidic Lake

Water is crystal clear.

Algae, moss, fungus are all that grows in the lake. It looks like Astroturf!

Acid in the water breaks down the bones of fish. Soon fish die.

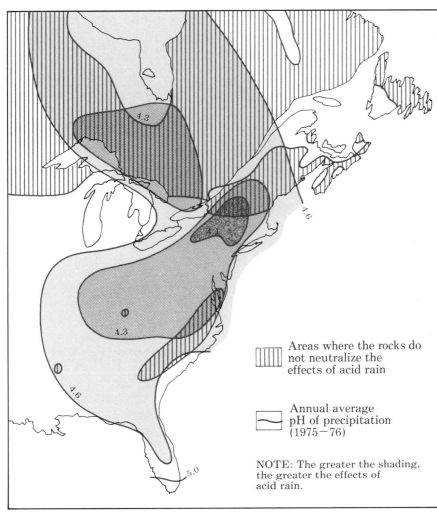

Figure 9.38 Factors Affecting the Distribution of Acidic Lakes in Eastern North America

Areas where the rocks do not neutralize the effects of acid rain

Annual average pH of precipitation (1975–76)

NOTE: The greater the shading, the greater the effects of acid rain.

The causes of acid rain are sulphur dioxide and the nitrogen oxides. Smelters, automobiles, electrical plants, and the burning of fossil fuels are the chief sources of these pollutants. They mix with rain, snow, or fog to form acid precipitation.

Acid rain is blown by prevailing winds across provincial and national boundaries, thereby causing political as well as environmental problems. The U.S. produces 25 700 000 t of sulphur dioxide each year, compared with 5 000 000 t produced by Canada. Because of prevailing winds, it is estimated that 50% of Canada's acid rain originates in the U.S. About 10% to 15% of the acid rain in the U.S. originates in Canada. The 381-m superstack (large smokestack) at a nickel smelter in Sudbury, Ontario, is the world's single greatest source of sulphur dioxide pollution. Improved pollution control has reduced the total to 2500 t/d from 7000 t/d. Further pollution control, at a cost of $500 million, would cut the present pollution levels in half.

If nothing is done to decrease acid rain, 48 000 Canadian lakes

Figure 9.39 The Effects of Acid Rain on Plants and Soil

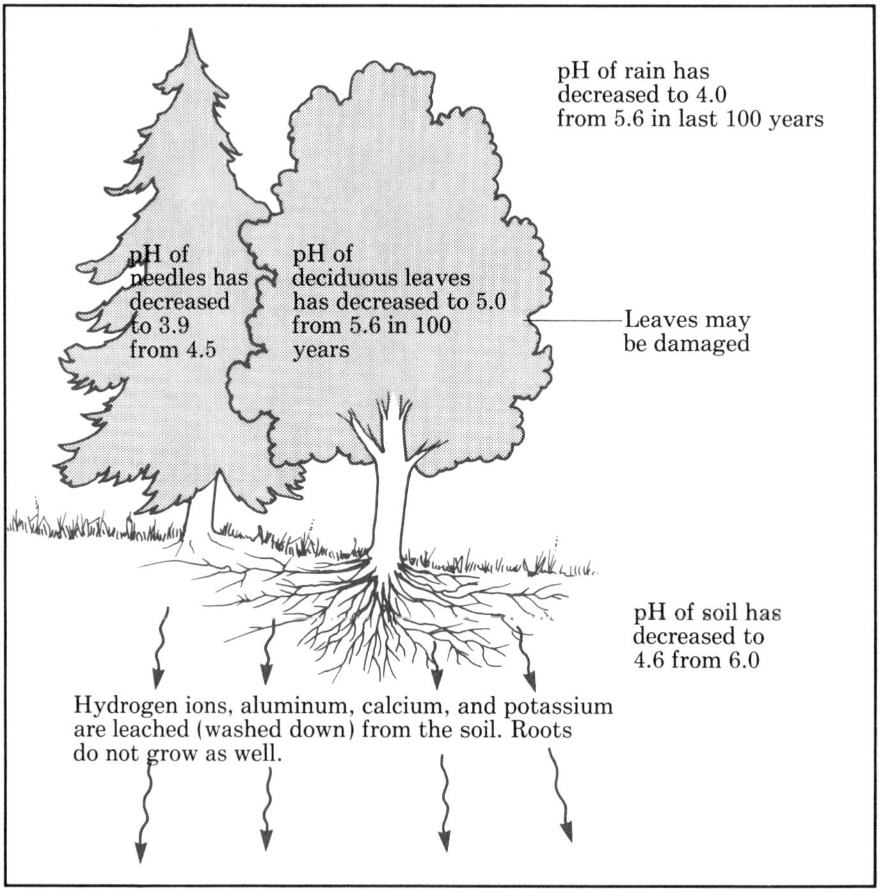

pH of rain has decreased to 4.0 from 5.6 in last 100 years

pH of needles has decreased to 3.9 from 4.5

pH of deciduous leaves has decreased to 5.0 from 5.6 in 100 years

Leaves may be damaged

pH of soil has decreased to 4.6 from 6.0

Hydrogen ions, aluminum, calcium, and potassium are leached (washed down) from the soil. Roots do not grow as well.

will contain no life by the end of the century. Already 2000 to 4000 of Ontario's lakes are too acidic to support trout and bass.

Acid rain is known to affect the health of plants and the chemical make-up of the soil. It may therefore also affect future food supplies. (See Figure 9.39.)

41. **Why do you think that it has been difficult for Canadians to persuade people in the U.S. to decrease the acid rain that they produce?**

Thermal Pollution

Thermal pollution is the term used to describe the damage that is caused by the discharge of hot or warm water into a body of water. It often occurs next to power plants and factories (Figure 9.40). Heating the water may make it impossible for fish and other life to live in the water. It may also alter the time of freeze-up. Birds, for example, may be misled into staying for the winter and then not be able to survive the cold air in January and February.

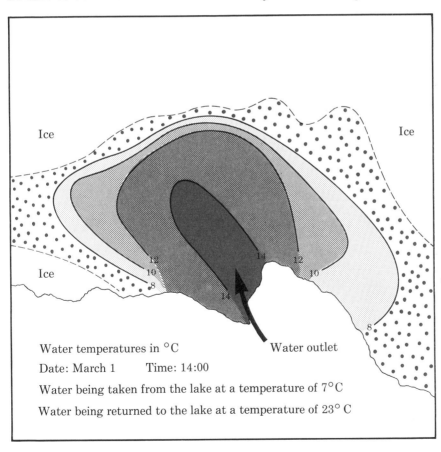

Figure 9.40 Thermal Pollution from a Typical Nuclear Power Plant

Ice

Ice

Ice

12

14

12

10

10

8

14

8

Water temperatures in °C

Water outlet

Date: March 1   Time: 14:00

Water being taken from the lake at a temperature of 7°C

Water being returned to the lake at a temperature of 23° C

42. What two uses could waste hot water be put to? Explain.

43. Write an essay of 500 words on water pollution. Discuss
    (a) the impact on the environment
    (b) the financial problems involved in trying to prevent it
    (c) the political problems generated by pollution that crosses international boundaries

44. Assume that you are the mayor of a city that is experiencing a number of pollution problems. As mayor, you must make decisions about which problems to address first, as well as the order in which they should be dealt with. The problems follow.
    (a) Noise from an expressway is disturbing local residents.
        Proposed solution: installing a sound barrier, in the form of an 8-m-high concrete wall along the expressway
        Cost: $750 000
    (b) Toxic dyes from an old leather tannery are being emptied into a local creek.
        Proposed solutions: (i) tax break to the tannery so that it can buy equipment to stop polluting the stream; (ii) continual monitoring of levels of pollution from the tannery
        Cost: $530 000
    (c) A city incinerator is emitting smoke and noxious odours.
        Proposed solution: installation of new burners, with limited recycling of glass and aluminum
        Cost: $1 100 000
    (d) Intense noise is being produced by aircraft using a municipal airport.
        Proposed solution: building a new and improved airport runway
        Cost: $1 200 000
    (e) An ugly junkyard, filled with cars, occupies city-owned land next to a new housing development.
        Proposed solution: building a 5-m fence around the yard to hide it from view
        Cost: $270 000
    (f) On the outskirts of the city is an old but little-known toxic chemical dump, which has not yet leaked poisons into the underground water supply.
        Proposed solution: digging up of the chemical storage drums and shipping them to a disposal site
        Cost: $1 600 000

(g) Old city-owned public works trucks are noisy and uneconomical to run.
Proposed solution: replacement with new, quieter, more energy-efficient trucks
Cost: $850 000

(h) An aged municipal pier and warehouse are an eyesore and are overrun with rats.
Proposed solution: replacement of pier and conversion of warehouse into restaurants and shops
Cost: $700 000

(i) A sewage disposal plant is out of date and overloaded. Some sewage empties into the ocean and pollutes the beaches.
Proposed solution: expansion of existing facilities to accommodate extra sewage
Cost: $670 000

(j) The city has acquired a run-down, abandoned factory because the owners failed to pay their taxes. This eyesore is near the city hall.
Proposed solution: tearing down the factory and converting the land into a park
Cost: $350 000

The total budget available per year for these projects is $2 million. Not all of that money needs to be spent every year, but that budget cannot be exceeded.

(i) Set out a four-year budget to include as many of these projects as possible. Pay particular attention to the order in which the projects will be undertaken.

(ii) For each project, explain why you decided to complete it when you did.

(iii) Write a short letter to a city resident who has asked you to get the fence around the junkyard built. Explain what you have done about the project.

VOCABULARY

aesthetic	contaminate	precipitator
algae	hazardous wastes	sanitary landfill
allergy	inversion	shanty town
botulism	Minamata disease	still birth
carcinogen	particulate matter	tailings
conservation	photochemical fog	thermal pollution
conserver society	pH scale	
consumer society	plume	

RESEARCH QUESTIONS

To answer these questions, you will probably need to refer to library resources and other sources of information.

1. Write a short essay of between 200 and 300 words, explaining why environmental specialists are worried about plans to drill for oil in the Arctic. Describe some precautions that might reduce dangers to the Arctic environment.

2. From the following list of types of pollution, choose one that is a problem in or near your city or a city in your area.
   - air pollution
   - thermal pollution
   - acid rain
   - pollution from hazardous wastes, such as dangerous chemicals
   - pollution from radioactive wastes

   For your topic, find out
   (a) the main cause or causes of the pollution
   (b) who is mainly affected by the pollution
   (c) whether government, citizens' groups, or industry has tried to reduce the pollution, and if so, by what means

   Discuss your findings in 400 to 600 words.

10

Global Environmental Concerns

Introduction

Although pollutants remain most concentrated near their source areas, air and water currents eventually spread them around the globe. Similarly, the cutting of the world's forests has worldwide as well as local effects. Both air pollution and the cutting of forests are believed to be accelerating global changes in climate. Because air pollution and forest clearance affect climate, they also will affect the supply of water and therefore of food. These are but some of the major concerns about the world environment.

Ocean Pollution

Almost all hazardous materials that pass into the rivers eventually collect in the oceans. Similarly, much airborne pollution ends up in the oceans, which cover almost 70% of the earth's surface. Of course, some pollutants are dumped directly into the oceans.

The most dramatic examples of water pollution are the oil spills that occur when **supertankers** carrying oil sink or run aground. Supertankers are very large ships that carry oil. In one such accident, in March 1967, 95 000 t of crude oil were released from the *Torrey Canyon* when it ran aground 24 km west of Land's End, England (Figure 10.1). The spilled oil killed much marine life, including birds and fish. It also coated beaches in England and France with a thick, black tarry layer. The costs to the fishing

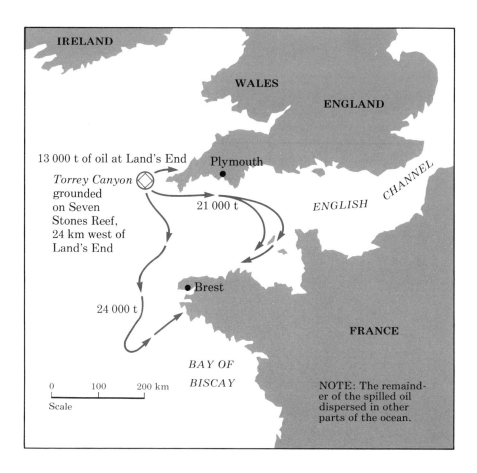

**Figure 10.1
Path of the Oil
Spilled by the
Torrey Canyon in
1967**

IRELAND

WALES

ENGLAND

13 000 t of oil at Land's End

Plymouth

Torrey Canyon
grounded
on Seven
Stones Reef,
24 km west of
Land's End

21 000 t

ENGLISH

CHANNEL

• Brest

24 000 t

FRANCE

0   100   200 km

Scale

BAY OF
BISCAY

NOTE: The remaind-
er of the spilled oil
dispersed in other
parts of the ocean.

industries of both countries were enormous. Clean-up operations in important resort areas were also expensive.

There are over 20 000 supertankers in operation today. Because of their size, they are very difficult to manoeuvre. Eighty percent of tanker accidents occur close to shore, where ship traffic is dense and where damage is greatest.

1. (a) **Turn to a world trading map in an atlas. Mark the most important oil-trading routes on a blank map of the world.**
   (b) **Using a red pencil or marker, shade in the ocean areas where you think that supertanker spills are most common.**

Pollution from oil products doubled between 1970 and 1980. Human sources produce eight times more oil pollution in water than natural sources. Although tanker accidents are the most obvious source of oil pollution, they account for only 10% of all the oil pollution in the ocean from human sources. Figure 10.2 illustrates

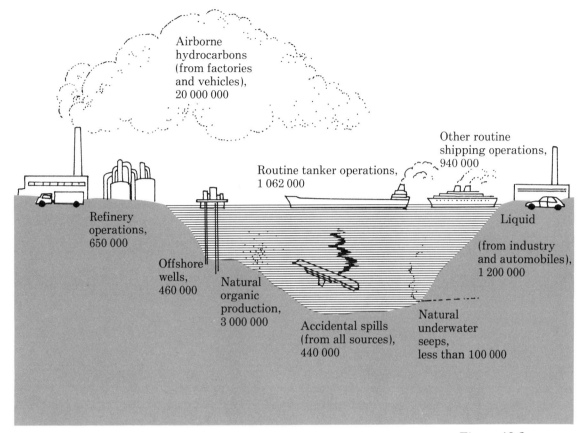

Airborne hydrocarbons (from factories and vehicles), 20 000 000

Other routine shipping operations, 940 000

Routine tanker operations, 1 062 000

Refinery operations, 650 000

Liquid (from industry and automobiles), 1 200 000

Offshore wells, 460 000

Natural organic production, 3 000 000

Accidental spills (from all sources), 440 000

Natural underwater seeps, less than 100 000

Figure 10.2
Sources of
Oil Pollution
in the Oceans
(In tonnes
per year)

the sources of oil pollution in the world's oceans.

The oceans of the world are also being used as a giant dumping ground (Figure 10.3). Sewage and garbage are routinely disposed of in the oceans. For example, millions of tonnes of garbage from New York City have been dumped into the Atlantic Ocean. On a number of occasions, ocean currents have brought up sludge from the garbage that has settled on the ocean floor. Several beaches on Long Island received this sludge as it washed up on the sand.

In addition, a number of hazardous wastes have been dumped into the sea intentionally, in attempts to avoid the problem of their disposal on land. Dangerous chemicals that kill plankton, a basic food for marine life in the oceans, have been detected even in the Arctic Ocean. They have been traced to the wastes from the plastics industry that were dumped into oceans off the coasts of Europe and North America.

Because of drainage patterns, the oceans of the world also receive a high proportion of the hazardous waste on land. Twenty-

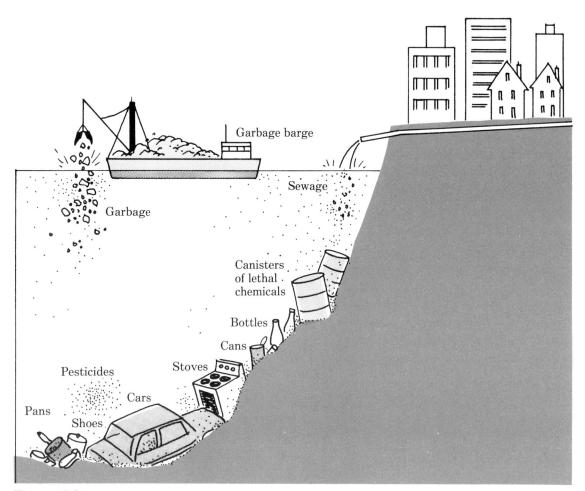

Figure 10.3
Wastes Dumped
into the Oceans

five percent of all PCBs, 50% of all other chemicals such as household cleaners, and up to 50% of all pesticides used on land eventually find their way into the oceans.

2. (a) List the items that you see in the ocean in Figure 10.3 and
   their probable sources.
   (b) What effects would these wastes in the ocean have on
       • people who live in the city?
       • fishing workers?
       • people who use beaches and swim?
   (c) What impact would this pollution have on the ocean's plants,
       animals, and fish?

3. Why do some people feel that dumping wastes in the ocean is
   more suitable than dumping wastes on land?

As people become more aware of the problems of ocean pollution, more can be done to solve these problems. Various solutions have been suggested or tried, including

- recycling waste products
- development of chemicals that break down after use
- use of methods other than chemical spraying of pesticides to control pests on farms
- more reliable equipment on supertankers to better enable them to avoid accidents
- increased coast guard activity concentrated on the interception and arrest of illegal polluters.

Global Water Supplies

Droughts occur in many areas of the world and though they have a more devastating effect on areas that are dependent on agriculture, they can also cause problems in industrialized areas. In 1980, such a drought affected Western Europe. People were not allowed to water their gardens or wash their cars, and they were asked to reduce their use of water for hygiene. In some places, water supplies to houses were discontinued and people had to carry water from a central supply faucet.

4. Imagine that the water supply to your home was discontinued. What items in your home would no longer function?

5. If you had to travel to a central faucet to collect water for household use, and you were permitted 5 L per person per day, how would your habits change? Remember that everyone must drink 2 L of water a day to remain healthy.

6. Assume that the drought occurred in August. What other activities in your community would be affected? Discuss at least three.

In some areas of the world, lack of water poses a problem (Figure 10.4). In other areas, rainfall is adequate but water supplies are polluted.

The United Nations estimates that about 650 million people in the world had inadequate or polluted water supplies in the period between 1970 and 1980. Water-related diseases kill about ten million people each year. Children are particularly vulnerable, and make up one-half of this total. Consider these cases:

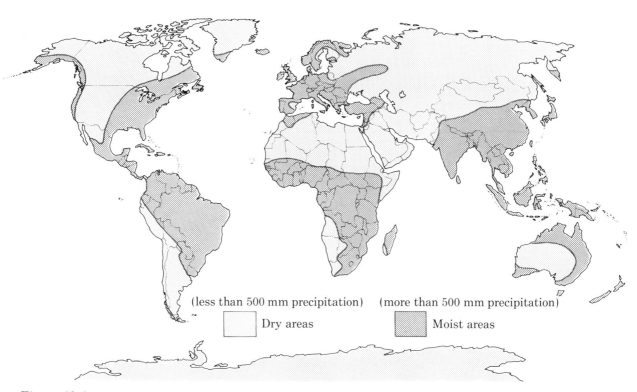

(less than 500 mm precipitation)   (more than 500 mm precipitation)

Dry areas   Moist areas

**Figure 10.4
The Dry and
Moist Areas of
the World**

**Figure 10.5
Child Carrying a
Water Jug in the
Sudan**

1. Augustina Ramos, a 14-year-old girl who lives in a small village in Honduras, gets up before dawn to collect water for her family. She treks along a difficult mountain path, through tropical growth, to the nearest river. Then she returns with the heavy jug. She does this seven times each day. She worries because she knows that the water she brings is polluted. A younger sister and brother died last year as a result of drinking the polluted water, but the river is their only source.

2. Carrying water is often more important for children than an education (Figure 10.5). Often 10- or 11-year-olds are taken out of school to collect water. In the dry season in Bolivia, schools are officially closed in the morning so that village children can haul water.

3. A school teacher in Bangladesh has reported that many of his students are absent all day because of water-linked illnesses. Even the children who stay in school all day have no water to drink. There is no source of clean water within 1 km of the school.

4. Droughts have been particularly severe in Africa and India in recent years. Crops have failed, cattle have died or been slaughtered, and many people have died.

Desertification

The driest areas of the world receive less than 250 mm of precipitation per year, and have little or no vegetation. These areas are referred to as **deserts**. The cold deserts of the world, such as the Arctic or the Antarctic, cover about one-sixth of the earth's surface, but contain little human settlement. They are therefore of less concern than the warm deserts, which contain a considerable number of human settlements. The warm deserts already cover about one-fifth of the earth's surface and are spreading.

The **semideserts** of the world usually receive 250 mm to 500 mm of precipitation per year. Under certain human and natural influences, semideserts can become deserts. In fact, many semidesert regions are delicately balanced between becoming desert and

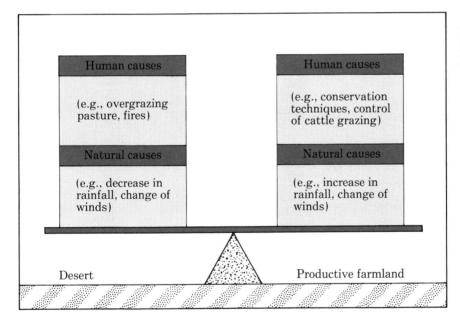

Figure 10.6
Factors
Determining the
Fate of a
Semidesert Region

becoming productive farmland (Figure 10.6). Whenever this balance is disturbed and a desert forms, **desertification** is said to have occurred.

7. What steps could be taken to limit the damage illustrated in Figure 10.6?

8. What would happen if human and natural forces of desertification occurred at the same time? Explain.

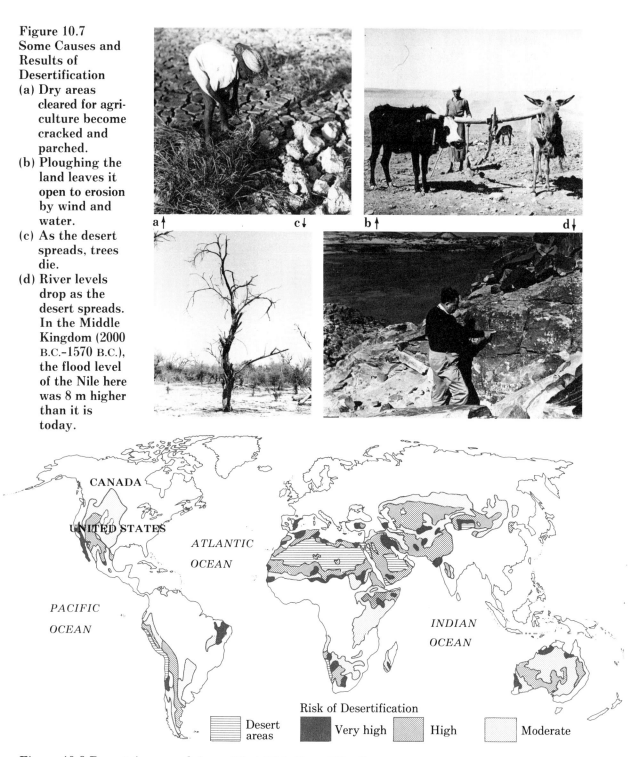

Figure 10.7
Some Causes and Results of Desertification

(a) Dry areas cleared for agriculture become cracked and parched.

(b) Ploughing the land leaves it open to erosion by wind and water.

(c) As the desert spreads, trees die.

(d) River levels drop as the desert spreads. In the Middle Kingdom (2000 B.C.–1570 B.C.), the flood level of the Nile here was 8 m higher than it is today.

a ↑   c ↓   b ↑   d ↓

Risk of Desertification

Desert areas   Very high   High   Moderate

Figure 10.8 Desert Areas and Areas That Risk Desertification

Most often, desertification occurs as the result of human activities. Clearing the land for agriculture, ploughing the land, and cutting firewood all increase the rate of erosion and the rate of water evaporation. These cleared areas then dry out and become desert (Figure 10.7).

9. (a) Examine Figure 10.8. What parts of the world have few, if any, areas that risk desertification?
   (b) What is the standard of living of the areas in (a)?

10. (a) List six areas of the world that have a high risk of desertification.
    (b) What is the standard of living in most of these areas?
    (c) Why would it be difficult for areas with a great risk of desertification to try to improve the situation?

Wise use of land can turn very dry, semidesert, and even desert areas into productive farmland or even forest. This has occurred in Israel. When the country was established in 1948, Israel had a high proportion of desert land. Figure 10.9 illustrates some steps that were taken to improve that land.

Figure 10.9 Steps Taken to Reclaim the Desert in Israel

11. Assume that you are appointed a representative of the government in the Sudan, Africa, to conduct a preliminary survey in

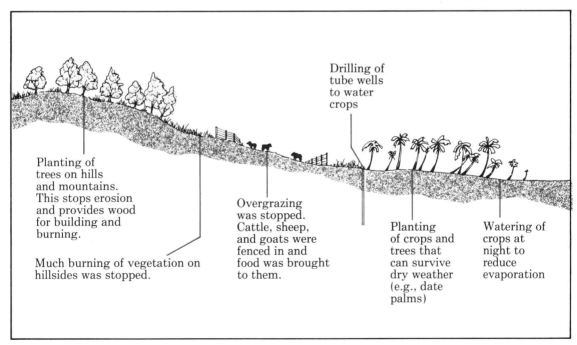

Drilling of tube wells to water crops

Planting of trees on hills and mountains. This stops erosion and provides wood for building and burning.

Much burning of vegetation on hillsides was stopped.

Overgrazing was stopped. Cattle, sheep, and goats were fenced in and food was brought to them.

Planting of crops and trees that can survive dry weather (e.g., date palms)

Watering of crops at night to reduce evaporation

**Figure 10.10
Selected Superdams
and Proposed
Superdams
around the World**

a semidesert area. Your assignment is to determine whether or
not there are signs that the desert is spreading in that area.
(a) Design a chart of things that you will investigate when you
     are flown to the area. You should look for at least eight
     items.
(b) Suggest at least ten scenes that you could photograph to
     support your answer to (a).

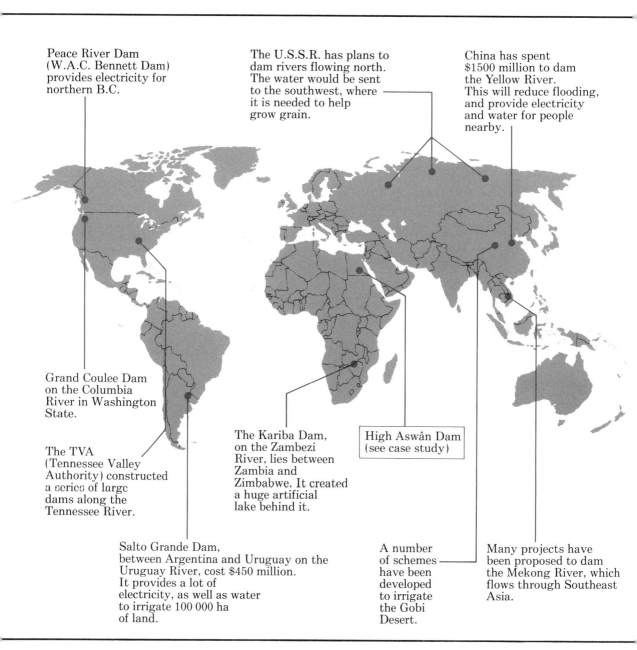

Peace River Dam
(W.A.C. Bennett Dam)
provides electricity for
northern B.C.

The U.S.S.R. has plans to
dam rivers flowing north.
The water would be sent
to the southwest, where
it is needed to help
grow grain.

China has spent
$1500 million to dam
the Yellow River.
This will reduce flooding,
and provide electricity
and water for people
nearby.

Grand Coulee Dam
on the Columbia
River in Washington
State.

The TVA
(Tennessee Valley
Authority) constructed
a series of large
dams along the
Tennessee River.

The Kariba Dam,
on the Zambezi
River, lies between
Zambia and
Zimbabwe. It created
a huge artificial
lake behind it.

High Aswân Dam
(see case study)

Salto Grande Dam,
between Argentina and Uruguay on the
Uruguay River, cost $450 million.
It provides a lot of
electricity, as well as water
to irrigate 100 000 ha
of land.

A number
of schemes
have been
developed
to irrigate
the Gobi
Desert.

Many projects have
been proposed to dam
the Mekong River, which
flows through Southeast
Asia.

Superdams

As the demand for water increases throughout the world, many large and very expensive dams—called superdams—will be built. Figure 10.10 shows superdams that have been built or proposed.

CASE STUDY

High Aswân Dam

The High Aswân Dam on the Nile River was designed to provide solutions to many of the problems of Egypt. A poor country, Egypt is overcrowded and cannot supply proper food for its people. Its climate is very hot and very dry. Apart from the Nile River, it has no reliable source of water for human use. In the past, the Nile would flood for a few weeks each year. During the flood, however, the Nile brought a new layer of rich soil to the fields in the valley.

Figure 10.11 Problems Caused by the Building of the High Aswân Dam

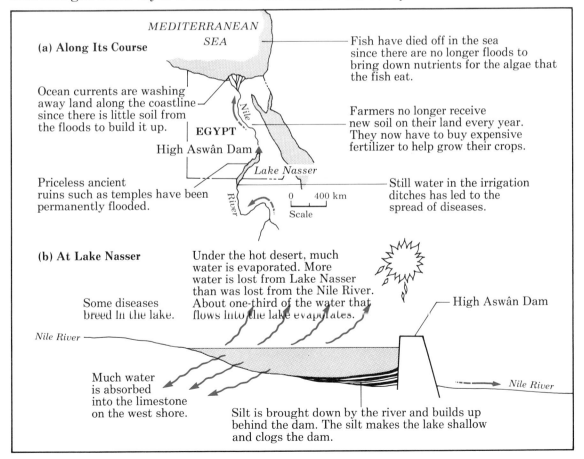

(a) Along Its Course

MEDITERRANEAN SEA

Fish have died off in the sea since there are no longer floods to bring down nutrients for the algae that the fish eat.

Ocean currents are washing away land along the coastline since there is little soil from the floods to build it up.

EGYPT

High Aswân Dam

Farmers no longer receive new soil on their land every year. They now have to buy expensive fertilizer to help grow their crops.

Lake Nasser

Priceless ancient ruins such as temples have been permanently flooded.

0   400 km
Scale

Still water in the irrigation ditches has led to the spread of diseases.

(b) At Lake Nasser

Under the hot desert, much water is evaporated. More water is lost from Lake Nasser than was lost from the Nile River. About one-third of the water that flows into the lake evaporates.

Some diseases breed in the lake.

High Aswân Dam

Nile River

Nile River

Much water is absorbed into the limestone on the west shore.

Silt is brought down by the river and builds up behind the dam. The silt makes the lake shallow and clogs the dam.

The High Aswân Dam was designed to prevent this annual flooding, and to provide electricity for the entire country and water for irrigation of the desert.

Although the building of the dam has solved some problems, it has created some new ones. Figure 10.11 shows some of the problems that have developed since the dam was completed.

12. **Of all the problems created by the building of the High Aswân Dam, choose the three that are most important from your point of view. Give reasons for your choices.**

13. **Instead of a superdam, many wells and smaller dams could have provided water and electricity. Why do you think the Egyptian government decided to build a superdam?**

14. (a) **Use an atlas to discover additional information about Egypt such as birth rate, death rate, types of industry, and average food intake per person. Compare Egypt with Canada under these headings.**

    (b) **The High Aswân Dam cost millions of dollars. Suggest other ways in which this money could have been spent for the betterment of the country.**

**Figure 10.12
Selected Water
Supply Problems
in the United
States**

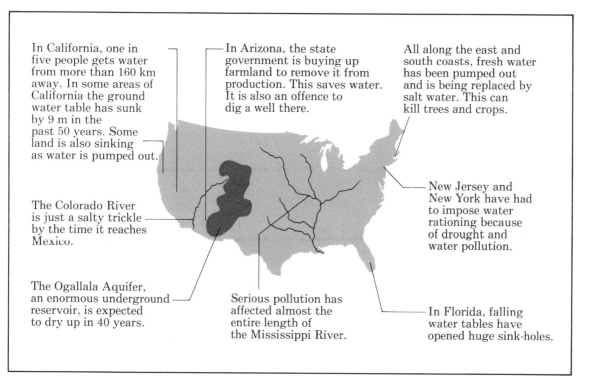

In California, one in five people gets water from more than 160 km away. In some areas of California the ground water table has sunk by 9 m in the past 50 years. Some land is also sinking as water is pumped out.

In Arizona, the state government is buying up farmland to remove it from production. This saves water. It is also an offence to dig a well there.

All along the east and south coasts, fresh water has been pumped out and is being replaced by salt water. This can kill trees and crops.

The Colorado River is just a salty trickle by the time it reaches Mexico.

New Jersey and New York have had to impose water rationing because of drought and water pollution.

The Ogallala Aquifer, an enormous underground reservoir, is expected to dry up in 40 years.

Serious pollution has affected almost the entire length of the Mississippi River.

In Florida, falling water tables have opened huge sink-holes.

15. Do you think that Egypt has benefited from the building of the High Aswân Dam? Write one-half page to explain clearly your point of view.

North American Water Supplies

Droughts are also a danger faced by some Canadian farmers. The Prairie provinces, central British Columbia, and southern Ontario are among Canadian farming areas affected by lack of rainfall. Although Canada contains 9% of the world's fresh water, it is not always available where it is needed.

Much of the agriculture in the United States depends on irri-

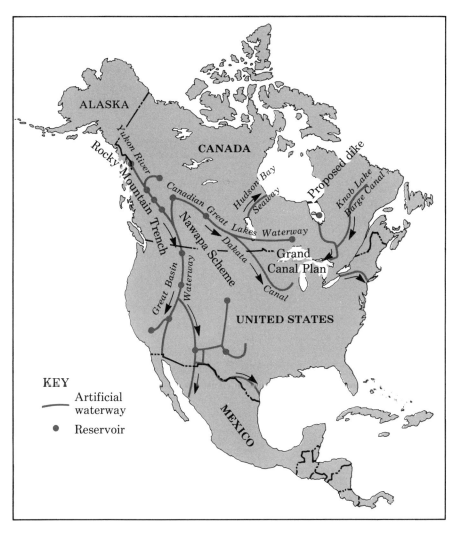

Figure 10.13 Continental Schemes for the Distribution of Water

gation. As more water is used, rivers shrink, **water table** levels fall, and wells sometimes go dry (see Figure 10.12).

Schemes have been proposed to move water from Canada and Alaska to the dry regions in the western United States. The routes suggested are shown in Figure 10.13. The costs would be very great, as would the damage to the environment. It could take 20 years and $600 000 million to make these plans a reality.

Deforestation

Deforestation is the cutting down of forests. Around the world, forests are being cleared at the rate of about 20 ha each minute. This means that an area the size of Nova Scotia and New Brunswick is cleared each year! There is increasing worldwide concern about the consequences of removing so many trees so quickly.

Clearing the Forests for Agriculture in Temperate Climates

Clearing the land increases the rate of soil loss. In southeastern Canada, 1.5 cm to 3.5 cm of topsoil are lost every 1000 years. Each year 870 000 000 t of soil are carried by the streams and rivers of the United States into the sea.

Figure 10.14 How Land Use Affects Soil Erosion

TREATMENT	TONNES OF SOIL LOST PER HECTARE PER YEAR	NUMBER OF YEARS TO ERODE ONE CENTIMETRE OF TOPSOIL
No crop; soil is ploughed 10 cm deep, cultivated regularly	104.0	1.3
Corn grown continuously	49.0	2.8
Wheat grown continuously	25.0	5.6
Crop rotation: corn grown one year, wheat the next, and clover the year after that	7.0	20.7
Dense cover of grass grown continuously	0.8	171.0

NOTE: Data were obtained over a period of 14 years in Missouri where the slope was about 3° and the average annual rainfall was 1000 mm.

16. **Look at the information given in Figure 10.14. What is the most important factor in determining the rate of soil erosion in this particular situation?**

17. In what ways do you think that
    - slope and
    - the type of soil
    might have an effect on the rate of soil erosion?

18. (a) Examine the following diagrams.
    (b) What do these diagrams show about conserving soil on the farm? Discuss each one separately.

Clearing the Forests for Lumber in Temperate Climates

Sir John A. Macdonald was one of the first to record concern about the future of Canada's forests. In 1871, in a letter to the premier of Ontario, he wrote, "The sight of the immense masses of timber passing my window every moment constantly suggests to my mind the absolute necessity there is for looking into the future of this great trade. We are recklessly destroying the timber of Canada, and there is scarcely a possibility of replacing it."

Few people took him seriously then, but now it is realized that forests will not last forever without reforestation. In Canada, 800 000 ha of forest currently are harvested each year. Of this, only 200 000 ha are reseeded or replanted. Natural regeneration or regrowth replaces 300 000 ha, resulting in a net loss of 300 000 ha each year. Forest fires and insects destroy additional areas. In 1980, the forest area burned was five times the area harvested, and by 1982 the spruce budworm had consumed five years' harvest in the areas infested.

A number of steps are being taken to salvage Canadian forests and the industries that depend on them.

- An inventory to establish the current state of timber resources is being carried out. This is a vital starting point.
- Research is being conducted to determine whether trees from other areas would grow well in Canada, and to discover how Canadian species can be grown more efficiently.
- More people are being trained in forestry.
- More money is being given for fire and insect control.
- Provincial laws are being more strictly enforced to ensure better reforestation.

These initiatives are minor, however, compared to those taken in the Swedish forestry industry, where fertilizing, spraying, trimming, and thinning of forests has been going on for 80 years. The Swedes invest five or six times more money per hectare in their forestry industries than does Canada. Clearly, Canadians have much to learn about caring for their forests.

19. The production of one issue of a national newspaper uses about 3 ha of timber.
    (a) How much timber would one year's issues (six days per week) consume?
    (b) In what other ways could newsprint be produced for an issue besides using 3 ha of forest?

20. List five wood or paper products used by you or your family that are thrown away, or wasted. Explain how you could reduce this waste. Be specific.

Clearing the Tropical Forests

The problems facing the temperate world as a result of deforestation are minute compared with the impact that clearing the tropical forests will have on the whole world.

For example, tropical forests, which are shown in Figure 10.15, are home to an enormous variety of animals and plants. Norman Myers, author of *The Sinking Ark*, has estimated that, each day, one of the species in these forests becomes extinct.

Future food supplies and medical improvements may well depend on these plants and animals. Many grains, such as corn and wheat, were developed from wild grasses. Aspirin, morphine (a pain-killer), and hundreds of other valuable drugs were first found in plants. About 70% of the drugs currently being tested for use in curing cancer are derived from tropical forest vegetation. If these

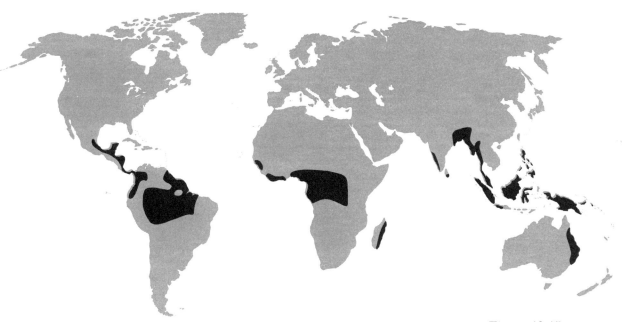

Figure 10.15
Tropical Forests
of the World

21. Copy the following table into your notebook. Fill in the table using the data in Figure 10.16.

LOCATION	COUNTRY	LATITUDE	AVERAGE TEMP. (°C)	ANNUAL RANGE OF TEMP. (°C)	TOTAL PRECIPITATION (mm)
Iquitos					
Colombo		SAMPLE ONLY			
Edmonton					

Figure 10.16
Climographs
from Forest
Environments

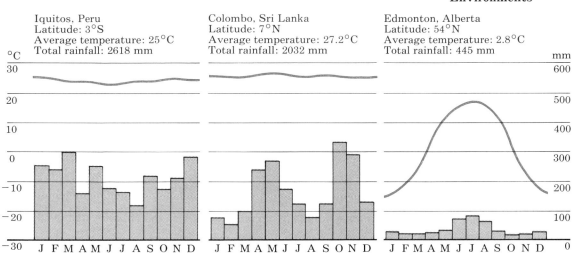

Iquitos, Peru
Latitude: 3°S
Average temperature: 25°C
Total rainfall: 2618 mm

Colombo, Sri Lanka
Latitude: 7°N
Average temperature: 27.2°C
Total rainfall: 2032 mm

Edmonton, Alberta
Latitude: 54°N
Average temperature: 2.8°C
Total rainfall: 445 mm

forests disappear, such potentially valuable resources will be lost.

Tropical forests differ greatly from temperate forests. By studying climographs (shown in Figure 10.16), the factors responsible for these differences can be determined.

22. **Use the completed table from question 21 to help answer these questions.**
    (a) **Describe the changes in temperature throughout the year for each of the three places.**
    (b) **Which station has the greatest change in temperature throughout the year?**
    (c) **What influence would this great change in temperature have on plant growth?**
    (d) **Would the changes in temperature affect plant growth in the other two stations? Explain.**

23. **Refer to the climographs in Figure 10.16 to answer this question and question 24. For how many months is the ground likely to be frozen in each of the three places?**

24. (a) **Describe how the precipitation varies through the year for each of the three locations.**
    (b) **How would this variation in precipitation, by itself, affect plant growth? Explain.**
    (c) **Greater precipitation in an area, increases the possibility of soil erosion. If precipitation is greatly concentrated in a few months, erosion also increases. Examine each of the three stations and rank them in order from those where the possibility of soil erosion is highest to those where it is lowest. In each instance, give reasons for your answer. Refer to your answers to 23 and 24 (a) and (b) for help.**

Deforestation has a great effect on the balance of nature. There is an important natural recycling of nutrients in a rain forest environment. Leaves fall and then decay on the forest floor. When it rains, the rain water carries the nutrients from the decayed leaves into the soil, where they are absorbed by the roots of trees and plants. Continuing the cycle, these trees again drop leaves to be turned into nutrients. Figure 10.17 (a) illustrates this recycling process.

Once the forest has been cleared, however, rain falls directly on the soil and can wash it away or **leach** it, washing valuable nutrients to lower levels of the soil. As Figure 10.17 (b) illustrates, these nutrients are often deposited just above the water table in a

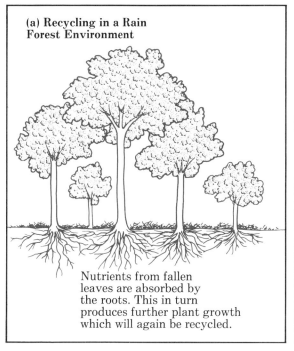

(a) Recycling in a Rain Forest Environment

Nutrients from fallen leaves are absorbed by the roots. This in turn produces further plant growth which will again be recycled.

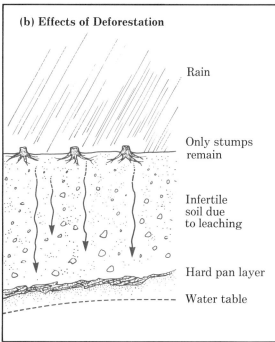

(b) Effects of Deforestation

Rain

Only stumps remain

Infertile soil due to leaching

Hard pan layer

Water table

**Figure 10.17
The Effects of
Deforestation in a
Rain Forest**

**Figure 10.18
Soil Erosion in
Tropical Areas.
These slopes in
Nepal, now useless
for agriculture,
were once covered
by forests.**

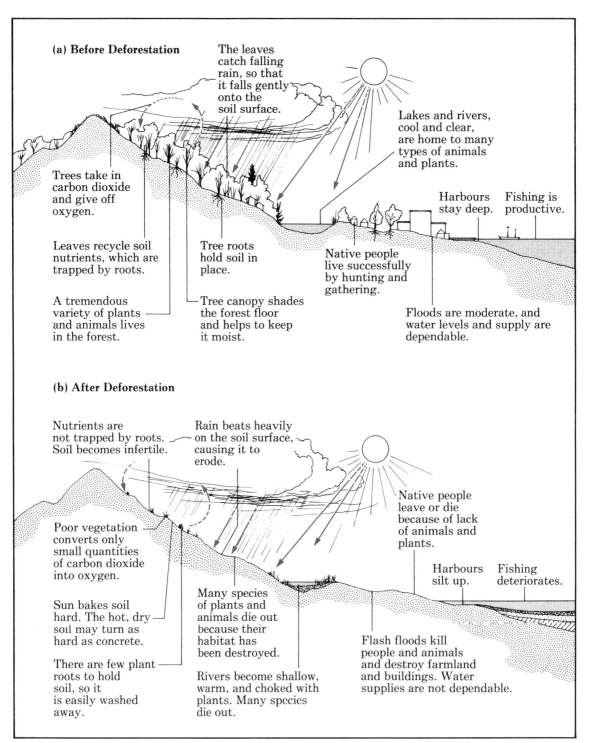

(a) Before Deforestation

The leaves catch falling rain, so that it falls gently onto the soil surface.

Lakes and rivers, cool and clear, are home to many types of animals and plants.

Trees take in carbon dioxide and give off oxygen.

Harbours stay deep.

Fishing is productive.

Leaves recycle soil nutrients, which are trapped by roots.

Tree roots hold soil in place.

Native people live successfully by hunting and gathering.

A tremendous variety of plants and animals lives in the forest.

Tree canopy shades the forest floor and helps to keep it moist.

Floods are moderate, and water levels and supply are dependable.

(b) After Deforestation

Nutrients are not trapped by roots. Soil becomes infertile.

Rain beats heavily on the soil surface, causing it to erode.

Native people leave or die because of lack of animals and plants.

Poor vegetation converts only small quantities of carbon dioxide into oxygen.

Harbours silt up.

Fishing deteriorates.

Sun bakes soil hard. The hot, dry soil may turn as hard as concrete.

Many species of plants and animals die out because their habitat has been destroyed.

There are few plant roots to hold soil, so it is easily washed away.

Rivers become shallow, warm, and choked with plants. Many species die out.

Flash floods kill people and animals and destroy farmland and buildings. Water supplies are not dependable.

Figure 10.19 Before and after Cutting the Tropical Forests

hard layer. This layer is so rich in iron and aluminum that it is mined as an ore or cut and dried to form building blocks.

As Figure 10.18 and 10.19 illustrate, deforestation in tropical areas has a great effect on plant, animal, and human life, as well as on the landscape.

In northern India, the massive deodar, oak, and pine forests that once covered the Himalayan foothills have been cleared. The topsoil has been washed off, rivers are clogged with silt, and serious **flash floods** result from sudden heavy rainstorms. In the plains below the foothills, the area frequently flooded has doubled from 20 000 000 ha in 1970 to 40 000 000 ha in 1980. Nearly six thousand million tonnes of topsoil are now being washed each year into the Bay of Bengal. A new area of land is forming beyond the mouth of the Ganges River.

Pressures to clear land covered by tropical forests are great. As the population of a country grows, there are more people who want to chop down the forests and farm the land. In many instances, this process can lead to disaster. Consider these facts:

1. Every year the world produces one and a half times the food needed to feed everyone on earth. Most poor countries produce plenty of food; but it is wasted, eaten by rats and other pests, or allowed to rot. There is therefore no real need to clear more land for farming.
2. Once hilly land is cleared of tropical forests for farming, it declines in value. Within two or three years, that land is often no longer suitable for farming. Even more land is then cleared for farming.
3. Some land is cleared for farming non-food crops. In the case of Kenya, much land is used to grow tobacco rather than food because tobacco brings in more money. Unfortunately, after a crop of tobacco has been grown, no other crop can be grown on that land for another three years. The tobacco must also be smoke-cured in small tobacco smoke houses. For every hectare of tobacco grown, three hectares of forest are cut down to provide wood to be burned in these smoke houses. Today, Kenya pro-duces all of its own tobacco, but many people go hungry. To compound the problem, more people in that country are smoking and contracting lung cancer than ever before.

25. (a) If you had a job in the government of Kenya, what might you do about the problem of losing forest to cure tobacco? Make two suggestions.
   (b) How might some farmers react to your suggestions?

As the remaining tropical forests of the world are cleared, the impact on the population is often severe. Figure 10.20 illustrates how the Indian tribes of the Upper Amazon River have suffered from the clearing of the Amazon forests.

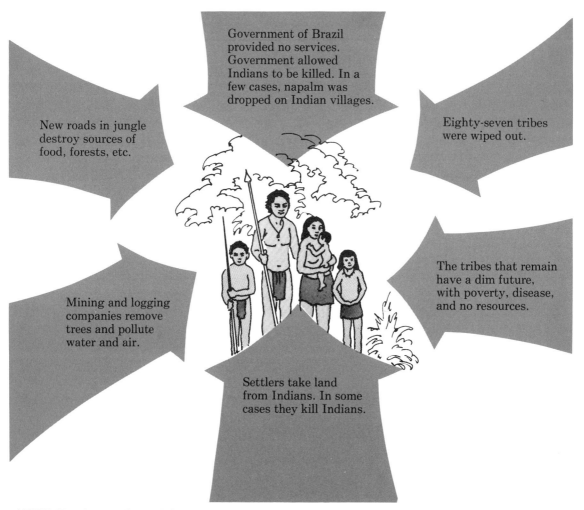

Government of Brazil provided no services. Government allowed Indians to be killed. In a few cases, napalm was dropped on Indian villages.

New roads in jungle destroy sources of food, forests, etc.

Eighty-seven tribes were wiped out.

Mining and logging companies remove trees and pollute water and air.

The tribes that remain have a dim future, with poverty, disease, and no resources.

Settlers take land from Indians. In some cases they kill Indians.

NOTE: Napalm is a chemical that severely burns the skin and can kill.

**Figure 10.20
The Effects on
Native Indians of
Clearing the
Amazon Forests**

There are a few encouraging signs concerning Third World forests. In the Philippines, for example, the government has a program that requires each person to plant one tree each month. In a small area of northern India, some replanting of trees has taken place in the mountains. As a result, there have been fewer flash floods, erosion has been reduced, and some trees can now be cut for fuel.

26. **Design a one-page advertisement to be placed in a Canadian newspaper. Using pictures or sketches as well as a written section, outline the problems that result from wasting Canada's forest resources.**

VOCABULARY

deforestation	flash floods	supertanker
desert	leach	
desertification	semidesert	

RESEARCH QUESTIONS

To answer these questions, you will probably need to refer to library resources and other sources of information.

1. Research an occurrance of a major oil spill in an ocean. Investigate the events that led to the spill and the consequences of the accident.

2. (a) Carefully explain how forest clearance affects world temperatures.
   (b) What would be the consequences of this change? Include the following topics in your account:
   - effects on agriculture
   - changes in sea level and their effects on land masses
   - effects on people
   - effects on the economies of the world

3. Describe, with simple diagrams, five ancient methods of obtaining water that are still in use today.

4. In the library, locate books and articles on the topic of soil conservation. Write two pages (about 400 to 500 words), including labelled diagrams, on methods used to conserve soil in Canada and the United States. List the sources of your information in a bibliography following your account.

SECTION V | The Future

Prospects for the Future

Introduction

Consider the following questions:

- What will my life be like in 25 years?
- Will the world's problems improve or become worse in the future?
- Is it a waste of time to think about the future?

1. **Without reading further in this chapter, write a half-page essay answering one of the questions above. Include ideas that come to your mind.**

2. **The English novelist John Galsworthy once said, "If you do not think about the future, you cannot have one." Do you agree or disagree with his statement? Give two reasons for your point of view.**

Major Concerns about the Future

Nuclear War

Millions of people around the world are concerned about the possibility of nuclear war. Because a nuclear war would destroy the world as we know it, some people believe it is the most serious of all concerns for the future. Figure 11.1 shows the countries that are known to have nuclear weapons or are suspected of having them.

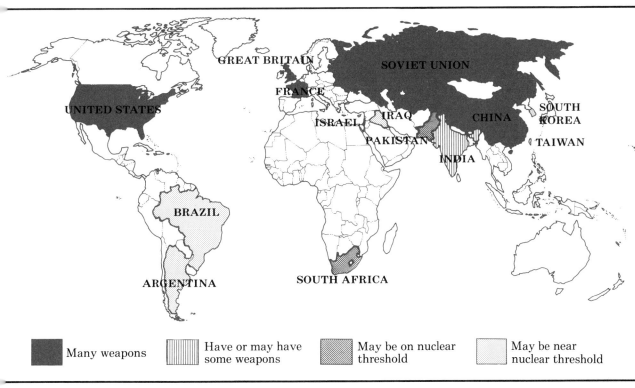

■	Many weapons	‖	Have or may have some weapons	▨	May be on nuclear threshold	▨ May be near nuclear threshold

Clearly, a nuclear war would not be limited to a few countries. The effects of a nuclear blast would be far greater than anyone could imagine. They include the following:

**Figure 11.1
Nuclear Weapons Around the World**

- millions of people killed instantly
- millions of others critically afflicted by the effects of radiation
- millions of others seriously burned, injured, and mutilated
- much of the earth's animal and plant life destroyed
- breakdown of the ozone layer in the earth's atmosphere. This would allow ultra-violet rays from the sun to reach the earth's surface, killing much life.

Carl Sagan, a respected American scientist, has described the threat of nuclear war in this way: "It is as if the people of the world are being held as hostages, while being threatened with terror."

3. Explain in your own words what you think Carl Sagan means.

People are concerned not only about the nuclear weapons held by the superpowers. They are also disturbed about the fact that nuclear capability is being acquired by other countries, some of which are governed by dictators or unstable governments. Such countries could build their own atomic bombs, using material from nuclear power plants. In spite of these risks, Canada has sold nuclear power plants to other countries. The construction of these power plants has benefited Canada because it created jobs for Canadians.

4. **Should nuclear power plants be sold to other countries? Give reasons for your answer.**

5. **Think of the possibility of terrorists acquiring a nuclear weapon.**
   (a) In what way could these terrorists use it?
   (b) What should countries such as the United States do to guard against these terrorists?

In the 1500s, the French physician and astrologist named Nostradamus made some amazing predictions. He wrote that the world would have a third major world war by the year 2000. This war would take place in Europe and the U.S.S.R. but would also involve China and the Americas.

L. F. Richardson, a British researcher, reached different conclusions. He studied the wars that took place between 1820 and 1945 and predicted that no nuclear war would occur before the year 2820 (Figure 11.2).

**Figure 11.2
The Richardson
Diagram**

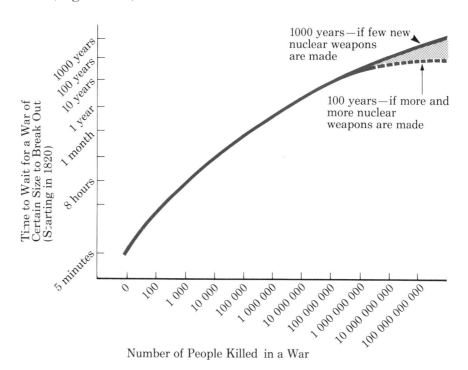

No one wants a nuclear war to occur. In fact, the prospect of a nuclear war is frightening. The real conflict develops over how to avoid that war. On one side of this conflict is the group of people who belong to the **peace movement**. They believe that only the destruction of all nuclear weapons will keep the world safe from nuclear war. Opposing that group are those who argue that there can be peace only through nuclear strength. They believe that a country will be afraid to start a nuclear war if the opposing country has equal nuclear strength. These two points of view are compared below.

PEACE MOVEMENT	PEACE THROUGH STRENGTH
1. Only the destruction of all nuclear weapons will prevent a war.	1. If the U.S. and U.S.S.R. have the same number of nuclear weapons, peace will reign. This is called a balance of power.
2. There are enough nuclear weapons to destroy the whole world 20 to 40 times. This is called **overkill** and is a major threat to the world.	2. Overkill is necessary in case some of the weapons are destroyed. Then there will be others to use.
3. Nuclear weapons are a waste of money. People could be helped, fed, or given medicine with the money now spent on nuclear weapons.	3. Money is well spent if it keeps peace through strength.
4. An atomic bomb might go off by mistake. The safeguards in place are insufficient.	4. Effective safeguards are in place to prevent mistakes.
5. No nuclear war can be "won". Who would want to be alive after a nuclear world war?	5. If you strike the enemy early and often, you can win a nuclear war.
6. If the dismantling (taking apart) of nuclear weapons does not start soon, it may be too late. The U.S. and the U.S.S.R. must learn to trust each other at least to some extent if they want peace.	6. The U.S. and U.S.S.R. do not trust each other. How can you know whether the other side actually dismantled its bombs?

6. **Examine both of the above points of view. With which do you agree? Explain.**

Handling Rapid Change in Our Lives and in the World

As was discussed in chapters 5 and 8, the amount of information in the world is increasing very quickly. The total amount of information in the world doubled during each time period shown below.

From	To
A.D. 1	1750
1751	1900
1901	1950
1951	1960

Now it doubles every three to five years.

7. **Examine the above figures again. Suggest three ways in which the information explosion has made your life different from that of someone living in the Roman Empire in A.D. 100.**

How can this rapid change be handled? What must be done in order to live in a world that changes so quickly? The answer to these two questions will shed some light on the future.

Sunrise and Sunset Industries

The changes in technology in the last quarter of this century are clearly affecting people. Employment is one area in which many changes have taken place. Industries that were once the backbone of the economy are shrinking in importance. The automobile and steel industries, for example, are employing fewer and fewer people. New machines are replacing people in these factories, and the products of these factories can often be made more cheaply in other countries. These industries are called **sunset industries** (Figure 11.3).

8. **Explain in your own words why the automobile and steel industries are called sunset industries.**

**Figure 11.3
An Example of a
Sunset Industry.
Steel plants across
North America are
being closed or
partly closed.**

9. What other industries can you think of that are sunset industries? Give reasons for your choice.

Other industries, called **sunrise industries**, are growing in importance. Sunrise industries provide new products that can save people time or money, or make their lives easier. Examples of sunrise industries include telecommunications, computer manufacturing, and the development of new energy sources (Figure 11.4).

The jobs being lost in sunset and other industries and in business are often those that require few or no skills. Bank tellers, cashiers, and auto workers are among those losing their jobs. In the future, more and more low-skilled workers will have difficulty finding jobs, particularly well-paying ones. Although there are many openings in sunrise industries, these positions often require a great deal of training. Canadians who are losing their jobs will need new skills to obtain new jobs.

Figure 11.4
An Example of a Sunrise Industry. This new factory produces computers.

10. Assume that you are the mayor of a city that has a large sunset industry. This industry has been important to the city for many years, but is now experiencing financial difficulty. It is your job to create plans to help the city. Write down six important ideas that you would include in a speech to the people of the city. Include plans for new jobs, etc.

11. Consider the following two lists of jobs, which reflect the major changes in North America's economy, and the information in this section of the text. What plans should you make for your future job? What should you focus on in your education?

JOBS OFFERING THE GREATEST NUMBER OF NEW OPENINGS IN THE NEXT TEN YEARS	JOBS OFFERING FEWER OPENINGS IN THE NEXT TEN YEARS
Service: janitor, beautician, transportation worker	Farmer
Professional/Technical: scientist, engineer	Farm worker
Management: manager, administrator	Secondary school teacher
Sales: insurance salesperson, real estate salesperson	College or university instructor
Retail: retail worker	Maid, servant
Trades: skilled craftsperson (e.g., carpenter)	Research assistant
	Typesetter

NOTE: There are likely to be many more small companies, more part-time workers, and more women in the work force.

Providing for the World's Population

The growth of the world's population (Figure 11.5) affects the quality of life around the world. This is largely because of the demands that a growing population places on food and water supplies and the other basic necessities of life.

Figure 11.5 World Population Growth

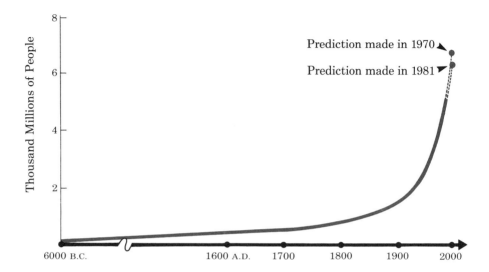

J. H. Fremlin calculated that, if present trends continue, in 900 years there will be 100 people for each square metre on the earth. The earth, of course, could not support such numbers. When too many people live in one area to allow an adequate standard of living there, a situation of **overpopulation** exists.

Not everyone believes that the world suffers from overpopulation. In fact, there are two differing points of view on overpopulation, as shown below:

1. The world suffers from overpopulation. There are too many people in the world, and as a result there are problems of overcrowding, pollution, crime, disease, and hunger.
2. There is no overpopulation. The problems of overcrowding, pollution, crime, disease, and hunger stem from poor management of people and resources, not from the fact that there are too many people in the world.

These two points of view are discussed in detail in the following sections.

Arguments Supporting the Overpopulation Theory

Consider these facts:

- Every second, four babies are born in the world.
- India's population is growing at the rate of one million people per month.
- China's population passed the one thousand million mark around 1980.
- At present, the **doubling time** of the world's population is 35 years. (Doubling time is the number of years necessary for a population to double in size.)

It seems that there are too many people in the world. Our cities are becoming more and more crowded. If there were fewer people, each person would have more room in which to live and work.

12. (a) **Have you ever been in a place that you believed was overcrowded? If so, describe it.**
    (b) **What was your reaction to the place referred to in (a)?**
    (c) **Name five specific indications of overpopulation in a country.**

The faster the world's population grows, the faster natural resources are used up. As non-renewable natural resources are used up, people will have to either plan to use alternative resources or face drastic changes in their lifestyle and standard of living.

In the same way, as the world's population grows, less and less food is available per person. In the case of Burundi, for example, the GNP per person is only $80 per year. Most of this money is spent on food.

As the world's population has grown, so has the amount of pollution dumped into the water and air, and onto the land. If there were fewer people on earth, there would be less pollution (see Figure 11.6).

Certainly the population of the world is growing more slowly than it used to. However, this slower rate of growth does not eliminate the problem of overpopulation. Conditions for many millions of people are getting worse. In fact, the death rates in some countries have already begun to increase, partly as a result of problems caused by overpopulation.

Some people have proposed that the world overpopulation problem could be solved by birth control. It has even been suggested that birth control should be mandatory in areas where overpopulation is an acute problem.

**Figure 11.6
Environmental
Pollution Has
Increased As the
Population has
Grown**

13. **Read through the section on overpopulation again. List the five key points that support the theory of overpopulation.**

Arguments against the Overpopulation Theory

Despite the large population of the world, much of the earth's surface is still largely uninhabited. If the human population were spread out more evenly, there would be little overcrowding. The entire population of the world today could fit into the state of Texas, with 180 m^2 of land per person. This area is about the same as the floor area of a large Canadian home.

14. Turn to these world maps in an atlas:
    • one that shows the distribution of population
    • one that shows the countries of the world
    Locate and list 15 countries that appear to have little or no
    population. The U.S.S.R., for example, is largely uninhabited
    because of a cold climate and inhospitable terrain.

It has been assumed that a large population results in resources
being used up more quickly. This does not have to be true. With
recycling and more use of renewable energy sources, this problem
can be reduced greatly. The sun's energy will continue to reach the
earth a long time, and its energy could be used more effectively
than it is now.

In the short run, children are expensive to society, and their
presence results in less wealth per person. When these children
grow up, however, they work and help produce new wealth. They
can also contribute new technology and new ideas. When these
children become adults, they usually contribute more to society
than they originally took from it.

As a population grows, markets for products increase, and
more workers are available to contribute their skills. A growing
population brings more people with new ideas into the world. In
fact, despite rapid population growth, less-developed countries
have increased their GNP per person as quickly as the First World.

Pollution, thought by some to result from overpopulation, is
actually the product of poor management of the environment.
Florida, for example, has grown quickly in population since 1960.
Yet, it has little air pollution, as its economy is based on tourism,
electronics, and other nonpolluting industries.

Almost all countries of the world are growing more slowly in
population than they were in 1970. India, Colombia, and China
are among those countries whose populations are still growing
quickly. The United Kingdom, Sweden, East Germany, and Austria
have populations that are relatively stable. West Germany has
had a declining population since 1970.

15. Examine Figure 11.7.
    (a) List eight major problems that exist on Habley Island.
    (b) Assume that the population is suddenly cut in half. Which
        problems in (a) would then be solved? Give reasons for your
        answers.
    (c) Considering your answers to (a) and (b), does Habley Island
        suffer from overpopulation? Explain your answer fully.

**Figure 11.7
Habley Island, an
Imaginary Tropical
Country**

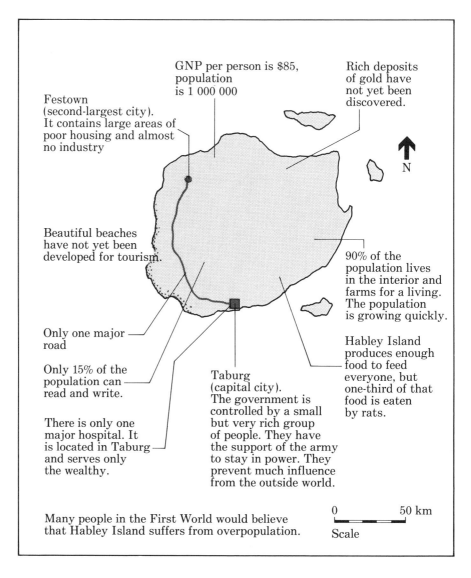

GNP per person is $85, population is 1 000 000

Rich deposits of gold have not yet been discovered.

Festown (second-largest city). It contains large areas of poor housing and almost no industry

N

Beautiful beaches have not yet been developed for tourism.

90% of the population lives in the interior and farms for a living. The population is growing quickly.

Only one major road

Only 15% of the population can read and write.

Taburg (capital city). The government is controlled by a small but very rich group of people. They have the support of the army to stay in power. They prevent much influence from the outside world.

Habley Island produces enough food to feed everyone, but one-third of that food is eaten by rats.

There is only one major hospital. It is located in Taburg and serves only the wealthy.

Many people in the First World would believe that Habley Island suffers from overpopulation.

0   50 km
Scale

16. **Do you agree or disagree with the theory of overpopulation? Write 200 words to explain why you chose that point of view.**

The Aging of Canada

In the 1970s, Canadians looked upon their population as largely a youthful one. The advertisements on television showed young people using a wide variety of products. In the 1980s, however, this emphasis has changed. The average Canadian has grown older, and Canadian families are smaller than ever before (see Figure 11.8). Television advertisements now use older actors. Baby products, such as shampoos and skin creams, are now shown as being used by the whole family. Although children are still featured widely in television advertisements, there are fewer children per adult now than twenty years ago. The large Canadian family of three or more children is disappearing.

17. **Give four possible reasons to explain the fact that Canadians are having fewer children, and explain your choices.**

The decline in the size of the Canadian family will have a number of effects on Canadian society. In 1980, 8.7% of Canadians were aged 65 and over. By the year 2000, this figure will be 13%,

**Figure 11.8
Why Canadians
Are Having
Fewer Children**

Children are expensive to raise.

Sometimes adults feel that children ignore their parents. Young couples do not want to have children who grow up to ignore them.

Adults look at teenagers who shoplift or take drugs, and decide that they do not want children.

Children change the lifestyle of parents. Fewer vacations, fewer nights out, and less freedom for parents are fears of many.

Many women feel that a career will be more fulfilling than raising children.

Some adults who had unhappy childhoods do not want children.

Birth control is available to Canadians. Adults now have the means to limit the size of their families.

Many people are concerned about overpopulation.

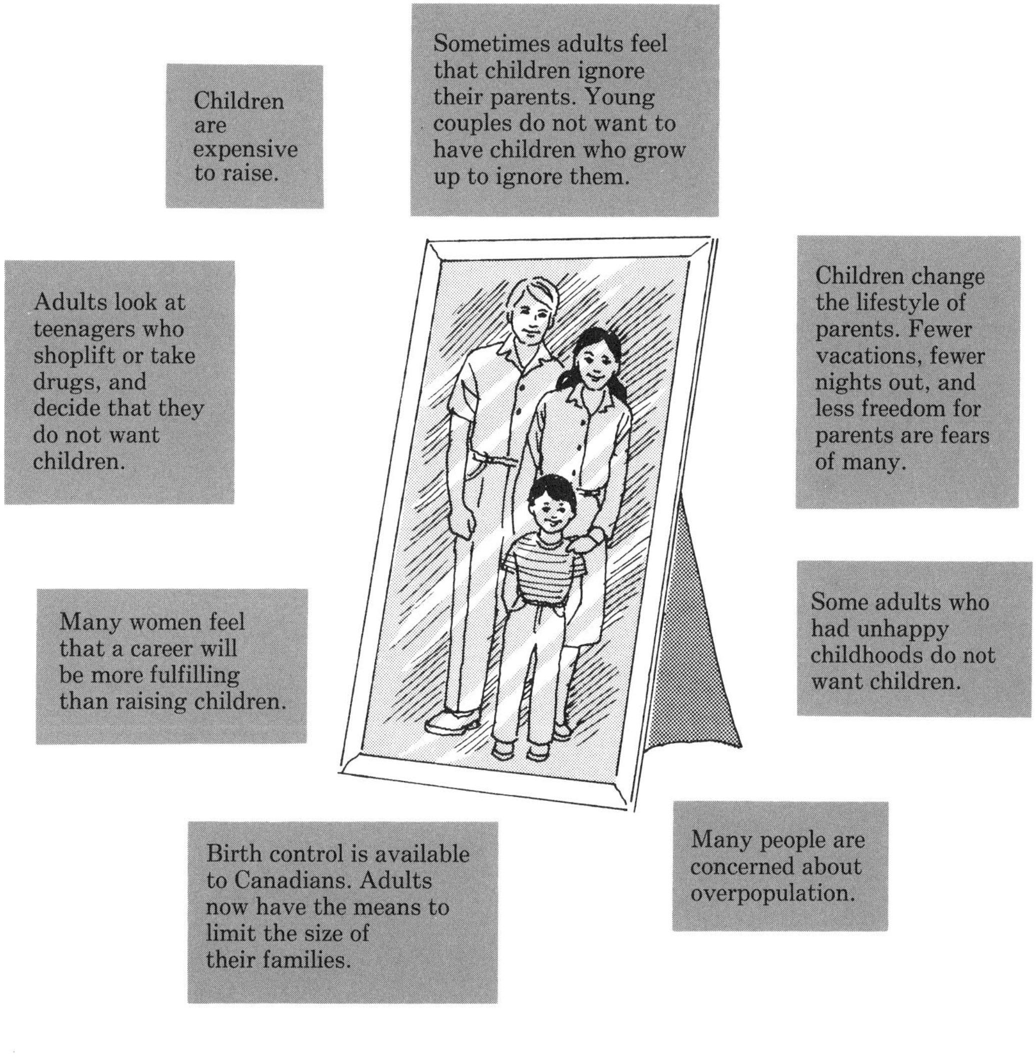

and by the year 2030 it will be 20%. As people grow older, they generally become more conservative and less open to change. In addition, people's needs change as they become elderly.

18. (a) In your local area, have you noticed any changes like the ones shown in Figure 11.9? List those that you have seen.
    (b) What will the pension plan problems mean to you when you go out to work?

Figure 11.9
Canada Will Change
As Its Population
Grows Older

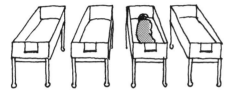

Some maternity wards will be closed.

Some schools will be closed.

Fewer baby products will be used.

More dental care and hospital wards for the aged will be needed.

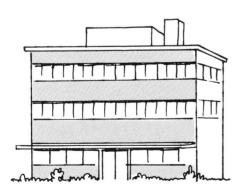

New senior citizens' homes will be built.

Problems will occur in our pension plan. In 1980, there were seven workers for every one pensioner. By 2003, there will be just over two workers for each pensioner.

(c) Think of the aging of Canada's population. What impact will this have on:
- advertisements on television
- government programs
- the age of people with whom you will work with
- the way in which people vote

Canada is similar to most other First World countries in its population trends. It appears that Canada will soon be faced with the problem of having too few people, not too many.

A Theory of Population Change (Demographic Transition)

The term **demographic transition** refers to changes in population growth. A theory has been developed to explain demographic transition (see Figure 11.10). In order to understand this theory, you should be familiar with several definitions. **Birth rate** is the number of live births per thousand population per year. **Death rate** refers to the number of deaths per thousand population per year. **Natural increase** is the difference between the birth rate and the death rate when the birth rate is higher. It is expressed as a rate per thousand population per year.

Example: India
Birth rate   42/1000 population per year
Death rate   21/1000 population per year

Natural increase   21/1000 population per year

This means that on the average, 42 babies are born and 21 people die for every thousand people now living in India. In one year, every group of 1000 people increases in size to 1021.

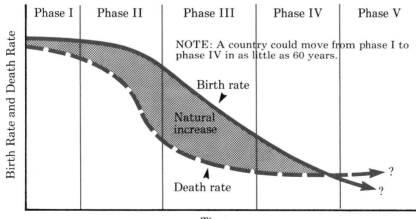

Figure 11.10
Changes in Population Growth (Demographic Transition)

The phases in Figure 11.10 refer to the following:

Phase I
- a traditional society
- high birth and death rates
- little natural increase
- people live for a short time only
- parents may have nine or ten children but only see two to three live to become adults
- parents may need larger families to help work farms, or to support them in old age
- e.g., parts of Africa today

Phase II
- rapid decrease in death rate, due to simple changes such as pit toilets, clean water supplies, or inoculation against diseases (measles, mumps, etc.)
- people still have large families, unsure of how many children will live to be adults
- great natural increase of population
- e.g., Mexico, Indonesia

Phase III
- birth rates begin to fall quickly as parents realize they cannot afford large families
- death rates still falling
- some birth control is available
- natural increase is shrinking
- e.g., China, India, Pakistan

Phase IV
- birth and death rates almost equal
- very little natural increase
- the more money parents have, the fewer children they have, so that they can keep their high standard of living
- e.g., Canada, United States

Phase V
- this phase may develop in certain countries
- the birth rate falls below the death rate and the population begins to shrink. This is called a **natural decrease**
- many older people
- e.g., West Germany

The countries of Western Europe have already passed through phases I to III and are in phase IV or V today.

19. If this theory of population change is correct for the countries of the world, what lies ahead for Mexico and China?

20. (a) What changes brought about the first drop in death rates?
    (b) Why would it be logical in phases I and II for parents to have a large number of babies?
    (c) What development would bring about changes in the thinking of the parents that you discussed in (b)?
    (d) Does it appear logical to enforce birth control in countries that are in phases II and III? Explain.

21. In what ways does this theory offer hope for people concerned about overpopulation? Explain your answer.

A Prediction Concerning the World's Population Growth

As you have seen, the rapid population growth in the world is beginning to slow down. Organizations such as the World Bank indicate that the world's population will stabilize within the next 100 years.

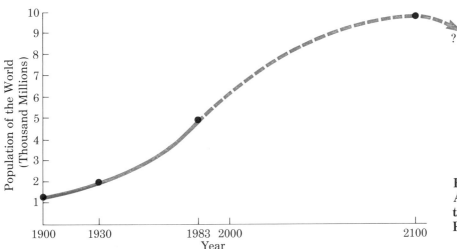

Figure 11.11
A Prediction of the World's Population

22. (a) Do Figure 11.10 and Figure 11.11 show the same thing?
    (b) If your answer to (a) is yes, where in Figure 11.10 does the prediction for the year 2100 occur?

The World at War

During the twentieth century, the world has never been completely at peace. In 1983, for example, one in every four countries was involved in a war of some kind.

Of course, some countries have never seen war in the twentieth

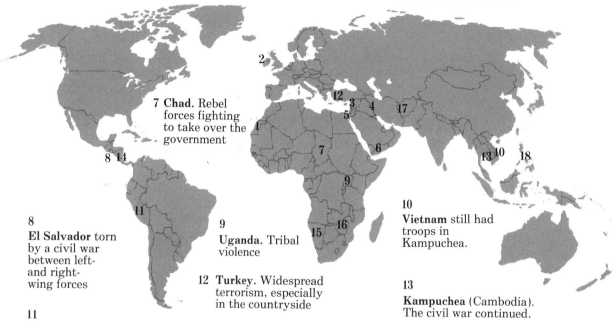

1

Western Sahara. Morocco involved in a war against Libya and Algeria over control of the Western Sahara

2 **Northern Ireland.** Violence and murder continued.

3 **Lebanon.** The civil war continued. Troops from Israel in Lebanon.

4 **Iraq** and **Iran** at war with each other

5 **Israel** experienced violence from time to time on the West Bank.

6 **South Yemen.** Civil war

7 **Chad.** Rebel forces fighting to take over the government

8

El Salvador torn by a civil war between left- and right-wing forces

9

Uganda. Tribal violence

10

Vietnam still had troops in Kampuchea.

11

Peru. The government engaged in a series of battles against communist rebels.

12 **Turkey.** Widespread terrorism, especially in the countryside

13

Kampuchea (Cambodia). The civil war continued.

14

Nicaragua. Guerrilla fighters trying to overthrow the government

15 **Namibia.** Guerrillas fighting South African troops for control of this country

16

Zimbabwe. Major conflicts in some outlying rural areas

17 **Afghanistan.** Troops from the U.S.S.R. constantly battling Moslem rebel forces who were trying to take back control of their country

18

Philippines. Guerrilla activity in mountains. Attempts to overthrow the government

**Figure 11.12
The World at
War in 1983.
Major conflicts
were in progress
on four
continents.**

century. However, the continual presence of local conflicts is a threat, in that these conflicts could spread to the rest of the world.

With nuclear weapons available, this threat is more serious than it once was. Some less powerful countries receive weapons from the U.S. and the U.S.S.R. If conflict between such countries spread, there would be greater danger of a major war than if the countries did not receive aid from these superpowers.

23. (a) Examine Figure 11.12. Which of the major conflicts shown there have you heard or read about?
    (b) Why do you think that you were not aware of the other conflicts that are taking place?
    (c) Which conflict is closest to Canada?

24. (a) Which area of the world appears to have the greatest number of conflicts?
    (b) What is the GNP per person for most countries in this area?
    (c) What human impact would there be on people living in a war zone?

Some of the countries of the world not directly involved in the wars of the world are indirectly involved, as they produce the arms used. Below is a table outlining the major arms exporters of the world.

COUNTRY	PERCENTAGE OF ALL ARMS EXPORTED IN THE WORLD
U.S.S.R.	44
United States	24
France	6
West Germany	4
United Kingdom	4
Czechoslovakia	4
Countries of Western Europe and Canada	4
Other countries of Europe	5
All others	5

25. Plot the information from this table on a bar graph. Label the bar graph fully and give it a suitable title.

26. Compare the bar graph of question 25 to the information in Figure 11.12. What does the bar graph show?

27. In your opinion, should Canada export arms to countries that might be at war? Explain.

28. What do Figure 11.12 and the table on arms exports show about the nature of people?

The Rich and the Poor

Most Canadians are aware of the great differences between their standard of living and that of many people in the Third World (Figure 11.13). It has been estimated that an average Canadian uses 50 times more energy than does someone in India. Consider also these facts:

- Over 100 million school-aged children in the world do not attend school.
- Nearly one-quarter of the world's population suffers from the lack of a proper diet.
- Many countries, such as Sri Lanka, are poorer today than they were in 1960.
- Thirty percent of the children born in the Third World die before the age of five from malnutrition and malnutrition-related diseases.

**Figure 11.13
A Home in the
Third World**

29. Design a poster to illustrate the differences between the Canadian way of life and that of most people in the Third World. Use the following guidelines.
   (a) Choose a theme or title for your poster.
   (b) Collect magazines and newspapers photos that relate to your theme.
   (c) Include some facts listed in this section or in other parts of the book. (Hint: Check the index at the back of the book for assistance in locating the facts that you need.)

Some people believe that the great gap between the rich and the poor in the world is the most serious of world problems. If these great differences are not eliminated, it is argued, a worldwide conflict could develop.

30. Compare this issue to the other issues discussed in this chapter. List them in order from the most important to the least important, in your view. Give reasons for your answers.

You and the Future

Many experts have been asked to predict the future for us. Predictions about and studies of the future are referred to as **futurology**. Institutes of futurology have been established. One such is the California Institute for the Future. Some of the predictions published in 1969 by this institute are summarized in Figure 11.14.

**Figure 11.14
Predictions
for the Year 1985
Made in 1969**

- Many machines will handle information.
- Information will also be stored in a few large machines at central locations.
- These new machines will be able to invade our privacy.
- Computer crime will be a problem.
- 300-km/h trains will be widely used.
- Non-polluting cars will be used.
- People will work on space stations that circle the earth.

- Transplants of organs (e.g., heart, kidneys) will be possible.
- Some artificial organs will be in use.
- "Banks" will store various organs for transplanting.
- There will be methods to immunize (protect) people against most diseases caused by bacteria and viruses.
- Personality changes will be possible through drugs. These will be used to control animals and to help the mentally ill.

31. (a) Discuss the items mentioned Figure 11.14 in a group of three or four other students.
    (b) Which of the changes do you consider to be beneficial? Give reasons for your answer.
    (c) Which of the changes do you think have caused problems?

**Figure 11.15
Predictions for
the Year 2025
Made in 1969**

- Intelligence will be improved by chemicals.
- It will be possible for the brain to be "plugged in" to a computer.
- Electricity will be transmitted without the use of wires.
- Cars will float over magnetic highways.

- Babies will be gestated outside the body. Parents will be able to choose the sex of their baby.
- New technology will allow doctors to stimulate the growth of new organs, arms, and legs.
- Life expectancy for people will be increased by 50 years through the use of chemicals.

32. (a) How old will you be in the year 2025?
    (b) Assume that all the predictions in Figure 11.15 come true. How will your life be different from that of a person who is now as old as you will be in the year 2025?

33. (a) Evaluate your predicted lifestyle for the year 2025. What will you like about your lifestyle? Give reasons for your answers.
    (b) What will you dislike about that lifestyle?

These are only a few of the predictions that have been made about the future. It is important not only to be familiar with predictions concerning the future of the world but also to develop goals for your own future.

34. Think ahead 20 years. What would you like your life to be like then? Consider the following factors:
    - job
    - type of home
    - family
    - hobbies
    - where you will live (province, city, etc.)
    - type of holidays that you will take
    - amount of education that you will have

35. Consider once again the issues that have been discussed in this chapter. What other issues of major importance to the world or to Canada can you think of? Briefly outline the nature of each one of those issues and explain its importance to the world and to you.

VOCABULARY

birth rate	natural decrease	peace movement
death rate	natural increase	sunrise industry
doubling time	overkill	sunset industry
futurology	overpopulation	

RESEARCH QUESTIONS

1. Use books, magazines, and newspapers in your library for assistance in answering this question.
   (a) Locate news items on three different events that relate to nuclear weapons or to the possibility of war. These events could have taken place at any time recently.
   (b) For each event identify
   - what was said or done
   - who said it or did it
   - the importance of the event
   (c) Write 200 words on the significance and meaning of all the events considered together.

2. Select four books in your library that focus on the way of life in Canada or the United States 40 years ago or more.
   (a) Choose one period of time for study (e.g., the 1920s/1930s).
   (b) Describe the way of life during that period. Focus your description on these items:
   - appearance of cities
   - types of jobs available to women and men
   - clothing styles
   - types of transportation
   - education available to women and men
   (c) In what ways has life changed since that time?

3. From your library obtain ten issues of a news magazine or one week's issues of a major daily newspaper. Search through the magazines or newspapers to find three items on different wars

or armed conflicts. Answer the following questions for each.

(a) In which countries are conflicts or wars taking place?

(b) Outline the major events described.

(c) Are other countries likely to be involved? If so, which ones?

(d) What impact does the conflict have on the people of the area and their lives?

4. Select several books or magazines on the U.S. space program. (Hint: Look for NASA in your library's card catalogue.)

(a) Outline the key details of the rockets involved in the program.

(b) What are the goals of the program?

(c) In your opinion, does the U.S. space program offer hope for our future? Explain your answer.

Glossary

Term	Meaning	Example
adherent	Someone who adheres to or supports—a religion, for example	The majority of people in Canada are adherents of Christianity.
aesthetic	Relating to beauty or general attractiveness	A drive along the Banff-Jasper highway in the Rocky Mountains is an aesthetically pleasing experience.
affluence	Material wealth of a person or a nation	Many Canadians enjoy great affluence.
algae	Plants that grow in water and look like slime when grouped together. As they decay, they deprive fish and other water plants of oxygen	Algae will grow quickly in water that contains high levels of human sewage.
alienation	The feeling of isolation or detachment from an activity or group of people	People sometimes feel alienation when they immigrate to a new country.
allergy	A negative reaction a person has to a certain substance	Thousands of Canadians suffer from "hay fever", which is an allergy to plants such as ragweed.
alluvial deposits	Layers of fine soil particles that settle on the beds of rivers or other bodies of water	Part of the city of Vancouver is built on alluvial deposits.
apartheid	A policy of racial separation in South Africa	On the African continent, the apartheid policy is unique to South Africa.
assembly line	Construction of a product by many people as the product moves along a track or conveyer belt	See Figure 3.14.
baby boom	The period between 1946 and 1961, when a great number of babies was born in North America and Europe	Those people born during the baby boom form the largest single age group in the Canadian market.
bilingual	Describes a person who speaks two languages or a country in which two languages are spoken	Canada is an officially bilingual country.

Term	Meaning	Example
birth rate	The number of live births per 1000 population per year	West Germany has one of the lowest birth rates of any country in the world.
black market	A system in which consumer goods are bought and sold illegally	Some people in the Soviet Union have purchased expensive stereos and videotape recorders on the black market.
botulism	A deadly form of food poisoning	Botulism is still a serious health problem in some countries of Africa.
bourgeoisie	A term used by Karl Marx to describe the class that dominates a society economically (from the French word bourgeoisie meaning "middle class")	According to Marx, the bourgeoisie gains profits at the expense of the workers.
break-of-bulk point	A city where freight is transferred from one form of transportation to another	Montreal, Vancouver, Churchill, and Halifax are all break-of-bulk points in Canada.
Buddhism	A religion based on the philosophy of Gautama Buddha, a fifth-century Hindu teacher; it focusses on three things: knowledge of oneself, meditation, and pure thoughts	Buddhism has spread across Asia to Japan since the time of Buddha.
bureaucracy	A work force employed by a government or corporation to run its programs	Large corporations such as General Motors have large bureaucracies to run their company
capital	Money used to invest in or build something	Banks lend capital to companies that want to build new factories.
carcinogen	A cancer-causing agent	The tars in cigarettes are suspected by medical researchers to be carcinogens.
Caricom	An economic and trading organization that includes many countries in the Caribbean area	Jamaica has been an important member of Caricom for a number of years.
cartel	An organization that controls the amount of production of an item and its price	One major cartel in the world is OPEC.

TERM	MEANING	EXAMPLE
caste system	A class system in India that is based on Hindu beliefs	The caste system developed over many centuries in India.
cellular radio	A modern mobile telephone system for cities in which each city is divided up into cells or districts, each with its own transmitter and receiver for telephone calls	See Figure 8.25.
censor	To restrict the information given to a person or group of people	The government censors the news that is broadcast in Hungary.
Christianity	A religion that developed out of Judaism; it is based on the teachings of Jesus Christ	Christianity has over one thousand million adherents in the world.
co-generation	The use of waste heat from industry for other purposes	Co-generation has become particularly common in West Germany because it saves industries money.
cold war	Hostility and sharp conflict in diplomacy, economics, etc., between states, without actual warfare	The Cold War between the U.S. and the U.S.S.R. almost became a full-scale world war several times.
collage	A grouping of pictures or other objects, pasted on a sheet of paper or bristol board, etc.	Some students decorate their classrooms with collages of scenes from around the world.
commodity	A good that is produced for sale	Wheat is one of Canada's main commodities.
COMECON	The Council for Mutual Economic Assistance: an economic organization of Communist countries	The Soviet Union has used COMECON to support its aims.
commercial radio station	A radio station that is operated for profit	Every major city in Canada has at least one commercial radio station.
commuter train	A train that carries people to and from work each day	Many commuter trains take people to and from work in London, England.

Term	Meaning	Example
conservation	The responsible use of a resource, such as energy	Most Canadians have reduced their home heating bills through conservation of energy.
conserver society	A society in which the standard of living is increased through the responsible use of resources	A conserver society recycles many of the goods that it uses.
consumer goods	Products for the personal use, such as radios and televisions	Most people in the Soviet Union have few opportunities to spend money on consumer goods.
consumer price index (CPI)	A measure that indicates the cost of living in a country	When oil prices go up, so does the consumer price index.
consumer society	A society in which the main standard of living is increased with little consideration of the wise use of resources	North America has built a strong consumer society.
contaminate	To pollute or infect, or poison (soil, water, food, etc.)	Industrial wastes have contaminated the Rhine River.
co-operative	Organizations owned by a group of people who share the profits	Co-operatives have become popular in certain parts of Africa.
cottage industry	Small-scale manufacturing in private homes	The spinning wheel was an important tool in the early Canadian cottage industry of textile manufacturing.
cross-breeding	Development of a new plant or animal from breeding two other plants or animals together	Wheat varieties have been cross-bred to produce a wheat strain that will grow well on the Canadian Prairies.
cultural baggage	The culture that immigrants bring with them to a new land	Folk traditions are part of the cultural baggage that Ukrainians brought with them to Canada.
cultural diffusion	The spreading of culture or ideas from one person to another	The spread of the French language is a good example of cultural diffusion.
culture	The way of life of a group of people	There are a wide variety of cultures in India.
culture hearth	Centre in which important aspects of culture were first developed	North America contains no culture hearth.

TERM	MEANING	EXAMPLE
culture realm	A large area throughout which the way of life is much the same	The influence of the North American culture realm extends around the world.
culture shock	The discomfort that affects a person or group when faced with people who have a different way of life	Most Canadians would experience culture shock if they went to live in a village in Indonesia.
death rate	The number of deaths per thousand population per year	Ethiopia has a high death rate.
deforestation	The cutting down of forests on a large scale	Deforestation of the Himalaya Mountains of northern India has led to serious soil erosion.
dehydration	Loss of water from the body	Dehydration is a frequent cause of death for children with diarrhea.
demographic transition	A theory developed to explain changes in population growth rates over time	A country's demographic transition can be determined by examining the number of births and deaths per thousand population during a certain time period.
dense	Compact or crowded (with particular reference to population in this text)	New York City is an area of dense population.
deported	Forced to leave a country	Sometimes people are deported from Canada because they have entered the country illegally.
desert	An area with little vegetation that has average annual precipitation under 250 mm	The Sahara is referred to as a hot desert, while parts of the Arctic are cold desert regions.
desertification	The spread of the deserts	Much of the Middle East is seriously affected by desertification.
dialect	A slightly different form of a language, usually spoken in a specific area	Many different dialects of English are spoken in England.

Term	Meaning	Example
dike	A wall built to prevent water from flooding low land	Although they are expensive, dikes have saved the Netherlands from many disastrous floods.
domestication of animals	The taming of animals for use by humans	The domestication of animals has allowed people to use them to carry heavy loads.
domestication of plants. *See* plant farming		
doubling time	The number of years necessary for something to double in size or quantity	The doubling time for the earth's population today is nearly 35 years.
economy of scale	Occurs when a large number of items can be produced quickly and the price per item therefore is reduced	Economies of scale have allowed the price of an automobile to decrease to the point that most Canadian families can afford to buy one.
eradicate	eliminate	Very few diseases in the world have been eradicated.
European Common Market. *See* European Economic Community		
European Economic Community (EEC)	An economic organization of ten European, non-Communist countries	The EEC competes with the United States in the manufacture and sale of many products.
exile	Being forced to live away from the country that a person regards as home	Living as an exile can be very discouraging for a refugee, who may have no money or job.
exploit, (exploitation)	To make use of a substance or a person for one's own purposes	Canada has been built on the exploitation of its forests, fish, and minerals. In the early Industrial Revolution, many factory owners became rich by exploiting their workers.

TERM	MEANING	EXAMPLE
fibre optics	A system of communication whereby a message is sent by a light beam along a thin glass strand	As more fibre-optics systems are built, their cost will decrease.
First World	Those countries that combine wealth with the most advanced levels of technology in the world, generally with liberal-democratic governments	Much of the international business carried on in the world involves countries of the First World.
Five-Year Plan	A plan in which goals are set for production and economic achievements over the five years to come	Five-Year Plans are used by many Communist countries in an attempt to organize their economies.
flash floods	Severe floods that result from sudden, heavy rainstorms	Flash floods in Las Vegas, Nevada, have sometimes carried cars out of parking lots into the middle of streets.
food surplus	Occurs when farmers produce more than enough food for themselves, and so can make food available to people who do not farm	The first food surpluses represented a major turning point in human history because they allowed the first towns and cities to develop.
forced migration	Occurs when people are forced to move to a new area to live	The slaves who were taken from Africa to Brazil were part of a large forced migration to the Americas.
fossil fuels	Sources of energy derived from the decay of plants and animals that also formed fossils in rock thousands of years ago. Most fossil fuels were formed under water	Oil and natural gas are the fossil fuels used to heat most Canadian homes.
free trade	Occurs when the trade among countries is carried out without tariffs	Free trade between Canada and the U.S.A. is the subject of much debate.
futurology	Predictions about and studies of the future	World conferences on futurology bring experts together who see both hope and doom for the future.

TERM	MEANING	EXAMPLE
GATT	General Agreement on Tariffs and Trade regulates the tariffs and trade for most of the international trading in the world.	GATT laid the groundwork for a great period of expansion of international trade by encouraging the decrease of tariffs.
geologist	Someone who studies rocks and rock formations	Geologists study rock samples to determine where a mine should be established.
ghetto	Area of a city occupied mostly by a minority group, sometimes isolated from the rest of the city	Few people from other parts of the city knew the way of life of people who lived in the ghetto.
Great Depression	The period from October 1929 until World War II, when there was a low level of economic activity and much unemployment	During the Great Depression, unemployed men rode across Canada on top of railway cars, hoping to find work.
gross national product (GNP) per capita	The average monetary value of goods and services produced in a country by each person in one year	The Comoro Islands near Africa have one of the lowest GNPs per capita of any country in the world.
hand-to-mouth existence	A way of life in which people have to eat food as soon as they obtain it	Even today there are groups of people who live a hand-to-mouth existence.
hazardous wastes	Waste products from industry, homes, and nuclear plants that are dangerous to people, plants, or animals	One hundred years ago, there were very few hazardous wastes in Canada compared with those that exist today.
hierarchy	A "vertical" ranking by size or importance	Paris is at the top of the urban hierarchy in France.
Hinduism	A major religion in India, one of whose tenets is reincarnation	Hinduism is one of the oldest religions in the world.
hunting and gathering	A method of obtaining food that involves hunting for animals and gathering vegetation	Very few Canadians are familiar with hunting and gathering as a way of life.
incentive	Something that encourages an activity	Interest-free loans are given to industries as an incentive to locate in certain areas.

Term	Meaning	Example
industrial linkage	The economic bonds among companies; for example, one company sells a product to another company, and the second company uses the product to manufacture another product	One important industrial linkage is the sale of steel to the car industry.
industrialization	Involves the widespread use of machines to perform work for people	The benefits of industrialization still have not reached many people in the world.
inflation	Increase in the money supply of a country, shown by rising prices and decreased purchasing power of the currency	Inflation is a particularly serious problem in much of South America.
information explosion	The rapid increase in knowledge and its communication in the world	The information explosion has resulted from technology that allows for increased instant communication.
inhospitable	Providing little shelter or sustenance	The Arctic is an inhospitable region of Canada.
interbreeding	Occurs when two people from different races have children	Interbreeding has helped to eliminate racial boundaries in Brazil.
internal migration	The movement of people from one area to another within a country	In Nigeria, there has been an important internal migration to the coast.
inversion	A weather condition in which cold (polluted) air is trapped below warm air	See Figure 9.12.
irrigation	The artificial watering of plants or trees, usually in order to increase crop yields	Irrigation allows farming to take place in southern California during the long, hot summers.
Islam	A religion based on the teachings of the prophet Mohammed	Mecca, in Saudi Arabia, is the holy city of Islam.
Judaism	The religion of the Jews, whose beliefs are contained in the five books of Moses and other writings	The spiritual centre of Judaism is the city of Jerusalem in Israel.

TERM	MEANING	EXAMPLE
language	The means by which people communicate with one another, using words	A young child usually begins to learn to speak a language at about the age of one.
language family	A group of languages that are similar	The languages spoken in Norway, Sweden, and Denmark belong to the same language family.
large scale	A large-scale map shows much detail of a small area.	A road map that shows an area of 2 km × 2 km is large-scale map.
leach	The dissolving and washing away of minerals from the soil	In some cases, the cutting down of forests in Brazil has left behind soil that is leached and soon becomes useless for farming.
leisure	Free time a person has that is not committed to work or school	Playing computer games is a popular way for some people to spend their leisure time.
lifestyle	The various activities that fill a person's time	A person's lifestyle is affected by his or her beliefs and wealth, among other things.
limited-access highway	A highway with at least four lanes which traffic can enter only at certain interchanges	
literacy	The skill of reading and writing	Literacy is important in helping people to learn.
literate	Able to use language in a written form	The Inca Empire of South America was not a literate one.
manufacturing	The process of producing consumer goods from the products of primary industries	Automobile manufacturing is one of the most important industries in Canada.
markets	Buyers; or the area in which a large number of buyers are found	New York City is a key market for manufacturers in North America.

TERM	MEANING	EXAMPLE
marshalling yard	An area of railway tracks where freight cars are organized to form trains	See Figure 6.5.
mass media (singular: mass medium)	The various means (such as television, radio, and newspapers) of transmitting information to a large number of people	Television and newspapers are mass media that have become an important part of life in Brazil.
mass production	The manufacturing of items in vast quantities, often using an assembly line and many workers, usually in a factory	Mass production provides a wide variety of consumer goods, from dolls to toasters.
mass society	An urbanized society with a dense population	The problems of living in a mass society can include loneliness and alienation.
megalopolis	A very large city formed when two or more cities grow outward and merge with each other	The first megalopolis in the world extended from Boston to New York to Washington.
midden	A pile of garbage or unused food left by people in early human settlements	By digging into a midden we can discover, through analysis of traces, what early people ate.
migration	A movement from one place to another	Early people migrated to new areas by following animal herds.
Minamata disease	Poisoning from a chemical called methyl mercury	Minamata disease usually affects people who eat fish contaminated by mercury.
monolingual	Describes a person who speaks only one language or a country in which only one language is usually spoken	A monolingual person may be at a disadvantage when travelling abroad.
moral values	Attitudes people have about what is right and what is wrong	An important moral value for conservationists is the preservation of the natural environment.
multifunctional	Having many functions; for a city, having many economic functions	London, England, is a multifunctional city since it includes governmental, transportational, financial, and commercial activities.

Term	Meaning	Example
multilingual	Describes a person who speaks more than two languages or a country in which more than two languages are spoken	Switzerland is a multilingual country in which four major languages are spoken.
multinational corporation	A company that has its head office in one country and a number of branches in other countries	Coca-Cola is a multinational corporation, with its head office in the U.S.A.
nationalism	Feelings of pride in one's country and unwillingness to allow outside influences to control the country's industry and culture	Nationalism has become a strong force in Pakistan in recent years.
natural decrease	The difference between the birth and death rates, when the death rate is higher	If the birth rate in a country is 15/1000 and the death rate is 17/1000, then the natural decrease is 2/1000.
natural increase	The difference between the birth and death rates, when the birth rate is higher	If the birth rate in a country is 47/1000 and the death rate is 25/1000, then the natural increase is 22/1000.
natural resource	A naturally formed material such as water, iron, timber, and minerals	Gold and diamonds are among the most important natural resources of South Africa.
natural selection	A process that evolutionists consider to take place by which living things that adapt to an environment survive, and those that do not adapt, do not survive	Natural selection has been proposed by some scientists as an explanation for the development of different human races.
network	A system of transmitting stations. Signals are sent along the air waves from one station to another, then retransmitted to the next station in the network, and so on	The CBC Radio Network transmits from coast to coast in Canada.
nomadic	A way of life in which people move from place to place, usually in search of food	A nomadic way of life is practised by the Bedouin Arabs and the Lapplanders, among others.
nomadic herders	People who depend on their animals for food and clothing and who follow their herds as they move to better pasture	The Tuaregs are a tribe of nomadic herders in the southern Sahara Desert.

Term	Meaning	Example
non-renewable resources	Resources that cannot be replenished once they have been used (e.g., oil and natural gas)	When we throw aluminum cans into the garbage, we waste a non-renewable resource.
OPEC	The Organization of Petroleum Exporting Countries	Some members of OPEC such as Kuwait have great wealth due to their extensive petroleum resources.
overkill	The capability of the world's nuclear weapons to kill many more people than actually live on this earth	At present, the overkill of the world's nuclear weapons is 20 to 40 times.
overpopulation	Occurs when there are too many people in an area to allow an adequate standard of living	Many people believe that India suffers from overpopulation.
package deal	A travel arrangement where a tour operator organizes details such as airplane travel and hotel accommodation	Many tourists travel to the Caribbean on package deals.
particulate matter	Tiny solid and liquid particles that stay suspended in the air	Inhaling particulate matter may cause coughing spells.
peace movement	A large group of people who want all nuclear weapons eliminated as a step toward peace	The peace movement has had a great influence on countries of the First World.
peasants	Poor farmers (usually not landowners) or farm labourers	Most of the one thousand million people in China are peasants.
petrochemical industry	An industry that involves refining petroleum to produce products such as gasoline, plastic, and jet fuel	The petrochemical industry is the source of plastic for the food-packaging industry.
pH scale	A scale used to measure the proportion of acid in water	Normal rain has a pH of 5.6.
photochemical fog	Occurs when the sun acts on air pollution such as automobile exhaust	In São Paulo, Brazil, the photochemical fog can turn a blue sky brown.

TERM	MEANING	EXAMPLE
pie graph	A circular diagram in which the "slices of the pie" represent the portions that are part of the whole	The World
piggyback	A form of transportation in which truck trailers are carried on the flat cars of trains	Truck trailer / Flatbed railcar →
plant farming	Involves the deliberate setting out of plants or seeds in the soil to be grown under human care	Plant farming changed the course of human history by increasing the ease with which food could be obtained.
plume	A volume of polluted ground water that moves and comes to a point somewhere underground	The plume of polluted ground water points in the direction in which that water is moving.
polder	Areas of reclaimed sea floor	The polders of the Netherlands are flat and fertile.
police state	A country in which the police and army are commonly used to control people opposed to the government	Vietnam is now a police state.
precipitator	A machine that removes many of the pollutants from smoke before it is released into the air	Precipitators prevent much dirt from entering the air and landing on cars and houses near large factories.
preventive maintenance	Maintenance (especially of roads) on a continuous basis to prevent major problems in the future	In New York City, little preventive maintenance of streets was done in the 1970s. The result has been that some important roads can no longer be used.

TERM	MEANING	EXAMPLE
priest-king	The political-religious leader of an early urban centre. Food and other supplies were often brought to this leader for redistribution throughout the settlement	The early priest-kings were the most powerful people in their societies.
primary industry	The removal of raw materials from the land or water. (Agriculture is a primary industry.)	The first primary industry in Newfoundland was fishing.
primary manufacturing	Is the first stage in manufacturing: processing raw materials (e.g., steel making)	Steel making has been an important primary manufacturing industry in Western Europe.
productivity	The number or value of goods that one worker produces in a certain period of time	If a worker can produce 40 hats per hour rather than 20, his or her productivity has doubled.
profit motive	The interest of a person or company in the amount of profit that can be made from an industry	The profit motive encourages industry to introduce new machines to manufacture their products.
profit sharing	A program whereby employees share in the profits of a company, possibly through owning shares	Profit sharing usually encourages employees to work harder, because they will share in the profits.
proletariat	The working class	According to Marx, the proletariat was exploited because it had to sell its labour to the ruling class.
protectionism	The policy whereby a country may impose high tariffs on goods imported from another country	When protectionism has been adopted by a number of countries around the world, it has often led to serious economic problems.
pull factor	Something that attracts, e.g., a person to a new country, or an industry to a new location	The freedom that Canadians enjoy has been a valuable pull factor for immigrants.
push factor	Something that encourages a person or an industry to leave a country or an area	Poverty was a strong push factor in Europe after World War II.
race	A large group of people who have physical characteristics in common, such as skin colour or hair type	The black race probably had its origin in central Africa.

TERM	MEANING	EXAMPLE
racism (racist)	Prejudice against someone on the basis of race; a person who is prejudiced in this way is called a racist	Racism is sometimes caused by ungrounded fear on the part of the racist.
refugee	Someone who has been forced to leave his or her home for safety or survival, especially in time of war	The wars in Southeast Asia led many refugees to flee to safety.
reincarnation	The belief that a person or animal will be reborn as another person or animal after death	Reincarnation is an important tenet (belief) of the Hindu religion.
religion	Usually involves: 1. a set of beliefs 2. rituals 3. literature and organization	A person's religion affects his or her thoughts and actions.
renewable resources	Resources that can be replenished once they have been used (e.g., fish, forests)	Renewable resources must be managed wisely if they are to be of value for hundreds of years.
resources	Something that people use for their benefit	Human abilities are a valuable resource for any country.
rituals	Activities that people carry out to demonstrate their beliefs	For many Christians, a church service is an important ritual.
root agriculture	The planting of fleshy roots or tubers in the ground which grow into new plants for food	The growing of potatoes, carrots, and parsnips is one example of modern root agriculture.
rotation (of crops)	The planting of a different crop in each of a number of fields, over a set period of time	In three-year rotation, corn may be planted one year, hay the second year, and wheat the third year.
rush hours	Hours in the morning and late afternoon when most people are travelling to and from work and transportation routes are crowded	Students are employed in Tokyo, Japan, during rush hours to physically push people into crowded subway cars.
sanitary landfill	A method of garbage disposal in which the refuse is laid down in layers that alternate with layers of soil	Sanitary landfill sites near large Canadian cities are being filled up quickly with the garbage from the cities.

Term	Meaning	Example
scientific management	Management based on scientific principles, to increase productivity	The assembly line was an early development in scientific management of the workplace.
Second World	Communist countries with a one-party system of government and state ownership of most aspects of the economy	China became a Second World country under the leadership of Mao Tse-tung.
secondary industry	The production of items by using the raw materials provided by primary industry (also called *manufacturing*)	An important secondary industry in Richmond, Virginia, is cigarette manufacturing.
secondary manufacturing	Is the second stage of manufacturing: processing the products of primary manufacturing to make more complex items, such as cars	Windsor, Ontario, depends largely on secondary manufacturing to provide jobs and revenue.
sedentary lifestyle	A lifestyle in which people do not have to move or travel to a great extent in order to obtain food	Most Canadians have a sedentary lifestyle.
seed agriculture	The planting of seeds in the ground to develop into a food crop, under human care	Crop yields from seed agriculture are often improved by the wise use of irrigation.
semidesert	An area where the average annual precipitation is between 250 mm and 500 mm	Along the southern edge of the Sahara Desert in Africa is an area of semidesert called the Sahel.
shanty town	An area of poor housing (outside or within a city) that has few of the modern services such as clean water and sewage disposal	Many major cities in the Third World have shanty towns.
site	The physical qualities of the area in which a city is located (e.g., hills, a harbour, or a river)	Cairo, Egypt, is located on the Nile River but is expanding into the desert area around it, making its site a very difficult one for the supply of water.
situation	The location of a city relative to other cities, and countries, natural resources, transportation routes, etc.	Singapore has an excellent situation for trade and is considered to be a crossroads of Asia.

TERM	MEANING	EXAMPLE
slave	A person who is the legal possesion of someone else, and must do what he or she is told to do (for no pay)	The slaves of ancient Rome did many jobs that machines do for us today.
slaver	Someone who bought slaves, transported them to a new area, and sold them for profit	A slaver had to watch closely for any signs of a slave rebellion.
socialism	An economic system whereby the community as a whole (or the government) owns the means of production and controls the economy, but in which personal freedoms are respected	For many Third World countries, such as Tanzania, socialism has proven to be very expensive.
soil erosion	The loss of soil resulting from the action of wind, moving ice, or water	Soil erosion is a serious problem in southern California during the winter rains.
sparse	Thinly scattered	The continent of Antarctica has a very sparse population.
stagflation	Occurs when a country experiences a stagnant economy with high employment and a high rate of inflation	Stagflation is a problem that is not easily overcome, even in the First World.
still birth	The birth of a dead baby	Modern medicine has reduced the occurrence of still births.
strike	The withdrawal of labour by a group of workers until a demand has been met by management	The demands of workers who go on strike are not always met.
sunrise industry	An industry that is rapidly growing in importance	The computer electronics industry is a sunrise industry.
sunset industry	An industry that is shrinking in importance relative to other industries and relative to its former role	The automobile and steel industries are often given as examples of sunset industries.
superpower	Refers to the U.S. and the U.S.S.R., which are the most influential and powerful countries in the world	The conflict of the superpowers has brought the world to the edge of war several times.

Term	Meaning	Example
supertanker	A large ship that carries a liquid cargo (usually oil)	Supertankers are usually as long as several football fields laid out end to end.
tailings	Solid waste products produced from mining	The tailings of uranium mining operations contain radioactive material.
tariffs	Taxes placed on imported goods	Canadian tariffs on imported Japanese cars have made these cars more expensive for Canadian buyers.
technology	Devices developed from people's application of their knowledge, skills, or resources, and used for some practical purpose	The bow and arrow used in hunting animals represent a low level of technology.
terracing	Building steps into the side of a mountain to allow for farming or the building of a home	Terracing is commonly used in Indonesia to permit rice farming.
tertiary industry	An industry that sells goods or provides services to people	The sale of clothing is an important tertiary industry in Paris, France.
textile	Cloth	The textile industry in Taiwan exports a large quantity of goods to the United States.
theme park	An entertainment park with rides and activities developed around a theme or central idea	Disneyland in Anaheim, California, was the first major theme park in the world, with film producer Walt Disney's cartoon characters providing the theme.
thermal pollution	An increase in the temperature of a body of water as a result of large volumes of hot or warm water being emptied into it.	Thermal pollution kills off certain species of fish and plant life in bodies of water.
Third World	Countries that do not have the technology to develop their economies fully. Some are therefore very poor; in others, one aspect of the economy brings in substantial revenue	Third World countries contain most of the people of the world.

TERM	MEANING	EXAMPLE
trade union	An organization that represents workers in dealing with their company's management	The United Auto Workers (UAW) is the largest trade union for workers in the automobile industry in Canada.
trade war	Occurs when a country enters into economic conflicts with other countries by increasing tariffs and thus decreasing or preventing the import of goods	In order to prevent a trade war, there must be co-operation and compromise between countries.
trading partners	The countries or other political groups with which a country or other political group trades	China is an important trading partner of Hong Kong.
two-way television	A system that connects a television studio by cable to a large number of homes with televisions. People in each home can send a message to the studio along the cable	See Figure 8.21.
underemployed	Refers to someone who is working at a job that requires less skill and ability than that person has	If a person who has a university degree works at a manual job, he or she is considered to be underemployed.
United Empire Loyalists	People who lived in the United States in the late 1700s but remained loyal to a united British Empire, and as a result, moved to Canada around the time of the American Revolution	United Empire Loyalists were proud of their British traditions.
untouchable	Someone who is outside the Hindu caste system in India	The untouchables often have the least desirable jobs.
urban	Used to describe a built-up area, such as a city or town	Most Canadians live in urban areas.
urbanization	A process whereby people move from the countryside to the cities, causing the cities to expand	The rate of urbanization has decreased in Canada and the United States since 1970.
Utopia	A perfect place in which to live, generally imaginary	Early settlers who came to the United States dreamed of setting up their own Utopia.

TERM	MEANING	EXAMPLE
voluntary migration	The large-scale movement of people to live in a new area as a result of a free decision that they made	Most people who moved to the U.S. did so freely, and were thus voluntary migrants.
water table	The point below which the soil is saturated with water	After long periods of drought, the water table drops.
welfare state	A country that has many government programs to ensure that everyone's basic needs are met	Many countries of Western Europe are welfare states.
World Bank	An organization set up to lend money to countries that cannot borrow from private banks	The World Bank's loans have made possible considerable progress in the Third World.
yield	Amount produced; in agriculture, the amount of food per hectare	The use of fertilizer on some Mexican farms has increased the yield of corn threefold.

Index

Credits and Sources

All photographs not specifically credited to another source are courtesy of the authors.

Cover Photo: Hong Kong Harbour: © Masterfile/ Sherman Hines

Section I Opener: EEC headquarters: Belgian Institute for Information and Documentation; Cliff village: UNESCO/Labordère; Floating island: UNESCO/B. Herzog; Stonehenge: B.A. Fretton;

CHAPTER 1

Photos: Figure 1.1: NASA; Figure 1.16: (left) Toronto General Hospital; (right) World Health Organization/ D. Henrioud; Figure 1.24: World Health Organization/ D. Henrioud; Figure 1.38(c): UNESCO/© J. P. Villot

Photos: Figures 1.15, 1.42: Based on statistics obtained from the Publications Board of the United Nations; Figure 1.17: The World Bank, *World Development Report, 1982* (New York: Oxford University Press). Reprinted with permission of the World Bank; Table entitled "Sources of Sulphur Dioxide and Nitrogen Oxides in North America" based on information obtained from the Pollution Probe Foundation

Section II Opener: Tractor: Massey-Ferguson Limited; Pipeline and Oil drilling: Government of Saskatchewan; Supertanker: Imperial Oil Limited

CHAPTER 2

Photos: Figure 2.4: R.C. Haskett; Figure 2.13: Australian Information Service/Dr. Kamminga

General Illustration: Figure 2.6: Based on statistics obtained from Statistics Canada

CHAPTER 3

Photos: Figure 3.10: Coca-Cola Ltd.; Figure 3.13: Historical Society of Western Pennsylvania; Figure 3.15: Ford of Canada Archives; Figure 3.16: Public Archives Canada C 29461; Figures 3.24, 3.25: Matsushita Electric; Figure 3.27: Ford of Canada; Figure 3.28: IBM

General Illustrations: Figure 3.4: *Abstract of the British Historical Statistics U.K., 1971;* Figure 3.9: Based on statistics obtained from the U.S. Department of Commerce, and B.R. Mitchell, *Facts on File,* 2nd edition, "European Historical Statistics 1750-1975; Figure 3.22: Based on information obtained from the United Nations and the Japanese Trade Centre; Figure 3.26: Based on information from Matsushita Electric; Figures 3.29, 3.30: Based on statistics obtained from OECD, Paris, France

CHAPTER 4

Photos: Figure 4.1: U.S.S.R. Embassy, Canada; Figure 4.12: R. Cheun; Figure 4.16(a): Roger Fredman; Figure 4.20: Belgian Institute for Information and Documentation

Cartoon Idea: Daniel Liebster

General Illustrations: Figure 4.2: Based on statistics obtained from *Keesings Contemporary Archives* (26 March 1976), p. 27641, and John L. Sherer (ed.), *U.S.S.R. Facts and Figures Annual,* 8, 1984; Figures 4.7, 4.9, 4.13, 4.17, 4.25: Based on statistics obtained from the Publications Board of the United Nations; Figure 4.19: World Bank, *World Development Report 1982* (New York: Oxford University Press). Reprinted with permission of the World Bank; Figures 4.22, 4.23: Based on information obtained from the U.S. Department of Energy

CHAPTER 5

Photos: Figure 5.19: Massey-Ferguson Limited

Cartoon Idea: Daniel Liebster

General Illustrations: Figures 5.2, 5.3: Based on statistics from various editions of *Canada Yearbook* (Statistics Canada, 1951-82); Figure 5.13: Adapted from *Manufacturing Industries of Canada* (Statistics Canada, 1976) CA IBS 31-209; Figures 5.14, 5.15: Adapted from *Summary of Canada's External Trade* (Statistics Canada, 1981), CA IBS 65-001; Figure 5.17: Based on statistics obtained from Statistics Canada; Figure 5.24: Based on statistics obtained from the Department of Employment and Immigration, Canada; Figure 5.25: Based on statistics obtained from Statistics Canada, CA IBS 62-002, CA IBS 62-010, and CA IBS 72-206

CHAPTER 6

Photos: Figures 6.6, 6.8(a): Canadian National Rail; Figure 6.23: Consulate General de France, Toronto

Cartoon Idea: Daniel Liebster

General Illustration: Figure 6.17: Based on statistics from the Canadian Automobile Association, *Car Costs 1984-85*

Section III Opener: Epcot: T. Ciccarelli; Floating home: UNESCO/C. Baugey; Mosque in Mali: UNESCO/A. Tessore

CHAPTER 7

Photos: Figure 7.5(b): Miller Services; Figure 7.8: Public Archives Canada PA-124423; Figure 7.13: Government of India Tourism Office

General Illustrations: Figure 7.9: Adapted from Statistics Canada, *Canada at a Glance, 1983;* Figure 7.20: Based on statistics obtained from the Publications Board of the United Nations

CHAPTER 8

Photos: Figure 8.6: Adapted from material obtained from Walt Disney Productions; Figure 8.15: Public Archives Canada C-27898